ADVANCES IN MANAGEMENT ACCOUNTING

ADVANCES IN MANAGEMENT ACCOUNTING

Series Editor: Chris Akroyd

Volumes 1–25: Marc J. Epstein and John Y. Lee
Volumes 26 and 27: Marc J. Epstein and Mary A. Malina
Volumes 28–30: Mary A. Malina
Volume 31: Laurie L. Burney and Mary A. Malina
Volume 32: Laurie L. Burney
Volume 33: Chris Akroyd
Volume 34: Chris Akroyd

ADVANCES IN MANAGEMENT
ACCOUNTING   VOLUME 35

ADVANCES IN MANAGEMENT ACCOUNTING

EDITED BY

CHRIS AKROYD

University of Canterbury, New Zealand

United Kingdom – North America – Japan
India – Malaysia – China

Emerald Publishing Limited
Emerald Publishing, Floor 5, Northspring, 21-23 Wellington Street, Leeds LS1 4DL.

First edition 2023

Reprints and permissions service
Contact: www.copyright.com

British Library Cataloguing in Publication Data
A catalogue record for this book is available from the British Library

ISBN: 978-1-83753-917-8 (Print)
ISBN: 978-1-83753-916-1 (Online)
ISBN: 978-1-83753-918-5 (Epub)

ISSN: 1474-7871 (Series)

INVESTOR IN PEOPLE

CONTENTS

LIST OF CONTRIBUTORS

Chris Akroyd	Department of Accounting and Information Systems, University of Canterbury, Christchurch, New Zealand
Mark Anderson	Haskayne School of Business, University of Calgary, Calgary, Canada
Kevin Baird	Department of Accounting and Corporate Governance, Macquarie University, Sydney, Australia
Abbie L. Daly	Department of Accounting, University of Wisconsin-Whitewater, Whitewater, WI, USA
Kevin E. Dow	College of Business Administration, The University of Texas at El Paso, El Paso, TX, USA
Andrea Drake	School of Accountancy, Louisiana Tech University, Ruston, LA, USA
Denise Frost	Waikato Management School, University of Waikato, Hamilton, New Zealand
Shahid Khan	Penn State Berks, Reading, PA, USA
Raj Mashruwala	Haskayne School of Business, University of Calgary, Calgary, Canada
Ella Mae Matsumura	Wisconsin School of Business, University of Wisconsin-Madison, Madison, WI, USA
Timothy C. Miller	Williams College of Business, Xavier University, Cincinnati, OH, USA
Nuraddeen Abubakar Nuhu	Department of Accounting and Corporate Governance, Macquarie University, Sydney, Australia
Winifred O'Grady	Kaipara, New Zealand
Sean A. Peffer	Von Allmen School of Accountancy, University of Kentucky, Lexington, KY, USA
Umesh Sharma	Waikato Management School, University of Waikato, Hamilton, New Zealand
Gary Spraakman	School of Administrative Studies, York University, Toronto, Canada

Dan N. Stone   Von Allmen School of Accountancy, University of
                        Kentucky, Lexington, KY, USA

Sophia Su   Department of Accounting and Corporate Governance,
                        Macquarie University, Sydney, Australia

Tyler Thomas   Wisconsin School of Business, University of Wisconsin-
                        Madison, Madison, WI, USA

Jeffrey Wong   College of Business, University of Nevada, Reno, NV,
                        USA

Dimitri Yatsenko   Department of Accounting, University of Wisconsin-
                        Whitewater, Whitewater, WI, USA

Zhimin (Jimmy) Yu   Marilyn Davies College of Business, University of
                        Houston-Downtown, Houston, TX, USA

STATEMENT OF PURPOSE

Advances in Management Accounting (AIMA) is a publication of quality, theoretical, and applied research in management accounting. The journal's purpose is to publish thought-provoking articles that advance knowledge in the management accounting discipline and are of interest to both academics and practitioners. The journal seeks thoughtful, well-developed articles on a variety of current topics in management accounting, broadly defined. All research methods including survey research, field tests, case studies, experiments, meta-analyses, and modeling are welcome. Some commentaries, research notes, and critiques will be included where appropriate.

Articles may range from purely empirical to purely theoretical, from practice-based applications to speculation on the development of new techniques and frameworks. Empirical articles must present sound research designs and well-explained execution. Theoretical articles must present reasonable assumptions and logical development of ideas. All articles should include well-defined problems, concise presentations, and succinct conclusions that follow logically from the data.

REVIEW PROCEDURES

AIMA intends to provide authors with timely reviews clearly indicating the acceptance status of their manuscripts. The results of initial reviews normally will be reported to authors within eight weeks from the date the manuscript is received. The author will be expected to work with the Editor and Associate Editors, who will act as a liaison between the author and the reviewers to resolve areas of concern. To ensure publication, it is the author's responsibility to make necessary revisions in a timely and satisfactory manner.

MANUSCRIPT FORM GUIDELINES

1. Manuscripts should include a cover page that indicates the author's name and affiliation.
2. Manuscripts should include a separate lead page with an abstract (not to exceed 250 words) and seven keywords.
3. The author's name and affiliation should not appear on the abstract.
4. Tables, figures, and exhibits should appear on a separate page. Each should be numbered and have a title.
5. To be assured of anonymous reviews, authors should not identify themselves directly or indirectly.
6. Manuscripts currently under review by other publications should not be submitted.
7. Authors should email the manuscript in two WORD files to the editor. The first attachment should include the title page with author details and the second should exclude the title page.
8. Inquiries concerning *Advances in Management Accounting* should be directed to: Chris Akroyd at Advances.In.MA@Gmail.com

INTRODUCTION

This volume of *Advances in Management Accounting (AIMA)* presents a diversity of management accounting topics, methods and author affiliations, which form the basic tenets of *AIMA*. Included are papers on planning, budgeting, costing systems, strategic management accounting practices and performance management. Topics analyzed include the new management accounting ecosystem, strategic planning and budgeting, complex cost accounting systems, non-monetary preferences and cost reporting, strategic management accounting practices, customer-centered strategy and relative performance information in remote work arrangements. The articles in this volume employ a variety of methods from experiments and case studies to surveys and a diversity in authorship with affiliations from Australia, Canada, New Zealand and the United States of America.

This volume begins with an article by the AIMA Editor and Associate Editors, Akroyd, Dow, Drake and Wong who argue that we need more cross-disciplinary research to bridge the gap between management accounting research and practice. They present an overview of the history of management accounting and show how research could be expanded to include external factors and information sources, which can be framed around the concept of the management accounting ecosystem. We encourage researchers to submit studies to *Advances in Management Accounting* that include the impact that external factors have on internal decision-making processes, evaluation of the effectiveness of new management accounting information sources and techniques in the broader ecosystem, and the use of new technologies to enhance the efficiency of management accounting practices.

The following three papers focus on issues around planning and budgeting. First, Spraakman and O'Grady examine how firms align strategic planning and budgeting. They interview management accountants at large, listed companies about how they achieve alignment between their strategic plans and budgets, both ex ante and ex post. They found that rather than using multiple strategic, planning, budgeting and forecasting processes these were all part of a single connected process. They show that alignment of strategic planning and budgeting are undertaken both prior to the beginning of the financial year as well as during the financial year. It is the alignments between these two mechanisms that enable these companies to accomplish their goals.

Sharma and Frost examine how social capital influences budgeting in a church organization. They argue that focusing on social capital can provide new insights into the construction of budgets and the social aspects which influence this process. They adopted a qualitative case study approach and carried out interviews of managers involved in the budgeting process, examined using an interpretive methodology. They found that budgeting was a social process that was influenced by the social capital of the participants.

Miller, Peffer and Stone examine participative budgeting. They carry out two experiments to investigate whether managers' judgments of fair behaviors are malleable and context-dependent, and if these judgments of fair behavior impact cost reporting misrepresentations. They found that managers deploy fairness beliefs around honesty or equality consistent with maximizing their context-relevant income. Hence, fairness beliefs constrain misrepresentations in predictable ways. In addition, the authors found that more accounting information is not always beneficial as the presence of this information can actually increase misrepresentations when managers are initially advantaged.

Matsumura, Thomas and Yatsenko examine complex cost systems. They argue that organizations that operate in highly competitive markets want to have more accurate cost systems as systems with greater complexity are potentially more accurate. However, the authors argue that even complex systems do not always provide accurate costings due to design or calculation issues. They found that greater cost system complexity resulted in greater confidence in the cost system. As the level of competition increased there was a decrease in managers' attribution of cost-system-driven adverse firm effects to the cost system. When cost system complexity and higher competition were combined, managers were less likely to attribute the cost-system-driven adverse firm effects to the costing system.

Su, Baird and Nuhu examine how organizational culture influences the use of strategic management accounting practices and competitive advantage. They collected data from 408 accountants in Australian businesses using an online survey questionnaire, which they examine using structural equation modeling. They found a positive association between the use of strategic management accounting practices and competitive advantage although this association was positively moderated by one cultural dimension, teamwork orientation. This indicates that the positive effect of strategic management accounting practices on competitive advantage is dependent upon the fit between the use of these practices and teamwork orientation.

Anderson, Khan, Mashruwala and Yu examine how managers acquire and develop specialized resources as they grow their firms which enable a resource-based competitive advantage. They argue that an important part of committing to a resource-based strategy is a willingness to keep spending on specialized resources during periods when sales and profits are down. They examine whether such resource-based commitments to a customer-centered strategy result in improved customer satisfaction. They find evidence consistent with their expectations that resource-based commitments are reflected in cost stickiness, which is an important dimension of creating and sustaining a resource-based competitive advantage.

In the final paper, Daly and Yatsenko seek to understand if relative performance information can improve performance in remote work arrangements. It has been argued that the use of relative performance information can improve employee performance; however, there may be differences in employees' remote work environments which could influence performance. In this study, the authors manipulate relative performance information across the sections of introductory accounting courses taught during the COVID-19 pandemic. The authors found that relative performance information improves performance in a remote work setting, as students receiving relative performance information achieved higher exam scores and increased their exam scores to a greater extent than students who did not receive relative performance information. The authors also found that lower performers improved performance more than higher performers in response to RPI, and the effect of RPI was more pronounced in those closest to meaningful thresholds. These results inform practice on the expected benefits of implementing relative performance information in a remote work setting.

The eight articles in Volume 35 represent relevant, theoretically sound and practical studies that extend our knowledge within the management accounting discipline. These articles manifest the journal's commitment to providing a high level of contribution to management accounting research and practice.

Chris Akroyd
Editor

THE NEW MANAGEMENT ACCOUNTING ECOSYSTEM: A RETROSPECTIVE VIEW AND PATH TO THE FUTURE

Chris Akroyd, Kevin E. Dow, Andrea Drake and Jeffrey Wong

ABSTRACT

In this paper, the editors argue that management accounting research should seek to expand to examine the broader ecosystem of information sources that influence organizational performance. The editors introduce the concept of the management accounting ecosystem as a means of linking discrete management accounting research topics to the broader environment in which organizations operate. By doing this, a stronger connection can be established between management accounting research and management accounting practice. The goal is to encourage more cross-disciplinary research that provides a better understanding of the ecosystem in which management accounting practitioners operate. The editors encourage researchers to submit studies to "Advances in Management Accounting" that evaluate the effectiveness of new management accounting information sources and the techniques used to analyze them in the broader ecosystem to enhance the effectiveness of management accounting practices. By exploring the wider information sources within the management accounting ecosystem, future management accounting research can become more innovative and better address the decision-making needs of organizational members.

Keywords: Management accounting ecosystem; practice-academic gap; IMA Competency Framework; cross-disciplinary; information; technology

Advances in Management Accounting, Volume 35, 1–18
Copyright © 2023 by Emerald Publishing Limited
All rights of reproduction in any form reserved
ISSN: 1474-7871/doi:10.1108/S1474-787120230000035001

INTRODUCTION

Management accounting aims to quantify, assess, and communicate financial and non-financial data to assist organization members in making informed decisions that align with the objectives of their organization (Horngren, Datar, & Rajan, 2012). As most of our economy's activity occurs within organizations, our aim as management accounting researchers should be to understand how organizations can better "coordinate complex activities" (Simon, 2000, p. 751). It has been suggested that

> management accounting and control systems are so important and ubiquitous today that if accountants and information people wrapped up their systems and took them home, the whole process of producing society's material goods and services along with the governance of social order would grind to a standstill. (Macintosh, 1994, p. 1)

Even though this quote is now almost three decades old, it remains just as relevant today as when it was made.

Historically, management accounting practice has focused on utilizing various techniques and analytical tools to aid organizations in planning, controlling, and enhancing their operational processes and financial performance. As industries have evolved, so too have the techniques and tools employed. Improvements in cost allocation, budgeting, and profit analysis have enhanced the effectiveness of internal decision-making. However, due to technological limitations, most of these improvements have focused on the data available within the organization, despite the knowledge that organizations operate in a broader "marketplace." Management accounting practitioners can now provide a more comprehensive understanding of organizational performance by systematically considering the broader ecosystem in which organizations operate and utilizing appropriate data and analysis. With the rapid pace of changes in the use of information technology in organizations (Spraakman, O'Grady, Askarany, & Akroyd, 2015), research is needed to support how firms can further advance how they use technology in their management accounting practices (Granlund, 2011).

This chapter introduces the concept of the management accounting ecosystem as a means of linking discrete, traditional management accounting research topics to the broader environment in which practitioners operate. A management accounting ecosystem can be thought of as the interdependency among entities in a complex network bound together to provide shared value to organizations and society. The management accounting ecosystem is a complex (and self-organized) network that includes an information source layer and an information technology layer (including computer science, statistics, math, machine learning, artificial intelligence, etc.) through which data and information move into the management accounting system where it is transformed into knowledge that is useful for decision-making. In essence, this ecosystem is how data and information sourcing, access, and flows are interconnected and enable efficient and effective communication between information sources and the management accounting system to help organization members make better decisions. While we do not purport to describe an overarching information management model in organizations, we strive to understand better the structural and functional information environment in which management accountants can help organizations create shared value. Thus, we view the management accounting ecosystem as a unifying conceptual model that illustrates the multi-disciplinary nature of management accounting practice that has always been, but also needs management accounting researchers to examine.

Organizations have always functioned within an ecosystem of competitors, partners, employees, and external market forces. However, a systematic consideration of the broader ecosystem using appropriate data and analysis has been limited. Accordingly, the conceptualization of a management accounting ecosystem recognizes the need for management accountants to use data from within the organizations they serve as well as from external sources.

Understanding what management accountants do in practice can help us bridge the gap between traditional management accounting research and the broader ecosystem where organizations now operate. This will enable us to connect traditional management accounting research topics with external factors influencing organizational performance. We aim to reduce the practice-academic gap and ensure that future research is relevant and accessible to a broader audience, including those from marketing, supply chain logistics, sociology, strategy, organization behavior, and psychology disciplines. By doing so, we hope to foster cross-disciplinary research that provides a more comprehensive understanding of the broader ecosystem in which management accounting operates.

As information technology rapidly transforms the business landscape, it has been argued that management accounting practitioners and researchers should leverage the opportunities at the intersection of technology and management accounting (Granlund, 2011). Therefore, we encourage researchers to submit studies to *Advances in Management Accounting* that examine the impact of external factors on internal decision-making processes, evaluate the effectiveness of new management accounting techniques in the broader management accounting ecosystem, and utilize new technologies to enhance the efficiency of management accounting practices. This approach will ensure that future management accounting research is relevant and accessible to a broader audience, thereby reducing the practice-academic gap. By exploring the intersection of information sources and management accounting practice we can gain a more comprehensive understanding of how these fields can complement each other, leading to the development of more innovative and effective management accounting practices and more relevant research.

The rest of this chapter is structured as follows. First, we present the IMA Competency Framework recently developed by the Institute of Management Accountants (IMA) along with the Data, Information, Knowledge, Wisdom (DIKW) Pyramid which we use to frame our discussion. We then provide a historical perspective on management accounting practice and an overview of what a management accounting system includes. Next, we introduce our new management accounting ecosystem, which serves as a first step toward identifying areas of interest to link management accounting practice with research. We then explore potential improvements to management accounting doctoral programs to overcome the practice-research gap and outline some areas for future research.

THE IMA COMPETENCY FRAMEWORK
AND THE DIKW PYRAMID

The IMA developed a Management Accounting Competency Framework (2022) based on extensive research on the practices of management accounting professionals (see Fig. 1). The framework consists of six broad domains linked to specific

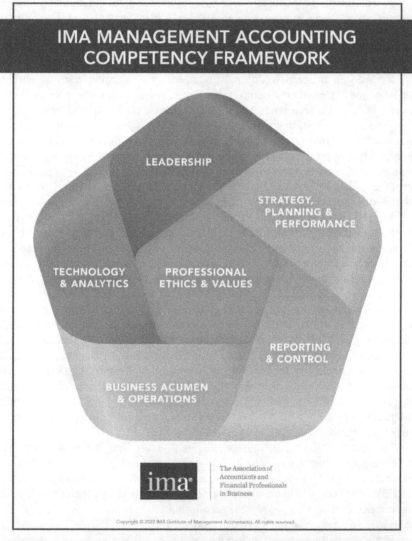

Fig. 1. IMA Management Accounting Competency Framework. *Source*: This graphic and its contents is used here with permission granted by IMA® (Institute of Management Accountants). Copyright© 2023 by IMA® (Institute of Management Accountants). All rights reserved. Further copying, modifying, reproducing or using without permission of the Institute of Management Accountants is prohibited.

skills and tasks that practitioners need to master to succeed in their careers, whether as new graduates or in the future. The IMA Competency Framework is useful for identifying areas of importance for practitioners and can guide further academic research to better understand how available methods and procedures can lead to better decision-making within the broader ecosystem in which they and their firms operate.

The strategy, planning and performance domain focuses on the visionary ability of management accountants to create and communicate strategic plans and performance metrics. This involves the ability to go beyond financial statements and focus on a wide range of stakeholders. The use of data analysis tools for strategy, planning and decision analysis is becoming increasingly critical to improve performance.

The reporting and control domain focuses on the stewardship function of management accounting which involves reporting on economic, environmental, social and governance performance. To do this, management accountants must know how to design internal controls and be able to use data analytics to communicate with stakeholders and work collaboratively with other departments.

The business acumen and operations domain is focused on management accountants as business partners. To become better partners, management accountants need to have knowledge of operations and be able to understand the drivers of revenue, cost and profitability. This requires the use of new business models and technology to analyze operations.

The technology and analytics domain is focused on the management accountant as a catalyst for change. This encompasses the necessary skills to effectively utilize technology, analyze data, which are necessary for making informed business decisions. Management accountants need to develop the ability to interpret data, identify patterns, and employ visual aids to communicate information effectively to stakeholders.

The IMA Competency Framework provides a comprehensive overview of the knowledge, skills, and abilities required to succeed as a management accountant. It emphasizes the importance of strategic thinking, effective communication, and collaboration with other departments. It also recognizes the importance of data analysis, risk management, and internal controls in ensuring that financial information is accurate and reliable.

As an example of how this relates to management accounting research can be seen in the strategy, planning, and performance domain. This domain includes the area of budgeting and forecasting, which has been the subject of many management accounting research endeavors. An expert practitioner in this area would, among other tasks "Lead collaborative forecasting efforts incorporating information from multiple internal and external expert sources and sophisticated modeling techniques" and "Design and lead the budget and financial planning process across multiple business units in a complex organization using advanced software tools" (IMA Management Accounting Competency Framework, p. 14).

Researchers in this area could use external sources of information, such as big data and analytics, to better understand these areas, which may not have been feasible to utilize in prior eras of management accounting research. Additionally, researchers should consider the planning process that can span multiple business units and the use of advanced software and modeling techniques to inform how organization members make decisions. These factors should be key considerations in designing budgeting and forecasting research studies, as they involve the broader aspects of the management accounting ecosystem.

To make decisions, management accountants use a variety of data sources, some of which are created internally and some of which can only be obtained from partners external to their organization. Raw data that partners have created must first be given the appropriate context to become useful information that can be shared with our organization. Management accountants then apply various analytical tools and techniques to reveal underlying patterns in that external information so that this knowledge can then be combined with internal data to form actionable intelligence. Thus, organization members can use their knowledge and experience to make better judgments and decisions to create shared value (Shields, 2015, 2018).

To apply the IMA framework and make it accessible to academics and practitioners, we need to understand how data flows. The IMA Competency Framework lays the foundation for management accountants to innovate and create new knowledge by addressing a broad set of essential core competencies. We posit that the IMA Competency Framework provides the foundation for understanding management accounting practice. But in order to examine how new information sources can be integrated into the management accounting ecosystem, we need to understand how to convert data into knowledge and wisdom, which is captured in the DIKW Pyramid (see Fig. 2). To do this, we apply a theory of knowledge management to help understand how data moves from individual information sources into the management accounting system (Alavi & Leidner, 2001).

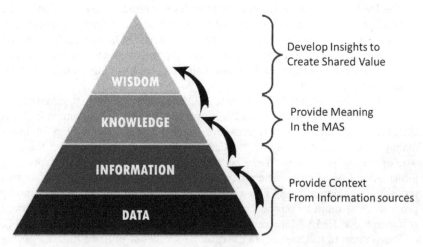

Fig. 2. The DIKW Pyramid and the Management Accounting System (MAS). *Source*: Hey (2004). Knowledge Commons – Revised by the Authors.

The DIKW pyramid is a hierarchical knowledge management model that explains how data can be transformed into knowledge and wisdom. According to this framework, data are the raw material collected from internal and external sources. These data are then transformed into information, which are organized and meaningfully structured. Information is then analyzed and interpreted to produce knowledge, which enables a deeper understanding of the information. Finally, wisdom is making good decisions based on knowledge and experience. The DIKW framework helps management accountants understand the steps required to convert data into actionable insights. By using this framework, management accountants can identify the types of data they need to collect, the tools they need to analyze it, and the processes they need to implement to ensure that knowledge and wisdom is generated and applied to enable shared value creation.

To bridge the practice-research gap, it is crucial to gain a comprehensive understanding of the practices of management accountants – what they do, who they do it to, why, where, when & how. The IMA Competency Framework is a useful tool for achieving this goal. Using this framework, along with the DIKW pyramid, we can inform the development of a new management accounting ecosystem and identify relevant research questions that would interest practicing management accountants. Since the activities of management accountants are diverse, it is necessary to encourage cross-disciplinary research. The ecosystem in which management accounting operates relies on a broad range of information, and technology is crucial for analyzing that information. In this sense, management accountants are operating in a new "era" of information and technology, and we must leverage these resources to advance our understanding of their practices. The following section briefly discusses a historical perspective on management accounting.

THE HISTORY OF MANAGEMENT ACCOUNTING

Common descriptions of management accounting emphasize planning for the future, controlling present operations, and evaluating past actions taken. Management accounting is driven by the need for organizations to create and interpret information that informs strategies for achieving a competitive advantage, and actions that implement those strategies. It is important to understand the history and development of management accounting in order to gain insights into its current state and future direction. The following historical perspective on management accounting, in Fig. 3, is not intended to be a comprehensive overview of the discipline's history, but rather aims to highlight some of the significant milestones over time and illustrate its adaptive nature.

Management accounting practices have evolved to meet the changing needs of decision-makers. Management innovations have been a key driver of this evolution, and advances in operations and information technology have enabled such innovations. While it is difficult to define distinct eras in the history of management accounting, certain developments can be associated with particular times, companies, and individuals. The following illustration (see Figure 3 below) and subsequent discussion highlight some of these key developments.

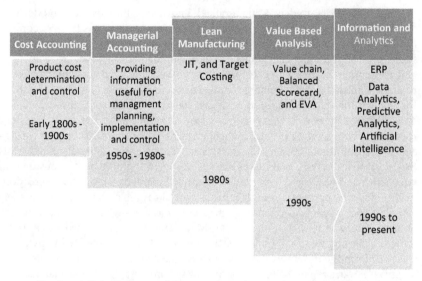

Fig. 3.   A Brief History of Management Accounting. *Source*: Authors.

Cost Accounting

Cost accounting became popularized during the Industrial Revolution, when the complexity of a company's operations necessitated the development of cost accounting systems to plan, control, and evaluate work processes (Kamal, 2015; Kaplan, 1984; Swain, 2021). Hierarchical management structures required information to evaluate performance, and effective management accounting systems of this era allowed managers to evaluate operations that may be remote from them. The late 1800s and early 1900s saw the emergence of the scientific management movement, which emphasized the use of standard costs and the measurement and allocation of overhead costs to products.

DuPont (early 1900s, circa 1914) identified the need for a more sophisticated management accounting system because of its vertical integration of different companies. The diversity of businesses in their supply chain required a unifying management accounting system. The company is credited with the DuPont Return on Investment (ROI) decomposition technique derived from a simple concept that ROI = Investment turnover × profit margin. The ROI analysis integrated cost management with asset management and allowed extensive key performance measures to be utilized.

Managerial Accounting

Managerial accounting is focused on providing information for management planning and control, primarily through methods such as responsibility accounting (Waweru, 2008, 2010). Managerial accountants support management through management control systems, which facilitate decision analysis and responsibility accounting (Kamal, 2015). An influential management movement that heavily influenced managerial accounting was Total Quality Management (TQM) that is thought to have originated in the 1950s with W. Edwards Deming teaching methods for statistical analysis and controlling quality to Japanese engineers and executives. TQM has become associated with a philosophy of a broad and systematic approach to managing organizational quality (https://asq.org/quality-resources/total-quality-management/tqm-history).

Lean Manufacturing

One of the most well-known examples of lean manufacturing is associated with the Toyota Motor Corporation. Toyota developed their Just-In-Time (JIT) process to make vehicles the fastest and efficient. It took Toyota 30 years to develop its methods to respond to challenges such as the lack of cash flow, land space, and natural resources. Many of these techniques spread in Japan during the 1970s and began to be adopted in the United States in the 1980s (Wilson, 2021). In the late 1980s, JIT was rebranded as lean manufacturing which included a broader supply chain focus. The supply chain struggles during the COVID-19 pandemic caused lean supply chains to struggle with the market's volatility. In the post-pandemic years, it remains to be seen how strong the influence of lean manufacturing will be.

Target costing is often seen as a cost management strategy used by companies to determine the maximum cost they can afford to produce a product or service while still earning a desired profit margin. But it has been shown to be a much broader organizational management tool (Kato, 1993). It has been argued that "Target Costing is neither accounting nor costing, rather it is frequent and mutual communicative act and strategy that enables comprehensive profit planning and management" (Okano & Suzuki, 2007, p. 1121). Target costing is often combined with value engineering, which is the process of reducing the cost of a product or service while maintaining or improving its quality and functionality (Tani et al., 1994). By setting a target cost upfront, companies can focus on designing and manufacturing products or services that meet customer needs while minimizing costs (Kato, 1993).

Value-Based Analysis

Michael Porter (1985) introduced the value chain concept, Competitive Advantage: Creating and Sustaining Superior Performance. The value chain is a tool that helps managers to analyze the key activities involved in delivering value to customers, enabling them to identify activities that do not add value to the process. Non-value-added activities can be eliminated, and resources can be redirected to activities that add value.

The Balanced Scorecard framework, introduced by Kaplan and Norton (1992), translates an organization's strategy into a set of performance objectives that can be measured, monitored, and modified as necessary. The framework considers organizational performance from four interconnected perspectives: learning and growth, internal business processes, customer, and financial.

Another value-based method of analysis is Economic Value Added (EVA). This variant of residual income was developed and marketed by Stern Stewart & Co., a New York consulting firm, to encourage value-maximizing behavior in corporate managers (O'Hanlon & Peasnell, 1998).

Information and Analytics

Managers see technology and data analytics as transformational forces in their businesses, facilitating data collection, analysis, and actionable information to support decision-making (Brands & Holtzblatt, 2015; Cokins, 2017; Ghasemaghaei, 2019; Nita, 2008). As management accounting is a discipline that supports decision-making, the link between information and analytics is natural. Furthermore, the integration of artificial intelligence into decision support technologies and operational processes has the potential to evolve the nature of management accounting further. Management accounting has adapted over time to suit the needs of organization members and will continue to change as operations become more complex and the sources of information become more diverse.

THE NEW MANAGEMENT ACCOUNTING ECOSYSTEM

As the evolution of management accounting practices described above indicates, organizational decisions have always been based on diverse information needs. Therefore, management accountants must fully identify, understand, and assess their information needs. As technology evolves and develops, the rise of new tools and technologies continues to drive a seemingly ever-changing information model. A natural ecosystem involves interactions between organisms and the environment for mutual benefit. Similarly, an information environment surrounding management accounting is analogous to a natural ecosystem where different species interact symbiotically as an individual community. This is why it is important to recognize that these technologies are not simply providing better and faster sets of information but are creating a new information environment that can be best conceptualized as a Management Accounting Ecosystem (see Fig. 4).

In essence, we posit that each individual information source contains raw data that might be useful to management, and management accountants can help organize the information so that it can be properly used by management. However, those data elements must be first converted into information in the technology layer of the ecosystem. Information is then moved into the management accounting system where management accountants can interact with it to form knowledge that the decision-makers can use. The outcomes of those organizational decisions form wisdom that then begets shared value.

At the core of our management accounting ecosystem lies the management accounting system (which consists of the fundamental areas of management accounting in which information is processed). As it is essential to base management accounting decisions on data, these data must be timely, nonrepudiatable, high quality, have integrity, and be reliable. This will help management

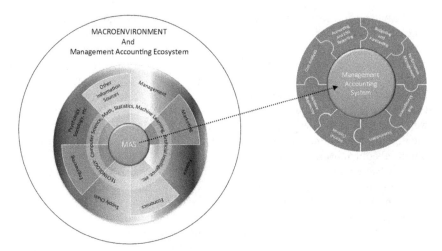

Fig. 4. The New Management Accounting Ecosystem. *Source*: Authors.

accountants communicate clearly to organizations members who make decisions to enable shared value creation. To this end, management accounting data must be combined with big data by utilizing each information source to show how technology can facilitate information flows.

Each information source in the management accounting ecosystem produces data useful if properly processed in the management accounting system. Once processed, these data are converted into information that can flow into the management accounting system. When management accounting expertise is applied to this information, useful knowledge is created. Within the management accounting ecosystem confines, management accountants must be more than technologically literate; they must have a functional understanding of how data can be processed into information and transformed into knowledge that organization members use to create shared value.

REDUCING THE PRACTICE-RESEARCH GAP

The gap between academic research and practice persists (see, e.g., Ferry, Saliterer, Steccolini, & Tucker, 2019; Mitchell, 2002; Tucker & Leach, 2017; Tucker & Lowe, 2014). To further address this problem, we offer some specific ideas on eliminating this gap. We posit that academic researchers, especially those still in their doctoral programs, should be familiar with the problems of practice and use that as a starting point for generating research ideas and projects. Thus, academics teaching doctoral seminars in management accounting should include articles from practice-oriented journals to encourage students to develop research projects that are based on the needs and interests of practitioners.

Many doctoral programs train students to understand and conduct rigorous scholarly research using sophisticated methodologies (i.e., well-designed experiments or surveys) and advanced statistical techniques. A primary way to accomplish this is to have students read a large number of scholarly articles, published in the top research journals. This is appropriate and necessary given the publishing requirements of most institutions. Conducting scholarly research suitable to (primarily) an academic audience is critical to their future success. However, we argue that it may lead to students generating their research ideas based on the potential for an incremental contribution to the academic literature, with the potential contribution to practice coming as an afterthought (or not at all). Thus, another "concrete" thing that academics that are teaching management accounting research seminars to doctoral students (or really any other area of accounting research) include practitioner articles to their reading lists.

For example, many doctoral students identify a particular academic article(s) that they are especially interested in, and then develop a project based on how to extend that article incrementally. Its impact on practice is not always a primary consideration, despite it being mentioned as a requirement for many journals. As an alternative, we posit that when identifying potential research topics, students interested in management accounting should first review the IMA Competency Framework and its associated tasks and procedures to identify specific areas that interest them. This ensures that their topic would be of interest to practitioners. Practitioner articles *and* academic articles should then be reviewed. Fruitful academic projects should then take that topic and explore what aspects of the broader management accounting ecosystem would impact that topic or task.

Management accounting researchers should start with topics highlighted in the IMA Competency Framework and then further develop their questions by considering the broader management accounting ecosystem outlined in this chapter. As noted, practitioners do not operate in a vacuum; researchers have to consider the other parts of the organization and relevant contextual and environmental factors (i.e., the ecosystem). Doing this will likely require the expertise of researchers in other areas such as marketing, economics, psychology, information systems, etc. Thus, we call for more cross-disciplinary research *and* research questions that are driven by the needs of practice. The underlying purpose of most projects should be how management accountants can help their organizations make better decisions related to the topic under study, again considering parts of the ecosystem that may have been previously ignored and not "considered related to accounting."

Broadening management accounting research to consider the wider ecosystem in which practitioners operate likely requires the use of diverse sets of information from non-traditional sources. For example, elements of consumer psychology that can enhance product quality and streamline the production process or how innovations in highway engineering ultimately impact intermodal transport and the efficiency of delivering goods to customers. These new research projects may also make co-authors from non-accounting and/or non-business disciplines extremely helpful. For example, including faculty from engineering disciplines on projects related to manufacturing costs would likely generate practical insights that would not evolve from research teams made up of accounting scholars alone.

A casual glance at author teams from many management accounting research articles reveals the makeup to be mostly accounting scholars, with occasional collaborations with scholars from related disciplines such as finance and economics. We argue that going forward, management accounting researchers should actively consider and search for co-authors from relevant disciplines outside of accounting or closely related business fields. Ultimately, academics from a wide variety of disciplines will become familiar with accounting research and how accounting scholars can contribute to their research streams. This will further the progress of management accounting research by engaging audiences outside of the traditional accounting research domain. Although accounting research may rely on other disciplines, such as economics, sociology, and psychology for theory or supporting findings, other disciplines rarely refer to accounting research for insights or support into their research.

We believe that management accounting has to become more interdisciplinary and inclusive. Our attempt to capture the management accounting ecosystem presently in place will provide an initial view that will help to reflect areas of research and practice in management accounting that may have traditionally been overlooked.

FUTURE MANAGEMENT ACCOUNTING RESEARCH

Future management accounting research should explicitly address topics identified by *practice* as being relevant. These topics can be identified broadly by considering the IMA Competency Framework. Once the management accounting topic of interest has been selected, research questions should be developed using the broader management accounting ecosystem developed in this chapter. The increased availability of information, from sources both internal and external to organizations, makes the development of cross-disciplinary research more feasible than ever. By including cross-disciplinary areas highlighted by the ecosystem, such as marketing and supply chain, management accounting research has the potential to become more relevant to a broader audience and have a greater impact.

Scholarly work focusing on the contribution to practice first, rather than the incremental contribution to academic research should be pursued and more highly valued. One could consider how a practitioner could use research to improve the performance of their organization or understand the "world" a bit better which may influence the decisions of other organization members. The need to broaden future research areas as motivated by the management accounting ecosystem introduced by this chapter suggests a broad array of topics for future research. Since the central purpose of this chapter is to introduce the concept of the management accounting ecosystem, examples of future research topics in two areas will be used: information technology and human resources.

The connections between information technology and management accounting research are numerous. Some examples of research topics that encompass both disciplines include:

- The impact of artificial intelligence on data analytics.
- Can data analytics or artificial intelligence improve budgeting practice.
- The value added by organizations using their information technology resources.
- The value of data quality on the usability and quality of information produced.
- Frameworks of domain knowledge that can guide data analytics.
- How management accountants can be the keepers of information within an organization.
- The willingness of management accountants and managers to rely on and work with emerging technologies such as artificial intelligence.

Increasingly, people are being recognized as the most important assets in organizations. Some examples of how human resources and management accounting research intersect include:

- The economics of employee training and its effect on retention and productivity.
- Quantifying the value of human assets.
- The hidden costs of turnover.

We need more research that binds the ecosystem. That is, we need:

1. Research on the technology layer to help management accountants get the information necessary for decision-making.
2. Research on how to get information from each information source to the management accounting system.
3. Research on human–computer interaction to facilitate information flows.

As noted above, budgeting/forecasting has been identified as a topic that is of interest to practitioners in the IMA Competency Framework. In examining the management accounting ecosystem, a researcher may note the importance of using information from other sources. A research question may be how much human managers are willing to rely on budgets developed using artificial intelligence (i.e., that construct budgets based on firm specific data coupled with outside economic data) versus those developed by human personnel?

Potential members of the research team could include faculty from the areas of psychology and computer science. Practitioners could be consulted on what they think may be other factors of interest, such as what may make their personnel more or less likely to rely on the AI created budgets. We also agree with Granlund (2011) that we need to expand the theories used to examine the management accounting ecosystem beyond agency theory, transaction cost economics, contingency theory, and social theories. While these theories provide

> some valuable insights..., they seem to push research into questions and problems that are many times far from the everyday practice of accountants and other producers and users of especially non-standardized accounting information. (Granlund, 2011, p. 15)

There is a need for a much wider range of theories that can enable us to better understand the multifaceted connections that are contained within the management accounting ecosystem (see, e.g., Pfister, Peda, & Otley, 2023).

CONCLUSION

Management accounting has long been a critical function in organizations, helping managers make informed decisions about operations and financial performance. However, as the business landscape has evolved, the traditional focus of management accounting on internal processes and data has become insufficient. Organizations operate within a broader ecosystem of competitors, partners, employees, and external market forces, and understanding and incorporating these factors into decision-making processes is essential to success.

To help bridge the gap between traditional management accounting and the broader ecosystem, we have presented a new framework: the management accounting ecosystem. This framework seeks to link discrete management accounting research topics to the broader environment in which practitioners operate. It aims to reduce the practice-academic gap and ensure that future research is relevant and accessible to a wider audience, including those from computer science, data analytics, supply chain, psychology, and marketing.

The management accounting ecosystem recognizes that organizations are not isolated entities but are part of a larger system of stakeholders and external factors. Thus, the framework considers the external environment, such as market competition, partner relationships, employee behavior, and market forces, and how they impact internal decision-making processes. By evaluating the effectiveness of new management accounting techniques in the broader ecosystem and utilizing new technologies to enhance the efficiency of management accounting practices, the ecosystem seeks to provide a more comprehensive understanding of organizational performance.

The information technology revolution has played a critical role in transforming the business landscape and has created new opportunities for management accounting practitioners and researchers. With the advent of new technologies, such as cloud computing, artificial intelligence, and machine learning, organizations have access to vast amounts of data and advanced analytics tools that were previously unavailable. This technology enables management accountants to analyze and interpret data in new ways, and to integrate it with external factors such as social media sentiment, environmental trends, and economic indicators. By incorporating this external data, management accountants can gain a deeper understanding of organizational performance and make more informed decisions.

To take advantage of these opportunities, management accounting practitioners and researchers need to collaborate and work across disciplines. Cross-disciplinary research is essential because the ecosystem in which management accounting operates relies on a broad range of information, and the use of technology to analyze that information is paramount. Researchers from diverse fields, such as computer science, data analytics, supply chain, psychology, and marketing, can provide valuable insights and perspectives on effectively integrating external data with internal management accounting practices.

The IMA Competency Framework serves as a useful tool for achieving the goals of the management accounting ecosystem. By using this framework, researchers can inform the development of the ecosystem model and identify relevant research questions. The IMA Competency Framework defines the core competencies that management accountants should possess, including planning and control, decision support, and analysis and interpretation of data. These competencies provide a foundation for the ecosystem model and guide the development of new management accounting practices and techniques.

By framing management accounting as an ecosystem can enable us to create "'usable knowledge', as opposed to academically self-referential knowledge" (Van der Stede, 2015, p. 173). "Thus, research *for practice* rather than research *as a practice*" as argued by Van der Stede (2015, p. 173, emphasis in the original). To do this, we need to "conduct properly executed academic studies on practice-relevant issues broadly conceived that yield potentially applicable insights" (Van der Stede, 2015, p. 173). The aim of the management accounting ecosystem is to show potential avenues for collecting data from different information sources that can be used to study important issues in practice in order to create shared value. To carry out this type of research management accounting academics need to be technologically literate, but also have a good understanding of how data are processed into information which can then be transformed into new knowledge about how shared value is created.

We believe that the management accounting ecosystem is a good start for bridging the gap between what has been traditionally considered management accounting research and the broader ecosystem in which organizations operate. By incorporating external factors such as market competition, partner relationships, employee behavior, and market forces and utilizing new technologies, we can conduct more impactful cross-disciplinary research. This will enable management accounting research to better understand organizational performance and better inform practice. As the business landscape continues to evolve, it is essential that management accounting practitioners and researchers embrace the opportunities presented by the ecosystem and work together to advance the field.

REFERENCES

Alavi, M., & Leidner, D. (2001). Knowledge management and knowledge management systems: Conceptual foundations and research issues. *MIS Quarterly*, *25*(1), 107–136.

Brands, K., & Holtzblatt, M. (2015). Business analytics: Transforming the role of management accountants. *Management Accounting Quarterly*, *16*(3), 1–12.

Cokins, G. (2017). Top 7 trends in management accounting. *Strategic Finance*, December 2013, 21–47.

Ferry, L., Saliterer, I., Steccolini, I., & Tucker, B. (2019). *The research-practice gap on accounting in the public services*, (pp. 9–31). Switzeland: Palgrave Pivot.

Ghasemaghaei, M. (2019). Does data analytics use improve firm decision making quality? The role of knowledge sharing and data analytics competency. *Decision Support Systems, 120*, 14–24.

Granlund, M. (2011). Extending AIS research to management accounting and control issues: A research note. *International Journal of Accounting Information Systems, 12*(1), 3–19.

Hey, J. (2004). The data, information, knowledge, wisdom chain: the metaphorical link. *Intergovernmental Oceanographic Commission, 26*(2), 1–18.

Horngren, C. T., Datar, S. M., & Rajan, M. (2012). *Costing accounting a managerial emphasis*. New York: Pearson.

Institute of Management Accountants (IMA). (2022). Retrieved from https://sea.imanet.org/career-resources/management-accounting-competencies

Kamal, S. (2015). Historical evolution of management accounting. *The Cost and Management, 43*(4), 12–19.

Kaplan, R. S. (1984). The evolution of management accounting. *The Accounting Review, 59*(3), 390–419.

Kaplan, R. S., & Norton, D. P. (1992). The balanced scorecard: Measures that drive performance. *Harvard Business Review* (January–February), *70*, 71–79.

Kato, Y. (1993). Target costing support systems: Lessons from leading Japanese companies. *Management Accounting Research, 4*(1), 33–47.

Mitchell, F. (2002). Research and practice in management accounting: Improving integration and communication. *European Accounting Review, 11*(2), 277–289.

Nita, B. (2008). Transformation of management accounting: From management control to performance management. *Financial Transformations in Business & Economics, 7*(3), 53–64.

O'Hanlon, J., & Peasnell, K. (1998). Wall Street's contribution to management accounting: The Stern Stewart EVA financial management system. *Management Accounting Research, 9*(4), 421–444.

Okano, H., & Suzuki, T. (2007). A history of Japanese management accounting. In C. S. Chapman, A. G. Hopwood, M. D. Shields (Eds.), *Handbook of management accounting research* (Vol. 2, pp. 1119–1137). Amsterdam.: Elsevier.

Pfister, J. A., Peda, P., & Otley, D. (2023). A methodological framework for theoretical explanation in performance management and management control systems research. *Qualitative Research in Accounting & Management, 20*(2), 201–228.

Porter, M. E. (1985). *The competitive advantage: Creating and sustaining superior performance*. New York: Free Press.

Shields, M .D. (2015). Established management accounting knowledge. *Journal of Management Accounting Research, 27*(1), 123–132.

Shields, M. D. (2018). A perspective on management accounting research. *Journal of Management Accounting Research, 30*(3), 1–11.

Simon, H. (2000). Public administration in today's world of organizations and markets. *Political Science & Politics, 33*(4), 749–756.

Spraakman, G., O'Grady, W., Askarany, D., & Akroyd, C. (2015). Employers' perceptions of information technology competency requirements for management accounting graduates. *Accounting Education, 24*(5), 403–422.

Swain, M. R. (2021). A brief History of management accounting. *Management Accounting Quarterly, 22*(2), 12–23.

Tani, T., Okano, H., Shimizu, N., Iwabuchi, Y., Fukuda, J., & Cooray, S. (1994). Target cost management in Japanese companies: Current state of the art. *Management Accounting Research, 5*, 67–81.

Tucker, B. P., & Leach, M. (2017). Learning from the experience of others: Lessons on the research–practice gap in management accounting – A nursing perspective. *Advances in Management Accounting, 29*, 127–181.

Tucker, B. P., & Lowe, A. (2014). Practitioners are from Mars; academics are from Venus? An investigation of the research-practice gap in management accounting. *Accounting, Auditing & Accountability Journal, 27*(3), 394–425.

Van der Stede, W. A. (2015). Management accounting: Where from, where now, where to? *Journal of Management Accounting Research*, *27*(1), 171–176.

Waweru, N. M. (2008). Predicting change in management accounting systems: A contingent approach. *Problems and Perspectives in Management*, *6*(2), 72–84.

Waweru, N. M. (2010). The origin and evolution of\management accounting: A review of the theoretical framework. *Problems and Perspectives in Management*, *8*(3), 165–182.

Wilson, G. (2021). Timeline: The history of just-in-time manufacturing. *Manufacturing*, December 01, 2021. Retrieved from https://manufacturingdigital.com/lean-manufacturing/timeline-history-just-time-manufacturing

STRATEGIC PLANNING AND BUDGETING: A SINGLE INTEGRATED PROCESS WITH EX ANTE AND EX POST ALIGNMENTS

Gary Spraakman and Winifred O'Grady

ABSTRACT

The purpose of this explanatory research was to understand how firms align strategic planning and budgeting both ex ante and ex post. After the literature review indicated that there was a shortcoming in explaining how the alignment was done, we interviewed management accountants at 20 large, profitable, stock-market listed firms with head offices in the Toronto area of Canada. To understand practice through interviews, we used qualitative, multi-case field research to address our research question, how do firms achieve alignment between their strategic plans and budgets, both ex ante and ex post? Our findings and contribution were that, rather than multiple processes (strategy, strategic planning, budgeting, and forecasting), strategic planning and budgeting are part of a single process. Alignment of strategic planning and budgeting is undertaken prior to the beginning of the fiscal year (ex ante) and during the fiscal year (ex post). Both provide opportunities to change ineffective strategies, strategic plans, and actions to minimize financial harm. Ex ante and ex post alignments enable the accomplishment of firms' financial objectives through explicit and verifiable decisions. With forecasting heretofore being an unclear and ambiguous subprocess, this chapter has made it transparent and manageable in assisting with accomplishing the strategy, strategic plan, and budget.

Keywords: Planning; budgeting; alignment; strategy; forecasts; multi-case methodology

---

Advances in Management Accounting, Volume 35, 19–44
Copyright © 2023 by Emerald Publishing Limited
All rights of reproduction in any form reserved
ISSN: 1474-7871/doi:10.1108/S1474-787120230000035002

INTRODUCTION

Although the literature specifies why strategic planning and budgeting are aligned, it does not, which is our purpose, explain how they are aligned prior to the start of the fiscal year (ex ante) and during the fiscal year (ex post). We are motivated to address this shortcoming and to propose a conceptual framework or theory explaining how the processes of strategic planning and budgeting are aligned. We expect this research to bring management accounting academic research and practice closer together (Tucker & Lawson, 2016).

We know that the accomplishment of the performance targets in the original budget for external (guidance) and internal (bonuses and incentive pay) reasons is why firms align strategic plans and budgets. Frow, Marginson, and Ogden (2010, p. 457) note that the commitment to the performance targets in the original budget continues for the entire fiscal year. Budgets appear to have a powerful influence on managers. That is what Marginson and Ogden (2005, p. 450) found in their study of a single firm, i.e.,

> [p]eople may commit to meeting pre-determined budgetary targets, not because of the threat of accountability or the promise of reward, but because budgets can offer structure and certainty in situations of high ambiguity and uncertainty.

They add, "the budget is being used as a coping [practice or] mechanism to counter or distort the experience of ambiguity" (p. 451). This suggests to us that with the ex ante alignment of strategic planning and budgeting the original budget is established as an anchor point.

Park (2022) has discussed the financial performance targets that firms set for themselves. He uses the consulting firm McKinsey's term, a treadmill[1] as a metaphor. The essence of the treadmill metaphor is that firms establish financial targets for themselves, generally in earnings growth terms, which "must" be met if the firm is to maintain market expectations and thereby prices of their stock. The underlying alignment of strategic plans and budgets is to maintain the belief that firms can control what happens in the marketplace to deliver expected earnings and sales growth and to signal that the firm is a good investment.

The CEOs of firms in our sample generally provide guidance in terms of earnings and sales growth to the market, i.e., to shareholders and interested analysts. The firms are profitable, shareholder owned, and stock market listed. As a result, the credibility of the CEOs and the value of firms are based on the achievement of the budgeted earnings and sales. That is the reasoning behind the careful preparation of and widespread commitment to original budgets. Moreover, respondents in 17 of the 20 firms self-declared that bonuses and incentive pay were based on the achievement of original budgets. Thus, firms are motivated to align strategic plans and budgets, prior to the start of the budget year and during the budget year, to meet the performance expectations of shareholders and analysts (external) and the bonus and incentive pay expectations of managers and employees (internal).

Despite our understanding of why the processes of strategic planning and budgeting are aligned, there is less clarity about how to align these processes. From the literature, we know firms have strategic plans which precede their budgets. Firms also have forecasts which update budgets. There are few explanations of whether and how forecasts are aligned with budgets and strategic plans.

The processes of strategic planning and budgeting, as noted by KPMG (2015), Deloitte (2014), and PwC (2012), recognize that before the beginning of the new fiscal year top-down strategy-based plans are implemented through bottom-up budgets.[2] As the actual performance that evolves during the fiscal year is often different from what was expected by the strategic plan and original budget, forecasts of the most likely future outcomes may be necessary in clarifying the potential gap developing between expected results and the original budget. In this context, the contribution of our research is a conceptual framework that explains how strategic planning and budgeting are aligned on an ongoing basis, with extant literature – i.e., Abernethy and Brownell (1999); Becker, Mahlendorf, Schaffer, and Thaten (2016); Blumentritt (2006); Erhart, Mahlendorf, Reimer, and Schaffer (2017); Grant (2003); Kannan-Narasimhan and Lawrence (2018); Peters, Gudergan, and Booth (2019); and Spee and Jarzabkowski (2011) – and our empirical research.

There are five more sections to this chapter. In the next section, we review the literature to understand what is revealed about the ex ante and ex post alignment of strategic planning and budgeting, and what is missing. This section also specifies the research question. The following section describes the research setting and our method for answering our research question. The subsequent section presents and discusses the findings from the empirical research that augments the literature. Next, a conceptual framework is proposed for an integrated strategic planning and budgeting process which indicates how ex ante and ex post practices/mechanisms align strategic planning and budgeting.

LITERATURE REVIEW

The accounting academic literature recommends that firms align their strategic plans and budgets to improve performance (Abernethy & Brownell, 1999; Becker et al., 2016; Blumentritt, 2006; Erhart et al., 2017; Grant, 2003; Kannan-Narasimhan & Lawrence, 2018; Peters et al., 2019; Spee & Jarzabkowski, 2011). When firms fail to maintain alignment between strategic plans and budgets, there is the risk of losing touch with the marketplace, failing to make necessary strategic changes, or developing financially unsound strategies (Blumentritt, 2006). To avoid these potentially adverse effects, it is important to understand how firms achieve this alignment. A review of selected literature on strategic planning and budgeting was conducted to identify practices/mechanisms used by firms to achieve and maintain alignment between strategic plans and budgets both before (ex ante) and after (ex post) the beginning of the fiscal year.

Practices/Mechanisms for Ex Ante Alignment

Many firms operate annual, sequential strategy, strategic planning, and budgeting processes. In this rational approach, corporate strategies and strategic plans are typically developed first then used to guide the subsequent, bottom-up development of budgets. Strategic plans and budgets are reviewed, sometimes revised, then approved by the board of directors. This description is typical of the processes observed in major oil companies (Grant, 2003). The practices/mechanisms used in this approach to ensure strategic plans and budgets are aligned at the start of the fiscal year (ex ante) include using strategic plans to guide budget preparation and the review and approval of strategic plans and budgets by the board.

Since the 2008 financial crisis, European firms are increasingly focused on ensuring the ex ante alignment of strategic plans and budgets (Becker et al., 2016). Accordingly, it would be helpful to identify further practices/mechanisms that help achieve this alignment.

The literature indicates that during the annual strategic planning and budgeting cycle, budgets can influence the development of strategic plans, in addition to their use for implementing such plans (Erhart et al., 2017). More specifically, "controllers can actively shape strategy formation in their organizations" (Erhart et al., 2017, p. 48). Similarly, Erhart et al. (2017, p. 36) reported the bidirectional influence of budgets with strategic plans. Certainly, budgetary input to strategic planning can help ensure the plans are financially viable. What is not fully explained in the literature are the specific practices/mechanisms that firms use to create ex ante alignment.

Practices/Mechanisms for Ex Post Alignment

Firms must maintain alignment between their strategic plans and budgets, i.e., they must have practices/mechanisms for reviewing and challenging existing budgetary allocations (Blumentritt, 2006). Yet the literature provides few examples of specific practices/mechanisms to maintain alignment between strategic plans and budgets. Grant (2003) investigated major oil companies and found that higher levels of environmental turbulence increased the uncertainty of strategic plans necessitating in-year changes to budgets through "coordination and performance managing." The practices/mechanisms involved in performance managing are not explicitly discussed, thus it remains unclear how these firms (re)aligned strategic plans with budgets as they responded to unexpected oil price fluctuations.

Budgets can motivate changes to strategic plans during the fiscal year. Abernethy and Brownell (1999) examined the impact of the budget style, i.e., interactive or diagnostic (Simons, 1995) and strategic change (i.e., low or high) on performance in large Australian hospitals. More specifically, they hypothesized that "the contemporaneous relationship between the level of strategic change under way and organizational performance will be enhanced when budgets are used interactively" and "where an organization is undergoing little or no strategic change, we expect diagnostic use of budgeting to continue to show performance-enhancing effects" (Abernethy & Brownell, 1999, pp. 191–192). The authors found that an interactive budget style supported ex post (re)alignment necessitated by changes to strategies, i.e., "top management use budgeting in an interactive mode ... [to] ... better serve the needs for learning and adaptation required when strategic change is underway."

Managers are known to adjust strategic plans and budgets during the year. Frow, Marginson, and Ogden (2005) considered how managers in one multinational firm balanced the need to achieve predetermined financial targets with the need to pursue strategic initiatives. Managers in the subject company were expected to commit to the firm's strategic priority of meeting deadlines for new product launches irrespective of budget variances; budgets could not be used as an excuse to miss pre-arranged deadlines. Accordingly, managers might "within their overall budget ... decide to reallocate resources between programmes funded by that budget, with products closest to launch taking priority" (Frow et al., 2005, p. 279). Managers relied on informal face-to-face discussions, reinforced and facilitated by formal control procedures, to build co-operation with other managers to achieve the firm's strategic priorities. Additional details of the specific practices/mechanisms for maintaining alignment between budgets and strategic plans were not provided.

Further evidence of how firms make changes to strategic plans and budgets throughout the year is provided by Kannan-Narasimhan and Lawrence (2018). The authors investigated how changing or reframing strategic plans and resources facilitated successful innovation. They found that how resources are (re-)framed (i.e., how the "story" is told), rather than total available resources, influences the success of strategic innovation. While this study confirms there can be ongoing changes to strategic plans and budgets during the year, once again it is unclear as to what specific practices/mechanisms were used to maintain ex post alignment.

Forecasts appear to be intimately related to strategic planning and budgeting and may be key practices/mechanisms for maintaining ex post alignment of budgets and strategic plans. Peters et al. (2019) argue that budgeting, forecasting, and results-reporting routines operate as a single interactive profit planning systems (PPSs) and can be integrated through shared learning processes. Additionally, the authors indicate that budgeting systems are typically used alongside forecasting systems during a budget year. Accordingly, we considered the relevant literature on forecasting to identify how this process contributes to the alignment of strategic plans and budgets.

Hennttu-Ano (2018, p. 331) suggests there are two types of (rolling) forecasts. The first is when a month or quarter is added to the budget each time a month or quarter ends, thus maintaining a consistent, say 12 month, budget horizon. The second is when the remaining months or quarters of the original budget horizon are recast (Merchant & Van der Stede, 2007). Hennttu-Ano (2018, p. 352) found most sampled firms developed forecasts for the remainder of the fiscal year and used the forecasts in conjunction with the original budget which was retained as a "frozen forecast ... from which targets were set."

Frow et al. (2010, p. 456) discussed "continuous budgeting[3]" which they viewed as a practice/mechanism enabling managers to maintain alignment between strategic priorities and budgets. Continuous budgets, like forecasts, indicate whether current strategic plans are likely to deliver the performance targets set in original budgets or whether they need to be modified. Through continuous budgets, managers "constantly engaged in reviewing what was happening to their performance" and "look[ed] at different ways of achieving ... targets" (Frow et al., 2010, p. 457). Frow et al. (2010) found that continuous budgeting supported the broader "processes of strategic implementation rather than the more-narrow focus of simply ensuring pre-set budgetary targets are actually achieved" (p. 460).

Jordan and Messner (2020) examined the use of rolling forecasts in one large European firm. They noted that at the beginning of the year the annual operating plan (AOP),[4] i.e., budget, and rolling demand forecast are aligned but as the year progressed the figures diverged:

> the [Distributor Annual Operating Plan] DAOP is a document that has got a list, key strategic initiatives that the distributor is going to take for the following year, but it has got also a plan, in terms of how many units for every [product] model they are targeting to sell for the following year. So, there is a moment in time in which this plan should be consistent with the forecast ... Then as we move forward, the target remains fixed, but the forecast, the demand plan every month can change. (Jordan & Messner, 2020, p. 352)

The authors do not extend their discussion to explain how the divergence between forecast and budget figures is addressed, or how the budget figures are (re)aligned with the strategic plan.

It is clear from the reviewed literature that firms, especially those operating in turbulent conditions, work to align their strategic plans and budgets at the start of the fiscal year (ex ante) and to maintain this alignment during the fiscal year (ex post). Common methods for ex ante alignment include using strategic plans to guide budgets and having review and approval processes for strategic plans and budgets. The practices/mechanisms used for ex post alignment are less clear but likely to involve some form of forecasts. Our study addresses the shortcoming in the theoretical understanding of the practices/mechanisms involved in integrating and aligning strategic planning and budgeting by asking the following research question:

RQ. **How do firms achieve alignment between strategic plans and budgets, both ex ante and ex post?**

RESEARCH APPROACH

The processes of strategic planning and budgeting consist of multiple practices/ mechanisms. Arguably one would expect some practices/mechanisms that align one with the other. This understanding is not presented in the literature. While employees in firms may understand how strategic planning and budgeting are aligned, there is insufficient detail in the literature for us to develop a survey to identify how the practices/mechanisms are used by actual firms.

To understand strategic planning and budgeting sufficiently to answer our research question, we need a methodology that puts us in contact with management accountants involved with the processes of strategic planning and budgeting. A qualitative, multi-case methodology is appropriate for our exploratory research (Eisenhardt, 1989; Eisenhardt, & Graebner, 2007; Keating, 1995; Northcott & Doolin, 2008; Vaivio, 2008) because:

> [C]ross-sectional field studies can deepen our insights into the constructs and relations commonly studied empirically. Compared with studying management accounting phenomena in individual cases, cross-sectional field studies can broaden our understanding by detecting cross-case patterns in specific issues that are otherwise embedded in detailed case write-ups. (Lillis & Mundy, 2005, p. 122)

Additionally,

> Multiple cases enable comparisons that clarify whether an emergent finding is simply idiosyncratic to a single case or consistently replicated by several cases (Eisenhardt, 1991). Multiple cases also create more robust theory because the propositions are more deeply grounded in varied empirical evidence. Constructs and relationships are more precisely delineated because it is easier to determine accurate definitions and appropriate levels of construct abstraction from multiple cases. (Eisenhardt et al., 2007, p. 27)

The interview protocol utilized open-ended questions to allow us to follow up on emerging lines of inquiry to help build a more detailed understanding of strategic planning and budgeting (Eisenhardt, 1989; Eisenhardt et al., 2007).

Our sample included a cross-section of firms that were large, profitable, stock-market-listed, and – for cost-control reasons in conducting the research – with head offices in the Toronto area of Canada. Firms included in the sample were expected to have formal processes for strategic planning and budgeting. See Table 1 for the demographic details of our firm sample.

We elected to conduct interviews with management accountants. We recognize that operational managers are responsible for implementing strategic plans and budgets. However, it is the firms' chief financial officers (CFOs) with the assistance of their management accounting subordinates who tend to provide staff support to strategic planning and budgeting processes. The management accounting subordinates would be able to provide knowledgeable responses to our interview questions. According to a respondent from one of our sampled firms (2),[5] "the general manager ultimately is accountable for the numbers, and the finance people are there to help her/him put the budget together."

We mailed letters to CFOs at 55 selected firms to explain our research and to ask for a 60-minute meeting with management accountants involved in the firms' strategic planning and budgeting processes. For some firms, the interviewee was involved with both strategic planning and budgeting while in others there were two interviewees – one from strategic planning and the other from budgeting. After sending the letters, those CFOs[6] were subsequently asked by telephone to

Table 1. Descriptive Statistics for the Sample.

	Population of Interest	Non-responding Firms	Sample of Responding Firms
Number	55[b]	35	20
			36% response rate
Sales Range[a] (in millions)	$200 – 46,635	$200 – 46,635	$200 – 19,015
Sales Mean[a] (in millions)	$6,132	$7,806	$3,201
Sales Median[a] (in millions)	$1,152	$1,365	$747
Standard Deviation[a] (in millions)	$11,343	$13,431	$5,353

Notes: Responding firms were on average smaller in terms of sales than non-responding firms.
[a]Canadian dollars.
[b]Nine firms were eliminated from the population of interest because: (1) firm ceased operations – one firm; (2) firm did not have its head office in Canada – one firm; and (3) we were unable to contact the CFO – seven firms.

provide contact details for their strategic planning and budgeting management accountants, who would be invited to participate. As a result, within 3 months, we were able to schedule interviews with 20 firms (36% of the total number of firms that were contacted). Our requests stopped when the number of scheduled firms reached 20, which was considered a reasonable response rate. Table 2 provides respondent attributes. The industries covered differ significantly in terms of their main activities and underlying technologies.

At the start of each interview, all prospective respondents were asked to read and sign an informed consent form to ensure they understood the project and interview protocols. All respondents signed, making explicit their agreement to participate. Data were collected with semi-structured interview questions administered to 28 respondents representing 20 firms. Respondents were specifically asked, based on their personal experiences, to describe their understanding of strategic planning and budgeting, and how they were aligned. Based on their formal positions, the respondents were knowledgeable, and thus likely to be limited in biases (Eisenhardt et al., 2007, p. 28). The questions used to guide the interviews are listed in the Appendix. All interviews were audio recorded, transcribed by the same research assistant, and returned to the appropriate respondents for verification. None of the respondents from the 20 firms requested changes to the respective transcripts suggesting the collected data were reliable.

An open coding approach was used to analyze the transcriptions. Interview data presented in the transcriptions were repeatedly reviewed to identify specific practices/mechanisms relating to the strategic planning and budgeting processes. The initial analysis revealed that forecasting practices/mechanisms were tightly linked to the strategic planning and budgeting processes. Practices/mechanisms were arranged into groups to reflect those used to align strategic plans and budgets before (ex ante) and during (ex post) the fiscal year. The resulting groupings synthesized our understanding of how practices/mechanisms were used to align strategic plans and budgets on a continuous basis.

To develop confidence in our interpretation of the evidence, transcriptions were independently analyzed by both authors, and their analyses were compared

Table 2. Profile of Respondents.

Industry	Firms	Interviewees	
		Male	Female
Manufacturing and Processing	7	4	4
Mining	3	5	1
Financial	2	2	1
Property	2	1	1
Services	2	3	1
Entertainment	1	0	1
Pharmaceutical	1	2	0
Retail	1	1	0
Telecommunications	1	1	0
Total	**20**	**19**	**9**

and reconciled. These interactions between co-authors occurred during all stages of data analysis and writing.

FINDINGS

This section will discuss the evidence in five parts: the first and second describe the strategic planning and budgeting processes, respectively. The third and fourth discuss the practices/mechanisms used for, respectively, ex ante and ex post alignment of strategic planning and budgeting. The last part discusses insights from cross-case analyses.

Strategic Planning

All firms had a top-down strategy that they translated into financial expectations in the form of a yearly income statement and a balance sheet for the next three or five years. This process involved refreshing the existing strategy and updating and extending the prior year's strategic plans. There was diversity among the strategic planning activities described by respondents. However, the one common feature was the involvement of one or more members of senior management, such as the chief executive officer (CEO), chief operating officer (COO), CFO, and senior vice presidents in strategy-related processes. Most but not all firms had the board formally approve the strategy and then the strategic plan. In addition, a few firms tried to involve more employees by soliciting their ideas for strategic initiatives. A respondent from one of these participatory firms stated:

> Every department is involved. We have strategic planning even if we are an accounting team... anybody, you can be working on the frontlines – anyone can put forth suggestions ... whatever you think. These ... questions go to the strategic planning team. (7)[7]

The level of detail in strategic planning varied. At the least detailed end of the spectrum, there might be simple guidance in the form of a targeted growth rate for the coming years (20, 16), a prioritization of strategic initiatives suggested by business units (15, 11), or broad strategic points to be fleshed out in strategic plans developed by operational units (3). Alternately, an example of a more detailed strategy and strategic plan is provided by a retailer:

> We have a template that we give each of the business units to fill out ... There is a strategic plan with a set of strategic initiatives which are grouped into strategic imperatives. There are three or four imperatives, they have their focus areas for their business, and a set of probably 10-15 initiatives. Each of those initiatives should have operating metrics against them, and also financial metrics including capital and earnings targets. (5)

Budgeting

Firms prepare annual bottom-up budgets. According to the respondent for one firm (4), budgets were distinguished from strategic plans based on Microsoft tools, "the strategic plan is essentially a PowerPoint document, while the budget is an Excel document." In other words, budgets contained more detail than strategic plans. For all sampled firms, the annual budget was developed within the context of the strategy and the related strategic plan. The budget was a detailed document, typically for the next fiscal year, although some firms prepared two-year budgets (12, 14, 20); if there was a second year, it was done with less detail and less commitment. Three firms converted the first year of the strategic plan into their budget (2, 5, 19) merely by inserting additional detail.

Budget participants for all firms can be classified into two categories. One comprised the budget owner – i.e., operating or line manager – responsible for financial targets. This group included CEOs, COOs, senior vice presidents, vice presidents, and a range of managers including general, group, divisional, and unit. The second category, generally management accountants, provided support during budgeting such as providing timeframes, templates, reviews of drafts, and consolidations.

Some firms relied mainly on the management accounting team to provide this support while others establish specialist budget preparation and analysis support. This range of roles included for example, controllers (3, 11), finance teams (4, 19), financial planning and analysis (FP&A) specialists (5, 8), and corporate budget teams (8, 7). The resulting budgets had realistic but demanding performance targets, which accommodated strategic initiatives and met or exceeded the first year of the three- or five-year strategic plan. Balancing top-down strategic plans with bottom-up budgets was a consistent challenge according to our respondents. For example, respondents from 12 firms mentioned, without prompting, that market expectations influenced budget targets, and respondents from 17 firms noted that developing realistic budget targets was crucial because manager and employee bonuses and incentives depended on their achievement. In this regard, one respondent remarked:

> If you end up with an unrealistic budget and you do not get a bonus payout that does not sit very well with people. As a result, [you get] a lot of turnover. (17)

Respondents revealed that budgeting can take anywhere from two (15) or more and typically four (11, 10) to six (20) months prior to the start of the fiscal year. During this period, tentative versions of the budgets are subject to comprehensive and rigorous scrutiny and revision. Feedback at any review stage leads to budget revisions (13). This feedback involves multiple management levels and numerous stakeholders operating at different organizational levels before ultimate presentation to the board, generally by the CEO and/or the CFO, for a final review and approval. We found budgeting to be highly interactive, as described by Frow, Marginson and Ogden (2010). Consider, for example, the feedback review conducted by a property management firm:

> It starts at the district level where you have the district manager and controller. They work from the bottom-up perspective, starting from expenses, line-by-line. They forecast for all of next year. That gets reviewed at the division level, and then from division level it gets reviewed at a regional level, and then to corporate. All that happens in a short period of time, probably a month. (16)

The approved budget was generally in effect from the first day of the new fiscal year, which meant budgets were approved before the current year's final financial results were known. All firms in our sample relied on forecast figures for current year permanent accounts when preparing their budgets for the next fiscal year. As the annual financial results became known, the firms refined the starting numbers for their new fiscal-year budgets.

Practices/Mechanisms for ex ante Alignment

The sampled firms use a variety of practices/mechanisms to align, ex ante, strategic planning, and budgeting. Accordingly, prior to the start of the new budget year, strategic planning and budgeting are aligned through back-and-forth reviews of budgets as they go from the lowest responsibility centers to the highest and ultimately to the board. Although there was some variation in the alignment of the first year of the strategic plan with the budget, the most common approach was the stringent reviews undertaken by occupants of various organizational levels before approval by the board. These reviews enabled discrepancies or inconsistencies to be identified and resolved. An example from one firm is described as:

> We typically start with some high-level planning where we focus on what we need to do from a growth perspective, how we would achieve that and how that all fits with our overall strategy. ... Each of our divisions is required to submit a plan for the year ... Then we do an initial review of these plans ... We generally take a first look and assess does it make sense? and does it line up with what we said we need to do at the corporate level? There are many discussions back and forth, meetings and presentations of the plans. Once that is finished and the high-level numbers are approved by the Board, then the plans are converted into detailed budgets. (4)

Our respondents' evidence revealed widespread awareness that the budget needs to align with the first year of the strategic plan. For example, a respondent from a firm operating in the property management industry explained:

> The planning influences the budgeting. If I say that I am going to have an initiative, to have a new program ... it should have a budget and be taken into account because we are going to have to spend money – on marketing or whatever. (7)

Similarly, a respondent from a manufacturing firm acknowledged:

> If your plan is to grow by X, or if your plan is to be in a certain market, then your budget assumptions have to reflect what that means. For example, if you are planning to [open in] India next year, you are going to have a capital expense, you are going to have to hire people, you are going to have some kind of an idea of how much sales [you will have]. Your budget has to reflect those assumptions, otherwise there will be a big disconnect. (2)

Finally, note the explanation from a respondent in a services firm:

> We usually have an off-site ... where ideas are discussed, and then they are ranked within the leadership team. Those are the ones we're going to strategically plan for the remainder of the current year and the following year which will be backed into the budget. (15)

We found the main practice/mechanism for eliminating gaps between strategic plans and budgets to be interactive and iterative budget reviews. Our findings, although for budgets, mimic the findings of Spee and Jarzabkowski (2011), who reported strategic plans are developed through "talk and text"; here we see budgets are also developed through "talk and text." This interaction occurred with all sampled firms as a series of reviews and revisions as the budgets move from the lowest responsibility levels to the board through consolidations and approvals. For example, respondents from a manufacturing firm (13) reported it was not uncommon to revise the budget numerous times as new, better, or different information became available and that the alignment of strategic plans and budgets happened through these reviews both before and after the budget got finalized and approved by the board. Reviews enable individuals with pertinent information to scrutinize and challenge budget figures so that the final budget is realistic and can be met or exceeded during the first year of the strategic plan; the intention is to stretch performance. While respondents from a range of firms (e.g., 13, 17, 18) indicated there is a healthy back-and-forth to set the budget, disaster would strike if executive management or the board set performance expectations which could not be accomplished by those with budget accountability.

An additional practice/mechanism for aligning strategic plans and budgets was demonstrated by a human resources consulting firm. The planning and budgeting staff groups worked closely together from the beginning of both processes to create constant alignment and thus shorten the time required to complete the strategic plans and budgets. According to a respondent from this firm:

> at the beginning part of the process, the [planning] and the finance business partners were working together. The front-end of the whole process is where they said, "okay these are the initiatives that we are going to do." Then we do not have to go through any of those reiterations in the later months when it is crunch time. The time is too precious to be going back and forth. (15)

This firm also adopted an additional practice/mechanism. To further avoid delays inherent with an iterative review process, the firm co-located the workspaces of planning support and budgeting support for them to work together from the start of each process. More specifically, when the senior leadership team identified strategic initiatives and assigned them to specific lines of business, the

> strategy individuals will talk to the finance business partners for each of those specific line of business to make sure that those initiatives are backed into their budget planning system ... so then we do not have to go through any of those reiterations in the later months. (15)

A retail firm (5) used a similar practice/mechanism. The strategy was simultaneously translated into a strategic plan and a budget. The top-down and bottom-up occurred simultaneously. The annual budgeting exercises began after the board approved the three-year strategic plan. Then, FP&A teams worked with business units to translate the first year of the three-year strategic plan into a budget for the next fiscal year.

Mining firms had rigorous practices/mechanisms to ensure the alignment of the strategic plans and budgets (1, 10, 12). Their strategic plans, based on technical estimates of ore reserves, were called "life of mine plans" or something similar. Once approved, annual production plans were derived from the first year of the life-of-mine plan. Production plans determined the volumes and site mining activities and reflected market demand and prices as well as strategic factors. Annual budgets were created by overlaying financial models onto the production plans thus creating alignment between strategic plans and budgets. This was described by a respondent from one of the three mining firms as:

> We work jointly with the business strategy group in both developing the life of mine – which is our ... plan – and whittling it down to the one-year outlook – which is our budget. (1)

Another practice/mechanism assisting with the alignment of strategic planning and budgeting was having these two groups report to the same manager or vice-president. Often the CFO had responsibility for both strategic planning and budgeting. Some firms suggested their strategic planning and budgeting processes were highly integrated and therefore no additional alignment was needed. For example, respondents from a manufacturing firm (9) claimed their strategic planning and budgeting were integrated and aligned by having the same employees involved in both strategic planning and budgeting. Similarly, respondents from another manufacturer stated, "the way that we do our budgeting and strategic planning is that they are integrated" (4).

Practices/Mechanisms for ex post Alignment

Our sample of firms used various practices/mechanisms to realign budgets with strategic plans when strategy changes were required during the year. Our firms tended to introduce remedial activities when actual results for the year to date were below the planned level, and when expected results for the remainder of the year fell short of the original budget. Thus, firms used regular reviews of actual performance to budget not simply to explain why a gap existed, but also to instigate broader discussions of strategy, strategic plans, and budgets. The forecasts were key practices/mechanisms for re-examining whether prevailing problematic conditions necessitated changes to the existing strategy/strategic plan or merely tactical adjustments. The following quotes illustrate the discussions prompted by the monthly/quarterly variance analyses and diagnostic control processes (Simons, 1995) at our sample of firms:

> Within the year ... we will run a [monthly] forecast mainly for the current quarter and the next quarter... the focus is then ... where are we, what do we need to do to hit our numbers, are we good or bad on revenue, are we good or bad on profitability, and what are the different actions we need to take? (18)

> On a monthly basis we go through everything to see where we are. We look at our forecast, that is our moving EBITDA target, but also come back to planning all the time. We say 'here are our initial strategic goals, what is holding us up from moving forward?' or 'has the landscape changed that we need to change our strategic plan? (8)

> [M]onthly we have a future revenue meeting...We know we want to grow at least 10% per year... if anyone is falling short, as a leadership team we will recognize that someone will have a problem ... they are not going to hit their target. So, we need to over-deliver in another team or we need to create a new brand, buy a new license, make a new acquisition or find another solution to make sure that we are closing that gap. (19)

Our respondents told us that shortfalls revealed by the variance analysis were quickly addressed. While some respondents stated that strategy and/or strategic plans could not be changed in the short term (7, 8), others suggested this could be done (19). One mining firm (1) used its life of mine plan to anticipate when production was going to drop and filled the gap by bringing sufficiently material projects (i.e., known deposits) into production. Maintaining an inventory of ready-to-go projects was essential for this flexibility.

Other respondents revealed various approaches to ex post alignment of strategic plans and budgets in conjunction with variance analysis. The air cargo firm sought to distinguish the impact that different factors had on the gap between strategic plans and budgets, namely:

> we basically segregate what are one-time variances and what are permanent variances... we know that we have a variance from the budget [but is it] a permanent change... like a new customer is added or new capacity is added? (6)

The evidence also revealed the reciprocal influence that budgeting has on strategic planning. The insurance firm in our sample prepared budgets for a two-year period. During strategic planning, the first year of the five-year strategic plan was ex ante aligned against the second year of the most recent or current budget in a process referred to as "aligning back" meaning to compare back to a previous version of the budget. The practice/mechanism was described in this way:

> In December we will have our [budget] for [next year] and [the year after]. When we get to the spring of [the first year] and we are now starting [strategic planning] again. One of the steps is to align back and say 'how could the [next year] numbers change from the [budget] numbers you just handed me'... we spend a lot of time aligning back – [asking] what changed and why is that number no longer valid? (20)

Similarly, a respondent from the pharmaceutical firm referred to the role of forecasts in adjusting future strategic planning, i.e.,

> The forecast is driven mainly by volume and pricing... all the data feed up to [the forecasting team] so they can say "wow, we thought in this past quarter we were going to sell 10,000 units but it was 8,000," and how does that impact what we are going to push into our 12-month and ultimately our long-term plan ... We need to get that forecasting piece right so we can plan accordingly. (9)

Our findings reveal that ex post aligning of strategic plans/budgets with actual performance during the fiscal year involves complex and on-going actions prompted by multiple feedback loops as shown in Fig. 1. Ex ante alignment begins with the annual budget exercise and continues as ex post alignment during the year with variance analysis and forecasting. These actions ensure that strategic plans/budgets support the *intended* strategy; the variance analysis and forecasting further foster *emerging* strategies by encouraging creative thinking to identify new initiatives for achieving budget targets in the accomplishment of (*realized*) strategy. Our findings support the reframing anticipated by Kannan-Narasimhan and Lawrence (2018) on fiscal year ex post alignment of strategic planning and budgeting. These findings also provide evidence of intra-year reframing of strategies and resource allocations to ensure the original budget is accomplished.

Our evidence also supports only the second of Hennttu-Ano (2018) types of forecasting namely the production of forecasts for the remaining months

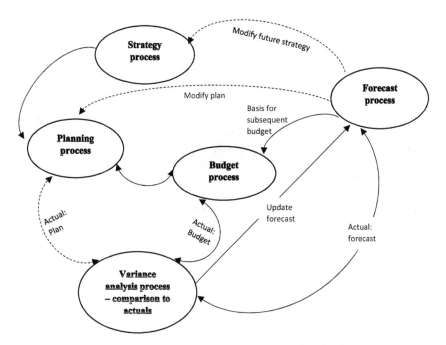

Fig. 1. Reconciling Strategic Planning and Budgeting.

or quarters of the original budget period. Rolling forecasts, involving adding a month or quarter each time a month or quarter ended, were done infrequently but not in conjunction with ex post alignment.

Cross-Case Patterns

The evidence of how strategic plans and budgets are aligned enabled us to develop additional and unexpected understandings of strategic planning and budgeting. This led to the identification of two cross-case patterns. The first is the frequent use of drivers for strategic planning and budgeting. The second pattern is the uniformity of practices/mechanisms used by firms to coordinate strategic planning and budgeting. Both patterns are shown in Table 3. Each will be discussed in the paragraphs below.

There was a variety of drivers underpinning the development of strategic plans and budgets. The most common driver was sales. The use of sales as a driver is problematic because of the confounding effects of inflation and product mix. Numerous firms attempted to improve the quality of their drivers. For example, some firms incorporated multiple drivers when developing their strategic plans and budgets. A parts manufacturer recognized that each of its 47 plants produced parts for established multi-year contracts. Growth came from new parts contracts with existing or new customers. In recognition of the source of growth, the firm used a research and development division to design new parts. Newly designed parts ready for production were awarded to existing plants on a competitive basis. Accordingly, the strategic plan and budgets for individual plants reflected estimates associated with the runoff of existing contracts as well as the introduction of new parts contracts. Strategic plans were developed around parts, the number of different parts, and the quantities of different parts.

The variety of drivers underpinning strategic plans and budgets was an unexpected cross-case pattern. Based on frequent references, it was apparent that our respondents were highly aware of their main performance drivers, e.g., mining firms (1, 10, 12) identified the number of tons of ore and the yield of precious metals from that ore; parts manufacturers (2, 4, 13) tracked contracts/orders; and property managers (14) managed with the number of buildings or units. The respondent at the telephone firm enviously noted that "all the driver-based or activity-based modelling that we do is at a much more granular level" (18).

As discussed, the mining firms (1, 10, 12) modeled their operational and financial from mining ore in the ground through to the financial parts of strategic plans and budgets. Similarly, the pharmaceutical firm modeled at a granular level all operational, marketing, and financial activities for each drug to generate strategic plans, budgets, and forecasts (9). Automobile parts manufacturers did "a full model of the entire product for its life cycle or however long they want it quoted for" (13). The property management firm had multi-year lease agreements with renters. The property leases were for various specified terms, but all were explained as expected flows of revenue with finite termination dates (14). The waste management firm and the telephone firm modeled their underlying operations to transparently show how inputs become outputs (16, 18).

A respondent from the retail firm lamented, "I would like to get a system where we have more of a driver-based model because that would allow us to do scenario planning a lot easier" (5). When granular drivers were not used, there was recognition of the missed advantages.

The second cross-case pattern is the comparable approaches used by our firms to coordinate strategic plans and budgets for the upcoming fiscal year. Table 3 specifies by firm the executive responsible for coordinating strategic planning and budgeting. The coordinating position was nearly always the CFO (17 out of 20). In the other three firms, another senior executive was responsible for coordination. In the 17 firms where the CFO was responsible for coordination, 6 had joint responsibility with the CEO.

The board had final approval and responsibility for strategic plans and budgets. The CFOs and other senior executives were supported in their coordinating responsibilities by operational and line managers, in addition to management accountants.

As we interviewed respondents from the sampled firms, we noticed that some indicated the use of a BSC for measuring performance. However, none of the firms used the BSC to align strategic planning and budgeting, contrary to the suggestions made by Kaplan and Norton (2001a, 2001b) that it could be used for this purpose. Moreover, none of the firms were practitioners of beyond budgeting (Hope & Fraser, 2003) in keeping with reported findings about the extent of beyond budgeting use in practice (Libby & Lindsay, 2010).

Table 3. Variations Among Firms Regarding Drivers and Coordination.

Mining firm (1)	Driver: ore processed Strategic planning and budgeting coordination: Board of directors supported by (1) CFO and (2) operating and engineering executives
Parts manufacturer (2)	Driver: sales Strategic planning and budgeting coordination: Board of directors supported by (1) CFO and president and (2) plant general managers
Winery (3)	Driver: sales Strategic planning and budgeting coordination: Board of directors supported by (1) CFO and (2) operating vice-presidents
Automation equipment (4):	Driver: sales Strategic planning and budgeting coordination: Board of directors supported by (1) CFO and (2) divisional general managers
Retailer (5):	Driver: sales Strategic planning and budgeting coordination: Board of directors supported by (1) CFO and (2) business unit executives
Air cargo operator (6):	Driver: sales Strategic planning and budgeting coordination: Board of directors supported by (1) senior planning managers (CEO, COO, CFO, marketing head) and (2) operational budget executives
Retiree housing operator (7):	Drivers: predictable lease revenues and capital expenditures Strategic planning and budgeting coordination: Board of directors supported by (1) CFO and (2) executives from operating groups and administrative departments
Movie theater operator (8):	Driver: attendance Strategic planning and budgeting coordination: Board of directors supported by (1) senior vice-president corporate development and (2) strategic business unit executives
Pharmaceutical (9):	Driver: products (drugs) Strategic planning and budgeting coordination: Board of directors supported by (1) CEO and CFO and (2) suppliers (all manufacturing, transportation, storage, marketing, etc. functions are contracted out)
Another mining firm (10):	Driver: ore body Strategic planning and budgeting coordination: Board of directors supported by (1) CFO and (2) operational and administrative executives
Power equipment (11):	Driver: existing and new products Strategic planning and budgeting coordination: Board of directors supported by (1) CEO, CFO and (2) department executives
Third mining company (12):	Driver: ore body Strategic planning and budgeting coordination: Board of directors supported by (1) CFO, technical committee and (2) business unit (mine) executives
Another parts manufacturer (13)	Driver: contracts for manufacture parts Strategic planning and budgeting coordination: Board of directors supported by (1) CFO and (2) business unit executives

(*Continued*)

Table 3.   (*Continued*)

Property manager (14):	Driver: returns on existing property plus net growth
	Strategic planning and budgeting coordination: Board of directors supported by (1) CFO, CEO and (2) budgeting executives
Human resource consulting (15)	Driver: sales plus initiatives
	Strategic planning and budgeting coordination: Board of directors supported by (1) CFO, executive vice-president (strategy) and (2) line-of-business executives
Waste disposal (16):	Driver: sales
	Strategic planning and budgeting coordination: Board of directors supported by (1) CEO, CFO and (2) regional executives
Packaging manufacturer (17):	Driver: sales from existing contracts plus new contracts
	Strategic planning and budgeting coordination: Board of directors supported by (1) senior executives and (2) operating executives
Telephone firm (18):	Driver: sales from existing products plus sales from new products
	Strategic planning and budgeting coordination: Board of directors supported by (1) CEO, CFO and (2) operating executives
Toy maker (19):	Driver: sales by product plus sales from new products
	Strategic planning and budgeting coordination: Board of directors supported by (1) vice-president financial planning and analysis and (2) global business unit executives
Life insurance (20):	Driver: sales
	Strategic planning and budgeting coordination: Board of directors supported by (1) CFO and (2) operating executives

The empirical evidence is clear that strategic planning and budgeting are interconnected; Fig. 1 summarizes the findings from our analysis highlighting the feedforward and feedback loops that provide multiple connection points. Strategic planning and budgeting can be described as a richly interactive nexus of information exchanges involving positive and negative feedback and feedforward information (Hoverstadt, Kendrick, & Morlidge, 2007).

This finding contrasts with Bedford's (2020) discussion of packages and systems in which strategic planning and budgeting were initially considered to have little or moderate interdependence. Our evidence from this empirical research strongly suggests that there is extensive interdependence between strategic planning and budgeting. The observed relationships suggest they can be better described as parts of one process rather than two. Many of the same employees are involved with both processes, strategic planning and budgeting are bi-directional each feeding into the other, the board approves each, the CEO and/or the CFO directs both, and each implements strategy. Some examples of interdependence were co-locating strategic planning and budgeting management accountants, assigning the same management accountants to both strategic planning and budgeting, and having the same executive management approve both strategic plans and budgets to ensure strategic priorities are resourced.

CONCEPTUAL FRAMEWORK FOR INTEGRATING STRATEGIC PLANNING AND BUDGETING

Our findings reveal practices/mechanisms used by firms to align strategic planning and budgeting as suggested in Fig. 1. These practices/mechanisms are closely interlinked and operate throughout the year to maintain alignment between strategic plans and budgets irrespective of the operating conditions that arise during the year. The extensive information flows between strategic planning and budgeting indicate they can be viewed as subcomponents of a single process rather than as separate processes as suggested by the literature. Table 4 depicts this single, integrated strategic planning, and budgeting process.

The conceptual model in Table 4 is based on relevant literature and tied together and augmented according to our empirical findings by practices/mechanisms. The relevant literature drawn upon for this conceptual framework can be succinctly described as: Abernethy and Brownell (1999), who found that an interactive budget style supported ex post (re)alignment necessitated by changes to strategies; Becker et al. (2016), who observed that European firms are cautiously placing more importance on ensuring strategic plans and budgets are aligned ex ante since the 2008 financial crisis; Blumentritt (2006), who argued that firms must maintain alignment between their strategic plans and budgets; Erhart et al. (2017), who found that "controllers can actively shape strategy formation in their organizations" and strategic plans and budgets are bidirectionally related; Grant (2003), who found that higher levels of environmental turbulence necessitated in-year changes to budgets; Kannan-Narasimhan and Lawrence (2018), who observed that what is important for strategic innovation is how resources are (re-) framed rather than total available resources; Peters et al. (2019), who argued that budgeting, forecasting, and results-reporting routines operate as a single interactive PPSs; and Spee and Jarzabkowski (2011), who reported strategic plans are developed through "talk and text."

Our conceptual framework indicates how strategic plans and budgets are aligned prior to the new fiscal year (ex ante), throughout the fiscal year (ex post), and between fiscal years. In brief, the five integrated, interactive, and iterative subprocesses comprising the framework shown in Table 4, are:

a. Strategizing: A firm's intended strategy is established before the start of the fiscal year under the leadership of the CEO and approved by the board.
b. Strategic planning: The intended strategy is implemented by the CFO/CEO with the help of management accountants through three- or five-year strategic plans. The top-down strategic plan would have been approved by the board.
c. Budgeting: Before the start of the fiscal year, the responsibility-center managers develop their bottom-up budgets with staff support from the CFO and management accountants. The strategic plan and the consolidated budget are aligned ex ante through interactive discussions that could produce changes to originally proposed strategic plans and budgets. Relatedly, the strategy may need to be changed. The consolidated budget is approved by the CEO and the board prior to the beginning of the new fiscal year. The budgeted figures must meet or exceed those contained in the first year of the strategic plan.

Table 4. Integrated Strategic Planning and Budgeting Conceptual Framework.

Subprocesses:	Strategizing	Strategic Planning	Budgeting	Intra-Year Reviewing (e.g., Variance Analysis and Forecasts)	Estimating Opening Balances for Permanent Accounts
Type of strategy	Intended strategy			Emergent strategy	Realized strategy
Time period	$t-1$	$t-1$	$t-1$	t	$t+1$
Responsibility	Board, CEO	CEO, CFO	CFO, management accountants	Management accountants, CFO	Management accountants, CFO
Approval	Board	Board, CEO	Board, CEO	CFO, CEO	CFO
Timing	Ex ante	Ex ante	Ex ante	Ex post	Ex ante
Focus		Align with strategy	Align with strategy and strategic plan	Maintain alignment with strategy, strategic plan, and forecast. Commitment remains with original budget	Use latest forecast in year t of ending values for permanent accounts as beginning values for year $t+1$
Alignment practices/ mechanisms	CEO responsibility for coordination of strategy and strategic plan	• Core executive group (or one individual) involved in review and approval of strategic plan and budget • Strategic plan precedes and feeds into budget • Simultaneous preparation of strategic plan and budget • Co-location of management accountants involved with strategic planning and budgeting, and FP&A and other special teams • CFO responsible for coordination of strategic planning, budgeting, and intra-year reviewing • Same management accountants in for all three subprocesses			Final forecast of permanent accounts used as opening values

d. Intra-year reviewing, e.g., variance analysis and forecasts: During the fiscal year, variance analyses and forecasts motivate corrective actions to ensure the actual performance accomplishes the original budget. These ex post alignment practices/mechanisms may lead to changes in the strategic plan and/or the strategy including the elimination of some strategic initiatives (unrealized strategies) or the introduction of new initiatives (emergent strategies).

e. Estimating values for next year's opening permanent accounts: Each forecast during the current year estimates the ending values for permanent accounts, and consequently the starting values for permanent accounts for the subsequent fiscal year. The latest forecast gets replaced by the actual values once the financial statements for the year are finalized.

Although the description of the integrated process appears to be linear, there are multiple opportunities for the process to cycle back on itself and to feed new information backwards or forwards as depicted in Fig. 1. The entire process is largely iterative. At any time, any of the above subprocesses can loop back to initiate a review of earlier subprocesses. Feedback loops initiated before the start of the fiscal year (ex ante) can produce changes to the strategy, strategic plan, and/or budget. Intra-year reviews operate mainly through practices/mechanisms such as variance analysis and forecasts and may initiate ex post adjustments and contribute to emergent strategy. This framework thus explains how strategic plans and budgets are implicated in modifying the intended strategy to produce the realized strategy.

The integrated conceptual framework reflects three temporal cycles in which alignment practices/mechanisms operate. Alignment efforts can operate before the fiscal year $(t - 1)$, within the fiscal year (t), and between the current fiscal year and the next fiscal year $(t + 1)$. The figures from the most recent forecast of the current fiscal year provide the starting point for strategic plans and budgets for the following fiscal year, until actual values are available for the ending fiscal year (t).

An incidental but important benefit derived from the operation of an integrated strategic planning and budgeting process is organizational learning and development. Strategic plans and budgets established at the start of the fiscal year reflect managers' understandings of the links between business activities and performance at that time. Ex post intra-year reviews comparing budgets to actual performance and to forecasts prompt managers to continually review their understanding of the drivers of performance. Additionally, as forecasts are based on the most recently acquired information and understanding of the business, they can be viewed as repositories of organizational knowledge about drivers of performance.

CONCLUDING COMMENTS

Our research considered subprocesses and practices/mechanisms used by firms to align strategic planning and budgeting. With qualitative research, it produced important insights on the subprocesses for aligning strategic planning and budgeting. Although there may be more, we at this time recognize four insights.

First, alignment is a continuous process with ex ante alignment of strategic planning and budgeting undertaken prior to the beginning of the fiscal year, and ex post alignment throughout the fiscal year. Both provide opportunities to change ineffective strategies, strategic plans, and budgets to minimize financial harm. Subprocesses and practices/mechanisms prompt organizational learning as managers seek to identify factors giving rise to gaps in performance. This learning enables managers to update the relationships underpinning their models of business performance. Second, improved performance through ex ante and ex post alignment practices/mechanisms better enables the accomplishment of CEO and senior management financial objectives though explicit and verifiable decisions. Third, with forecasting heretofore an unclear and ambiguous subprocess, this chapter has made its role in assisting with accomplishing strategies, strategic plans, and budgets transparent and manageable.

Fourth and more reflectively, qualitative research can reduce endogeneity which is often a concern with management accounting research, mostly with quantitative analysis (Chenhall & Moers, 2007). The endogeneity problem weakens research results when the explanatory variable on the right of the equation is related to the variables on the left. Qualitative analysis allows for understanding and describing complex relationship among variables as unexplained correlations are less likely to occur; endogeneity is largely solved with qualitative research, as noted in Table 4, which more explicitly describes the multiple relationships among variables (van Lent, 2007). Van Lent (2007) argues that the impact of the unknown and unknowable endogeneity can be reduced by focusing, as this research did, on a system of variables such as our conceptual framework. Van Lent's (2007) main concern was whether the conceptual framework makes sense rather than the behavior of individual variables that may or may not demonstrate endogeneity.

We have one contribution. In addressing the literature shortcoming in explaining the alignment of strategic planning and budgeting, we found one process rather than two separate processes. Strategic planning and budgeting are part of the single process as shown in Table 4, which also includes strategy on the left side and variance analysis with forecasting and the estimation of ending values for permanent accounts on the right. In effect, our conceptual framework explains how strategic planning and budgeting are integrated and aligned with strategy and variance analysis (with forecasts). This framework is useful for research especially the strategy, strategic planning, budgeting, and control literatures as well for pedagogy and practice.

Although the general findings have validity, the limitations of this research are that it is based on a relatively small and geographically restricted sample. Despite the respondents being highly knowledgeable, the interviews were somewhat limited in duration. To increase validity, future research could adopt a case study approach to undertake detailed investigations of fewer firms to thoroughly understand the specific practices/mechanisms used to integrate strategic planning and budgeting.

NOTES

1. Park (2022) cites McKinsey's *Valuation: Measuring and Managing the Value of Companies* as the source of the term treadmill.
2. As this academic research involves interviewing practitioners, we use terms familiar to them. KPMG (2015, p. 6) provides the following terms for use with integrative performance management, which is concerned with strategic planning, budgeting, and forecasting.

Strategic planning, "A top-down strategic plan ... defines the strategic aims of the [firm] and high-level activities required to achieve the goals of the [firm]." In this chapter, strategic plans refer to the top-level or firm-wide financial goals and targets, and their associated performance indicators.

Budgeting. "A budget ... enables resource allocation to be aligned to strategic goals and targets set across the entire [firm]." In effect, budgeting clarifies how resources are allocated to support activities intended to achieve the firm's strategies.

Forecasting. "A forecast ... tracks the expected performance of the business, so that timely decisions can be taken to address shortfalls against targets or maximizing an emerging opportunity."

3. Frow et al. (2010) term "continuous budgeting" is equivalent to "forecasting" as used in this chapter. For both terms, the financial performance targets are those established in the original budget.
4. Jordan and Messner (2020, p. 344) stated that operating plans were the name used for budgets.
5. To maintain the confidentiality of firms (and thereby respondents), all firms were assigned a number from 1 to 20, and references were made by their assigned numbers.
6. We did not ask to meet with CFOs. One CFO met with us; for the other 19 firms, we met vice presidents (5), controllers (7), directors (11), and managers (4).
7. As noted earlier, to maintain the confidentiality of firms (and thereby respondents), all firms were assigned a number from 1 to 20, and references will be made to firms by their assigned numbers.

ACKNOWLEDGMENTS

The authors thank the reviewers and editor for their beyond expected insightful and constructive contributions to this chapter. They also thank Diana Sheikham for her outstanding research assistance. Of course, the authors retain responsibility for all errors and shortcomings.

REFERENCES

Abernethy, M. A., & Brownell, P. (1999). The role of budgets in organizations facing strategic change: An exploratory study. *Accounting, Organizations and Society*, *24*(3), 189–204.

Becker, S. D., Mahlendorf, M. D., Schaffer, U., & Thaten, M. (2016). Budgeting in times of economic crisis. *Contemporary Accounting Research*, *33*(4), 1489–1517.

Bedford, D. S. (2020). Conceptual and empirical issues in understanding management control combinations. *Accounting, Organizations and Society*, *86*, 1–8.

Blumentritt, T. (2006). Integrating strategic management and budgeting. *Journal of Business Strategy*, *27*(6), 73–79.

Chenhall, R. H., & Moers, F. (2007). The issues of endogeneity within theory-based, quantitative management accounting research. *European Accounting Review*, *16*(1), 173–195.

Deloitte. (2014). *Integrated performance management: Plan, budget, forecast*. London: Deloitte LLP, UK.

Eisenhardt, K. M. (1989). Building theories from case study research. *Academy of Management Review*, *14*(4), 532–550.

Eisenhardt, K. M. (1991). Better stories and better constructs: The case for rigor and comparative logic. *Academy of Management Review*, *16*(3), 620–627.

Eisenhardt, K. M., & Graebner, M. E. (2007). Theory building cases: Opportunities and challenges. *Academy of Management Journal*, *50*(1), 25–32.

Erhart, R., Mahlendorf, M. D., Reimer, M., & Schaffer, U. (2017). Theorizing and testing bidirectional effects: The relationship between strategy formation and involvement of controllers. *Accounting, Organizations and Society*, *61*, 36–52.

Frow, N., Marginson, D., & Ogden, S. (2005). Encouraging strategic behaviour while maintaining management control: Multi-functional project teams, budgets, and the negotiation of shared accountabilities in contemporary enterprises. *Management Accounting Research*, *16*(3), 269–292.

Frow, N., Marginson, D., & Ogden, S. (2010). "Continuous" budgeting: Reconciling budget flexibility with budgetary control. *Accounting, Organizations and Society*, *35*(4), 444–461.

Grant, R. M. (2003). Strategic planning in a turbulent environment: Evidence from the oil majors. *Strategic Management Journal*, *24*(6), 491–517.

Hennttu-Ano, T. (2018). The role of forecasting in budgeting control systems: Reactive and proactive types of planning. *Journal of Management Control*, *29*, 327–360.

Hope, J., & Fraser, R. (2003). Who needs budgeting? *Harvard Business Review*, *81*(2), 108–115.

Hoverstadt, P., Kendrick, I., & Morlidge, S. (2007). Viability as a basis for performance measurement. *Measuring Business Excellence*, *11*(1), 27–32.

Jordan, S., & Messner, M. (2020). The use of forecast accuracy indicators to improve planning quality: Insights from a case study. *European Accounting Review*, *29*(2), 337–339.

Kannan-Narasimhan, R., & Lawrence, B. S. (2018). How innovators reframe resources in the strategy-making process to gain innovation adoption. *Strategic Management Journal*, *39*, 720–758.

Kaplan, R. S., & Norton, D. P. (2001a). Transforming the balanced scorecard from performance measurement to strategic management: Part I. *Accounting Horizons*, *15*(1), 87–104.

Kaplan, R. S., & Norton, D. P. (2001b). Transforming the balanced scorecard from performance measurement to strategic management: Part II. *Accounting Horizons*, *15*(2), 147–160.

Keating, P. (1995). A framework for classifying and evaluating the theoretical contributions of case research in management accounting. *Journal of Management Accounting Research*, *7*, 66–86.

KPMG. (2015). *Planning, budgeting, and forecasting: A KPMG and ACC thought leadership*. KPMG LLP, UK.

Libby, T., & Lindsay, R. M. (2010). Beyond budgeting or budgeting reconsidered? A survey of North-American budgeting practice. *Management Accounting Research*, *21*(1), 56–75.

Lillis, A. M., & Mundy, J. (2005). Cross-sectional field studies in management accounting research – Closing the gaps between surveys and case studies. *Journal of Management Accounting Research*, *17*, 119–141.

Marginson, D. E. W., & Ogden, S. G. (2005). Copying with ambiguity through the budget: The positive effects of budgetary targets on managers' budgeting behaviours. *Accounting, Organizations and Society*, *30*(5), 435–457.

Merchant, K., & Van der Stede, W. A. (2007). *Management control system*. Harlow: Prentice Hall Pearson Education.

Northcott, D., & Doolin, B. (2008). Qualitative research in accounting and management – The journey so far. *Qualitative Research in Accounting and Management*, *5*(1), 5–10.

Park, J. J. (2022). *The valuation treadmill: How security fraud threatens the integrity of public companies*. New York, NY: Cambridge University Press.

Peters, M. D., Gudergan, S., & Booth, P. (2019). Interactive profit-planning systems and market turbulence: A dynamic capabilities perspective. *Long Range Planning*, *52*, 386–405.

PwC. (2012). *Integrated business planning*. PricewaterhouseCoopers, pwc.com.au/consulting.

Simons, R. (1995). *Levers of control*. Boston, MA: Harvard Business School Press.

Spee, A. P., & Jarzabkowski, P. (2011). Strategic planning as communicative process. *Organization Studies*, *32*(9), 1217–1245.

Tucker, B. P., & Lawson, R. (2016). Moving academic management accounting research closer to practice: A view from U.S. and Australia. *Advances in Management Accounting, 27,* 167–206.

Vaivio, J. (2008). Qualitative management accounting research: Rational, pitfalls and potential. *Qualitative Research in Accounting and Management, 5*(1), 64–86.

van Lent, L. (2007). Endogeneity in management accounting research: A comment. *European Accounting Review, 16*(1), 197–2005.

APPENDIX: INTERVIEW QUESTIONS

1. What is your job title?
2. What do you do?
3. Please describe the various steps or stages with budgeting as you understand them.
4. Please describe the various steps or stages with strategic planning as you understand them.
5. Does your work involve strategic planning and/or budgeting? A yes or no is sufficient.
6. Please describe any computerized budgeting and/or strategic planning systems that tend to be used for these processes.
7. In your opinion, what IT knowledge and skills are needed for using budgeting and/or strategy planning systems?
8. In your opinion, what positions (or employees) tend to be responsible for budgeting? For strategic planning?
9. In your opinion, how are budgeting and strategic planning aligned and realigned? What activities and positions (i.e., employees) are involved?
10. In your opinion, what communications facilitate alignment and realignment? When and how does the communication occur?

Notes: The first eight questions set the context for Questions 9 and 10; Questions 1 and 2 reveal respondents' involvement with strategic planning and budgeting; Questions 3 and 4 provide a description of the stages of strategic planning and budgeting, respectively, and clarifies respondents' roles; Question 5 reveals that all of our respondents are actively involved in strategic planning and budgeting; Question 6 elicits a description of the largely Excel and ERP systems underpinning strategic planning and budgeting processes; Question 7 reveals that Excel is a required skill; and Question 8 finds that respondents are unanimous that line managers are responsible for strategic plans and budgets and that the role of the finance function is to provide staff support.

SOCIAL CAPITAL AND BUDGETING IN A LOCAL CHURCH

Umesh Sharma and Denise Frost

ABSTRACT

The purpose of this chapter is to examine the budgeting process in a local church from a social capital perspective. The social capital provides novel insights into the construction of budgets and its social aspects. A qualitative case study was adopted, with an interpretive methodology. Semi-structured interviews were used to interview 14 managers involved in the budgeting process at a local independent church. The interview data were supplemented by documentary evidence. Nahapiet and Ghoshal (1998) framework of social capital was used to analyse the data. The main finding was that budgeting was found to be a social process – that can best be explained by social capital theory. There may be an element of self-selection, as the church agreed to participate in the study and chose to allow a researcher to examine social aspects of its budgeting process. The chapter contributes to both social capital theory and church literature. Social capital provides novel insights into the construction of budgets and its social aspects. In addition, contemporary budgeting practices are studied in a church in a denomination and country not previously studied.

Keywords: Church; social capital; social process; budgeting process; budgeting; New Zealand

INTRODUCTION

The budgeting literature is broad, varied and has been studied from different research paradigms (Bower, 2017; Covaleski, Evans, Luft, & Shields, 2003; Kurt & Feng, 2019; O'Grady, Akroyd, & Scott, 2017). In this chapter, budgeting in a

Advances in Management Accounting, Volume 35, 45–71
Copyright © 2023 by Emerald Publishing Limited
All rights of reproduction in any form reserved
ISSN: 1474-7871/doi:10.1108/S1474-787120230000035003

church is examined from a social capital perspective. The church, Fountain Springs (FS),[1] is an independent Pentecostal church that was founded in the 1970s and is located in New Zealand. In a church, setting objectives, allocating of resources, and getting feedback on spending, contribute to the achievement of spiritual aspirations (Bower, 2017). In the process, budgeting fosters cooperative behaviour and both strengthens and reinforces social capital. Very little seems to have changed in how resource allocation in budgeting is discussed (Bower, 2017). Carmona and Ezzamel (2006) recognise the lack of exploration into accounting and religion by stating 'research on the relationship between accounting and religion or religious institutions is in short supply' (p. 117). McPhail, Gorringe, and Gray (2004) point out that accounting academe has neglected to take theology seriously. McPhail and Cordery (2019) also argue that the literature has yet to engage with the fundamental challenge that lies at the core of the accounting and theology. McPhail and Cordery (2019) also articulate that new paradigms should be utilised in analysing how religious organisations/spirituality approaches accounting and transforms it. The tendency has also been towards the use of Laughlin (1988, 1990) and Booth's (1993) orientation to view the phenomena of religion sociologically. In contrast, we use an interpretive paradigm and study budgeting from a social capital perspective to accomplish spiritual aspirations.

In the budgeting and social capital literature, three studies (Chenhall, Hall, & Smith, 2010, 2012; Vieira, Ha, & O'Dwyer, 2013) were located investigating social capital in management control systems (MCS). In these three studies, budgeting is covered as part of MCS, but the influence of social capital on the budgeting *process* is not specifically referred to. The actual process of budgeting using social capital to accomplish spiritual aspirations remains less well understood. Social capital includes the social connections, attitudes, norms and institutions that give church members a sense of belonging. Social capital is used in this chapter because it allows a group of people to work together effectively to achieve a common purpose of participation in the budgeting process. It allows a group of people to function together as a whole through trust and shared identity, norms, values and mutual relationship. Social capital is different from other forms of capital in that it resides in social relationships whereas other forms of capital can reside in the individual (Robison, Shmidt, & Siles, 2002). Social capital also emphasises on trust, norms and network, which are an essential component of social cohesion (Putnam, 1993). Other frameworks tend to emphasise relatively less on network ties, trust, norms, shared narratives which is amplified by social capital perspective. Nahapiet and Ghoshal (1998) define social capital 'as the sum of the actual and potential resources embedded within, available through, and derived from the network of relationships possessed by an individual or social unit' (p. 243). Social capital thus constitutes both the network and the assets that may be mobilised through that network (Bourdieu, 1986). There is an absence in the literature regarding the examination of the influence of social capital on the budgeting process (or vice versa) in a church. Social capital is a sensitising theoretical perspective and viewed as a 'skeletal theory'. The empirical evidence from the case study adds richness to the social capital perspective. Hopwood (1983) on a similar note calls for understanding accounting in the social context in which it operates. The social context entails relationships and is not merely technical. Also, significant emphasis seems to have been placed on Laughlin's (1988, 1990) and Booth's (1993) orientations in religious organisations. Laughlin (1988) examines the social and technical aspects that are amplified through a specific study of the accounting systems in the Church of England. Laughlin's (1990) study brings the literature on accountability closer to certain studies in accounting addressed to understanding the current practices in the organisational context in which they are exercised. Laughlin (1990) summarises the current 'skeletal' theoretical insights concerning accountability in practice and then 'fleshes' out this model by looking at the specific financial accountability practices at a Church. Booth's (1993) call for study on churches is deemed to add to our understanding of accounting as a situated practice. Booth (1993) proposes that the dominant position of religious beliefs be amplified in any attempts to understand organising and management of churches. This present study aims to examine the budgeting in a local church from a social capital perspective.

Boland and Pondy (1983) argue that accounting, and by implications budgeting, is both a natural and rational process, and that both processes are needed in organisations. However, management accounting textbooks tend to focus on the rational process, that is on the technical and normative aspects of budgeting. The natural and social aspects of budgeting show interactions between organisational participants in negotiating budgets (Meyers, 1996). We believe that the social aspects of budgeting are not largely explored in the extant literature, particularly in relation to social capital theory. Social capital, as discussed previously, is used in the chapter as it allows a group of people to work together effectively in relation to the calculative practice of budgeting process. Social capital theory has been considered in this study for its ability to shed light on the social aspects of budgeting. Our chapter aims to fill this gap in the literature.

The remainder of this chapter is structured in the following way. Section two introduces the relevant literature on budgeting. Section three explains Nahapiet and Ghoshal (1998) framework, and how their framework was adapted for this study. The research method is explained in Section four, and the case study organisation, FS, is introduced. In Section five, the case study findings are examined and analysed using the adapted social capital framework. The case study findings are discussed in the sixth section. Section seven concludes the chapter.

BUDGETING

Budgets are management tools most pervasively utilised in organisations for resource allocation decisions (Bower, 2017; Davila & Wouters, 2005; Lawrence & Sharma, 2002). The role that social aspects play in the budgeting process of organisations with varied scopes has been rarely researched (Parker & Kyj, 2006). Budgeting participation provides managers and employees with an opportunity to intentionally influence budget targets (Irvine, 2005).

The process of setting budgets is considered to be a cornerstone of MCS in most firms (Kramer & Hartmann, 2014). Budgets can be set as a target to be achieved and as a means of objectifying the vision of the organisation (Irvine, 2005). For instance, Irvine (2005) examines attitudes to budgeting in a local church and considers potential conflict between the 'sacred' agenda for the church and the 'secular' nature of accounting. She shows budgeting as an enabling and liberating contribution to a church's fulfilment of its spiritual mission. Budgeting has been shown to provide a valuable linkage between the conception of a church's goals for the coming year, and the resourcing of these goals (Lightbody, 2000).

Firms introduce MCS, including budgets, when they first invest in control (Gibb & Scott, 1985; Lyne, 1988; Sharma, Lawrence, & Lowe, 2010).[2] The choice of MCS manifests firms' strategies and shows that firms that choose and initiate MCS better suited to their strategy perform better than others (Nath & Sharma, 2014; Sharma, Lawrence, & Lowe, 2014; Sharma & Frost, 2020; Soobaroyen, Ntim, Broad, Agrizzi, & Vithana, 2019). In relation to control, individuals with difficult but attainable goals perform better than those who have less difficult goals (Kenno, Lau, & Sainty, 2018). The less difficult goals are chosen by managers to create budgetary slack (Davila & Wouters, 2005).

Merchant (1985) notes that the propensities to create budgetary slack are lower where managers participate actively in budgeting. The budget process might also lead to sub-optimisation within the organisation, as departmental managers often are too keen to improve their own department without considering how this may fit with the broader strategic goals (Hope & Fraser, 2003). Merchant (1990) notes that the pressure to meet financial targets can shape the manipulation of short-term performance measures and encouragement of a myopic, short-term orientation.

The critical literature, however, suggests that budgets can be used for political gains and for the purpose of control and domination by management (Kuruppu et al., 2016). The use of fair budgeting leads to improved subordinate performance. Libby (1999), for example, explained that a combination of voice and explanation by subordinates led to improved performance. In the budget-setting process, members may be able to negotiate their way through the budgeting process, which enhances social capital (Hauriasi, Van-Peursem, & Davey, 2016). Some commentators have examined a model of vertical information sharing between superiors and subordinates in the budgeting process (see Parker & Kyj, 2006). Upward information sharing embodied the re-creation of private information by subordinates to superiors. Superiors generally encourage participation when budget goals are used in the performance evaluation of subordinates, because of concerns about organisational justice (Parker & Kyj, 2006).

There have been studies carried out in the field of budgeting in religious not-for-profit organisations, specifically in denominational churches. Some of this work investigates budgeting practices in the head office of a denominational church (Lightbody, 2000, 2003), whereas others have studied the process of budgeting in a local church (Irvine, 2005; Kluvers, 2001). In contrast, Hauriasi et al. (2016) report on budgeting practices at all levels in the Anglican Church of Melanesia. Irvine (2005) and Lightbody (2000) view budgeting as an enabling and liberating contributor to a church's fulfilment of its spiritual vision. Kluvers (2001) considers power and control in budgeting as well as culture and change factors. Irvine (2005) analyses belief systems and the sacred-secular dichotomy in a church. In Irvine's (2005) study, 'the budget was never to take over as an end in itself, but always to be subservient to the vision' (p. 225). This study builds on this limited literature on budgeting in church. Very little seems to have changed in how resource allocation in budgeting is discussed and this chapter seeks to add to the budgeting process literature from a social capital perspective.

Positioning Our Study

Three papers were located that refer to social capital and budgeting in an organisation. However, neither of the three papers study social capital in the budgeting process, nor study social capital and budgeting in a local church. Chenhall et al. (2010, 2012) research social capital in MCS in an Australian nongovernment organisation. They adopt three taxonomies of MCS, two of which include budgets as a component of the MCS. Budgets are included as a part of a formal MCS (Chenhall & Morris, 1995), and as part of a diagnostic control system, one of Simons (1995) four levers of control (Chenhall et al., 2010). Chenhall et al. (2012) field study of non-government organisation examines how the debates, critiques and struggles over the choice of different metrics can have beneficial and damaging effects on social capital in non-government organisation. However, the focus of their study is on links between MCS and social capital, with budgeting addressed indirectly as a component of MCS. Vieira, Ha, and O'Dwyer (2013) investigate the interplay between MCS and social capital in a social enterprise in Vietnam. In doing so, they adopt a similar approach to Chenhall et al. (2010). Neither Chenhall et al. (2010, 2012) nor Vieira et al. (2013) address the budgeting process per se or the influence of social capital on the budgeting process.

Participative budgeting where relational aspects of the budgeting are shown has been in the literature (Covaleski et al., 2003). Covaleski et al. (2003) note that participative budgeting is where the employees communicate private information about local conditions to the owner and these reports influence the organisations' production plans and the employee's compensation. The owner has the choice as to whether to base the employee's compensation, in part, on the employee's communication about local conditions. In making this decision, the owner knows that the employee has superior information about local conditions, but the employee also has the ability and incentive to manipulate his report to create budgetary slack. However, more studies are needed to better understand the budgeting in the social context in which it operates (Hopwood, 1983). Thus, this present study examines budgeting practices in a local church from a different perspective to the commonly sacred-secular dichotomy – by drawing on social capital theory.

THEORETICAL FRAMEWORK

Social Capital Theory

Nahapiet and Ghoshal (1998) framework of social capital was used as a theoretical basis for the study as it allows the study of social capital within an organisation

(Subramanium, Stewart, Ng, & Shulman, 2013). Accordingly, Nahapiet and Ghoshal (1998) framework is suitable for studying the budgeting process in an organisation, as budgeting occurs internally within an organisation. Our application of social capital as a model to guide our analysis is a key contribution of this study. Nahapiet and Ghoshal (1998) framework has been applied empirically to a number of business forms such as family firms (Pearson, Carr, & Shaw, 2008), corporates (Hatzakis, Lycett, Macredie, & Martin, 2005), and small and medium enterprises (Fuller & Tian, 2006). In addition to the structural and relational dimensions of social capital, Nahapiet and Ghoshal (1998) framework includes a cognitive dimension. Nahapiet and Ghoshal (1998) indicate that the inclusion of a cognitive dimension covers aspects of social capital 'not yet discussed in the mainstream literature on social capital' (p. 244). This cognitive dimension allows for a more comprehensive analysis of social capital in an organisation, as it takes into account aspects of social capital arising from a shared context such as shared vocabulary and shared narratives. Nahapiet and Ghoshal (1998) framework can be viewed as a 'skeletal theory' (Laughlin, 1995, p. 81), requiring 'empirical flesh' to make it 'meaningful and complete' (Laughlin, 1995, p. 83).

Nahapiet and Ghoshal (1998) framework is displayed in Table 1. In their framework, social capital is viewed as occurring in three clusters or dimensions: the structural, the cognitive and the relational. They acknowledge that the three dimensions are not separate but are highly interrelated entities.

The structural dimension concerns 'the overall pattern of connections between actors – that is, who you reach and how you reach them' (Nahapiet & Ghoshal, 1998, p. 244). This dimension consists of three elements: network ties, network configuration and appropriable organisation. Network ties work on the premise that "'who [sic.] you know" affects "what you know"' (Nahapiet & Ghoshal, 1998, p. 252). Efficient network ties provide information benefits in terms of access (receiving valuable information and knowing who to pass it on to), timing (receiving information sooner than others) and referrals (the provision of information on opportunities to others in the network). Network configuration relates to the configuration of network ties and impacts the accessibility of information. Nahapiet and Ghoshal (1998) argue a sparse network of diverse contacts may provide more information benefits than a dense network of less diverse contacts. An appropriable organisation occurs when social capital such as ties, norms and trust developed in one setting can be transferred to another setting.

The relational dimension refers to 'those assets created and leveraged through relationships' (Nahapiet & Ghoshal, 1998, p. 244). This dimension is concerned

Table 1.   Nahapiet and Ghoshal (1998) Framework.

Structural Dimension	Cognitive Dimension	Relational Dimension
Network ties	Shared language and vocabulary	Trust
Network configuration	Shared narratives	Norms
Appropriable organisation		Obligations and expectations
		Identification

with personal relationships that develop over a period of time. There are four elements to the relational dimension: trust, norms, obligations and expectations and identification. Trust is the confidence that the end result of another person's intended action will be fitting from 'our' perspective. Norms represent 'a degree of consensus in the social system' (Nahapiet & Ghoshal, 1998, p. 255), and are an important aspect of social capital (Cohen & Prusak, 2001). Norms noted by Nahapiet and Ghoshal (1998) include openness, teamwork, cooperation, transparency and a tolerance of failure. Obligations involve 'a commitment or duty to undertake some activity in the future' (Nahapiet & Ghoshal, 1998, p. 255), and can be thought of as a 'credit slip' held by one individual to be fulfilled by another (Nahapiet & Ghoshal, 1998). Expectations are obligations that exist between two people, as there is an expectation that the 'credit slip' will be honoured. The fourth element, identification, relates to how individuals identify or 'see themselves as one' (Nahapiet & Ghoshal, 1998, p. 256) with others or with a group. Identification can occur through group membership, or where an individual adopts the values and standards of other people or groups. Identification results in a heightened concern for the group and may enhance cooperation.

The cognitive dimension has to do with 'those resources providing shared representations, interpretations, and systems of meaning among parties' (Nahapiet & Ghoshal, 1998, p. 244). This dimension focusses on those aspects of social capital that provide a shared context in an organisation, for instance, a shared language and vocabulary, and shared narratives (myths, stories and metaphors). Shared language such as shared terminology enables those in a particular field to communicate more easily. Shared narratives provide an interpretation of events and function to transfer tacit experience and knowledge.

Theorising with Social Capital

Nahapiet and Ghoshal (1998) framework was developed in the context of the creation and sharing of intellectual capital. Thus, it has been adapted for the purpose of studying the influence of social capital on the budgeting process (or vice versa). The adapted framework was developed to incorporate elements from both Nahapiet and Ghoshal (1998) framework and the wider social capital theory. Nahapiet and Ghoshal's (1998) three dimensions of social capital were retained. A shared view (a shared vision, purpose, understanding or goal among those in the organisation) (Nahapiet & Ghoshal, 1998), replaced shared narratives in the shared context dimension. It was considered that the concept of shared vision, purpose, understanding or goal, was directly relevant to the budgeting process in an organisation, as it promotes cooperation. In contrast, shared narratives, particularly the notion of myths, stories and metaphors, were not thought to be relevant to budgeting. In the structural dimension, network ties were seen as being either formal (as a function of job title) or informal (unrelated to job title). Knoke (2009) notes that formal job descriptions often outline who managers will interact with during the course of their job, thus influencing formal network ties. Network configuration was expanded to include bridging and bonding social capital (Adler & Kwon, 2002; Putnam, 2000). It was considered that bonding

Table 2.   The Adapted Framework.

Structural Dimension	Cognitive Dimension	Relational Dimension
Network ties	Shared language and vocabulary	Trust
• Formal		
• Informal		
Network configuration	Shared views	Norms
Appropriable organisation		Identification
Physical spaces for people to connect		

social capital in particular, was directly relevant to the budgeting process, as it is related to teamwork. Physical spaces for people to connect (Cohen & Prusak, 2001) were also added to the structural dimension. Cohen and Prusak (2001) note that organisations can make it easier for employees to connect by physically configuring workspaces to encourage employees to gather, talk and meet informally. The provision of staffrooms, alcoves and communal areas, where staff can meet, also promotes community. Obligations and expectations, particularly the notion of a '"credit slip' held by A to be redeemed by some performance by B' (Nahapiet & Ghoshal, 1998, p. 255) were omitted from the relational dimension as they were not considered relevant to the budgeting process. This adapted framework is shown in Table 2.

RESEARCH METHOD

A qualitative case study was chosen as the best way to arrive at examining the budgeting process in a local church FS from a social capital perspective. The case study method allowed for a detailed study of budgeting, and took into consideration the organisation's economic, historical, organisational and social context (Scapens, 1990). An interpretive methodology (Chua, 1986; Parker & Northcott, 2016) was adopted, as it was considered congruous with the subjective nature of social capital and assisted in understanding social capital from the subjective viewpoint of managers involved in budgeting. Data were collected primarily through semi-structured interviews, supplemented by documentary evidence, and evidence obtained from FS' website. Documentary evidence consisted of an annual budget for the 2021/2022 financial year, along with annual financial statements from the Charities Commission website.[3] A budget procedure manual was requested, but no such document existed. Likewise, minutes of Leadership Team meetings were requested, but were not made available to the researcher. Background information on FS was obtained from several sources: interviewees; an interview carried out with the previous Finance Administrator in 2019; Barry (2015); and the Charities Commission website.[4] The documentary evidence was used to formulate interview questions for the study.

The choice of interviews to collect data was consistent with the interpretive paradigm, as this method gathered information about interviewees' subjective views (Hopper & Powell, 1985) of social capital. Managers involved in the budgeting process were identified, and 15 interviews covering 14 interviewees were carried out over a 16-month period from May 2016 to August 2017. Interviews were carried out over a 16-month period. The participants for interviews were chosen on the basis of their input into the budgeting process. Participants from the Families Team and those on the Leadership Team were chosen. The Leadership Team was studied as they promote discussion on the budget and make the final decision on the budget. The Families' Team is the largest team at FS. Fig. 1 displays the interviewees and their position at FS. The interview questions were formulated from prior literature and primarily based on Nahapiet and Ghoshal's (1998) three dimensions of social capital: structural, relational and cognitive dimensions. The interviews were transcribed with Saldana's (2013) and Bazeley's (2013) methods of coding were adopted. The coded interview transcripts were entered into *NVivo*.

In order to identify the themes for the study, we followed Saldana's (2013) method of coding. The interview transcripts from the organisation have been coded and entered into NVivo (Bazeley, 2013). The 'describe, compare, relate' strategy developed by Bazeley (2013) was used when developing themes. The 'describe step' involved reading through coded text relevant to the theme and making notes. The 'compare' step entailed looking for similarities and differences between the theme under consideration and other themes, noting what was unique, and what was common (Bazeley, 2013). The 'describe, compare and relate' process of theme development led to the development of three themes for the study: valuing people, integrity and generosity.

The challenge was when the data were coded, far too many nodes came up. The potential conflict was to have many nodes where material in each node would be specific to that node, rather than lumped under one mega-node. Naming the node was a challenge as well as sometimes there was conflict with fine distinctions between the definitions of nodes. Later on, we brought together similar nodes, as often the difference between some nodes was minimal.

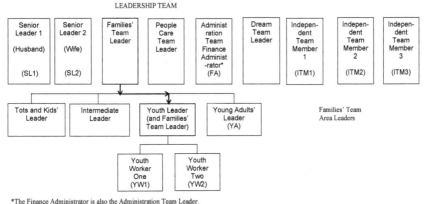

*The Finance Administrator is also the Administration Team Leader.

Fig. 1. High Level Organisational Chart.

One of the authors has a personal connection with FS, as, for the last 27 years, she has attended the church. During this time, she has developed an understanding of the history of the church, its values and its *modus operandi*. Hence, she could be viewed as an 'insider', raising the issue of reflexivity. The author's perception is that the association with the church resulted in interviewees speaking more openly. Corbin Dwyer and Buckle (2009) indicate that such an acceptance of the interviewer by interviewees provides the interviewer with 'a level of trust and openness' (p. 58) that may have not been present otherwise. Being an insider is the strength of this study as it relates to the cognitive dimension (shared context) of social capital theory which is an important element.

The Case Study – FS

FS is an independent Pentecostal church that was founded in the 1970s and is located in New Zealand. Each week, around 1,000 people attend a Sunday morning service, with around 400 attending a Sunday evening service. Through a related trust, the church provides a free, weekly Wednesday night meal for around 200 people.

In 2011, FS changed its governance structure, replacing the previous Leadership Team, made up of all staff, with four teams: 'the Families' team', 'the People Care team', 'the Administration team' and 'the Dream team' (see Fig. 1).[5] Each team has a team leader who is also on the new Leadership Team. The Families' team looks after pre-schoolers, children, and young adults up to the age of 25. The People Care team provides pastoral care. Those involved in the administration of the church are on the Administration team. The function of the Dream team is to provide creative input into the church.

FS is run by a Leadership Team of nine which meets weekly (see Fig. 1). Six of the Leadership Team members are church staff, and three are independent team members who are members of the congregation and have specialist skills. Independent team member 1 (ITM1) is a counsellor who has had previous church leadership experience. Independent team member 2 (ITM2) is a retired accountant who has also had previous church leadership experience, while independent team member 3 (ITM3) is a chartered accountant who works in a large accounting firm. The three independent team members were brought onto the Leadership Team at the beginning of 2012, and they serve on a voluntary basis.

Each of the four teams has a regular team meeting where team leaders report back to their team on relevant items raised during the weekly Leadership Team meeting. Items raised during the individual team meetings can also be taken on to the Leadership Team meeting. In addition, all staff attend a weekly staff meeting. ITM1 and ITM2 also attend the staff meetings. At the time of the interviews in 2016/2017, there were 21 staff in all at FS. This study involved examining the budgeting process in the Families' team, the largest team at FS, and at Leadership Team level. All nine of the Leadership Team were interviewed, as were three of the area leaders in the Families' team, and two of the staff in the youth area who were involved in budgeting.

FS is set up as a trust and is registered as a charity with the New Zealand Charities Commission. The financial year at FS runs from 1 April to 31 March. The annual accounts are prepared by an external, independent accounting firm and are professionally audited. In the financial year ending 31 March 2013, FS had income of around $1.26 million. In the same period, FS made a small deficit. FS relies heavily on donations from congregation members, with over 98% of its 2013 financial year income arising from tithes and offerings. Due to its reliance on donations, FS has limited options to increase revenue. Area leaders for the Families' team, the People Care team, the Administration team and the Dream team are allocated an annual grant to spend on activities taking place in their area. In the 2012/2013 financial year, the Families' team had a budgeted annual grant of $42,400, excluding salaries and wages.

The Budgeting Process at FS

The budgeting process is defined as the process of setting (planning), budget monitoring (control) and actions taken by managers to execute the budget and meet budget targets. The budgeting process at FS commences in mid-February when the Finance Administrator (FA) informs area leaders that their area budget is due in mid-March.[6] Area leaders differ as to how they prepare the budget for their area. For example, the Tots and Kids' leader, who has prepared her area's budget for 25 years, obtained 'last year's annual, actual figures, and ... the current year-to-date figures'. The year-to-date figures provide information for the current financial year up to January. She adds in expected expenses for February and March. The budget for the upcoming year is then prepared, taking into account 'What kind of extra activities that maybe we didn't do last year, but that we are considering this year?' (Tots and Kids' leader).

In contrast, the Intermediate leader, who at the time of the interview, was preparing her first budget, approached the budget preparation process quite differently. As her area had been newly created, she obtained the amount of her area's annual grant, or 'an amount to aim for' from the FA. She then spoke to the Young Adult's (YA) leader about how she prepared her budget:

> [The YA leader] showed me how she did hers and so I had a look at kind of the different areas she budgeted in to ... And saw the way that she set hers out and so I did something similar. (Intermediate leader)

The Intermediate leader also took advice from the Tots and Kids' leader, as the Intermediate area was previously looked after by the Tots and Kids' leader.

Once area leaders have completed their budget, the FA collates the area budgets and prepares a draft budget for FS. The FA then adds to the budget forecast income and other items of expenditure that are not area related. According to the FA, FS' income is 'fairly easy to forecast', as income from tithes is available on a monthly basis. In addition, 80% of tithes are paid either by automatic payment or eftpos. The FA indicated that expenses don't 'fluctuate much', so he sets non-area related budget expenditure around the same level as the previous year. He 'underestimate[s] the income to leave [a] gap' for unplanned expenses, such as a missions trip opportunity.

At this point in the process, the FA discusses any issues of concern arising from an area leader's budget with the leader concerned and makes adjustments to that area leader's budget. The draft budget is reviewed by ITM3, who is a chartered account- ant. The FA then outlines the main points of the budget to Senior Leader 1 (SL1).

The next step in the process occurs at a Leadership Team meeting. The FA explains the main points of the budget to the Leadership Team. The Leadership Team discusses the budget and make decisions regarding items of capital expend- iture. They decide on the priority to be given to capital expenditure items, and which capital expenditure items will be purchased.

> So capital expenditure, depending on if we've even got any surplus to work with, I just list along aside the operating budget and we throw those around in that same meeting. (FA)

Compared to the operating expenditure budgeting process, capital budgeting is a more informal and less structured process. Decisions on capital budgeting items are made by the Leadership Team.

The Leadership Team also decide how funding for missionaries will be distrib- uted, specifically which people or organisations will be funded, and how much each will receive. FS has a policy of setting aside a tithe (10%) of the previous year's income to support missionaries. 'We give away a portion to mission ... we always give away 10%. That's kind of an informal rule' (ITM3). Staff salaries are discussed, and any increases approved. According to Senior Leader 2 (SL2), 'We can't pay the market rates for wages ... And people coming in to work at the church know that they are not going to get a market wage'. After discussion, the budget is approved by the Leadership Team. It is then formally signed off by SL1. The FA then reports back to area leaders on the finalised funding for their areas. In a nutshell, the budgeting process is bottom up in nature with CAPEX and mis- sionary budgetary decisions done at the Leadership Team level.

The FA provides area leaders with individualised two monthly monitoring reports that outline how their actual spending compares against their budget. He provides them with information along the lines of 'This is how you're going. This is how much you've got left'. The FA informs area leaders if he has any concerns regarding their actual spending for the two-month period.

> [On] the odd occasion, I might say well you've spent 40% of your budget, we're only 20% of the way through the year, you're going to really watch that for the rest of the year. (FA)

The FA also provides the Leadership Team with monthly reports on FS' financial situation.

> My report back to the Leadership Team is far more detailed in terms of how we're tracking with expenses percentage-wise, based on the year before and what I've forecast as well. (FA)

The next section examines the case study findings.

CASE STUDY FINDINGS

The effect of social capital on the budgeting process (or vice versa) at FS can be illustrated through the influence of the structural, cognitive and relational dimen- sion of social capital.

The Structural Dimension

Network Ties – Network ties may be either formal (as a function of job title) or informal (unrelated to job title). With regard to formal network ties, preparing and monitoring the operating and capital expenditure budgets presented many opportunities for managers to interact, both in formal meeting and informally outside of organised meetings.

At FS, three of the Leadership Team referred to the way they interacted as 'a robust discussion'. According to the People Care Team Leader:

> A real camaraderie, a real close, quite a tight knit, very robust discussion. We're not afraid of conflict. We're not afraid of disagreeing with each other. We are, however, kind to each other despite disagreements.

Four of the Leadership Team members spoke of team members being free to disagree with each other. The Finance Administrator believed:

> I think we have a healthy balance between getting on and disagreeing. So, our meetings are not meetings where we all nod and go 'yes'. There is healthy amount of 'actually, I completely disagree with that'.

Budgets have been debated in an interactive way. This involved face-to-face interactions at formal meeting where it was intended to discuss plans, flag concerns and identify emerging issue relating to both financial and operational issues.

Network Configuration – An organisation can be described as having closure in that it is a social network, which has explicit social, financial and legal boundaries. Network ties provide the channels for information transmission. Closure is relevant to budgeting because closure in social networks in organisation is necessary for trust, information exchange and budget-related norms to be effective. Bonding social capital is relevant to budgeting, as it is likely to be a feature of close working relationships and information exchange among those involved in budgeting process. Bonding capital was obvious among the Leadership Team. FS brought three independent team members, who attended FS, but were not on the staff into Leadership Team. These individuals were able to bring in new skills to the budgeting process as they had expertise working for private companies.

Appropriable Organisation – Appropriable organisation occurs when elements of social capital such as ties, norms and trust developed in one setting, can be transferred to another setting. At FS, there was a close connection between senior staff members and the values. The formal values were closely linked to the personal values of senior leaders. Prior to working at FS, Senior Leader One worked at a church under a manager who was 'abusive' and 'in places dishonest'. After this experience, he determined to treat people in a way that 'reflected the character of Jesus' that is with 'dignity and honour' (Senior Leader 1). The values at FS arose out of this resolution.

Cognitive Dimension

FS had a formal set of organisational values which entailed shared language and vocabulary as well as the shared views of the cognitive dimension. FS is best described as a values-driven church where the focus is on operating and making decisions in a way that is consistent with its core values. The four core values are stated as: 'We value people', 'Integrity', 'Authenticity' and 'Vulnerability', and are described on FS' website as follows:

- 'We value people. God's supreme passion is people. This being so, any endeavour that bears His name must value and love people. We are careful at [FS] to ensure that people never become "the means to the end".
- We value integrity – we seek to function and communicate with truth and simplicity.
- We value authenticity – we value an atmosphere in which people can be honest and real.
- We value vulnerability – we are all on a journey. There are no "experts" here. The only reason any of us are here is the grace of God. We are honest about that'.

These four core values provide 'a degree of consensus in the social system' (Nahapiet & Ghoshal, 1998, p. 255) at FS. Staff described how the values were pivotal to the way FS operates. SL2 used the analogy of a pair of glasses to explain how she viewed the values. 'It's like having glasses on and we view everything through that'. In the opinion of the Dream team leader, the values

> Are woven through everything ... I think the way we do stuff, the way we talk in our Leadership Team, the way we want our staff to be treating their volunteers, these [values] are central to it.

There is an expectation that staff will adhere to the values in the way they work. 'It's kind of, for the lack of a better term, drilled into us that every decision we make must be made through the [FS] code of values' (YA leader). FS has a human resources policy of hiring staff who fit with the organisation's values. The Dream team leader, who also has a human resources role, stated:

> We don't necessarily advertise to a wider community. It's more about we see people that have the values and then maybe they're asked to go on staff because they have the values ... Because it's part of what they've bought into.

According to the People Care leader, the core values underpinned the budgeting process:

> So, although we're not literally going through each value with every question that we ask about budget, it is at the forefront ... We think about integrity when we're thinking about budget[s]. We are thinking about transparency, vulnerability, and all of that stuff when we're looking at budgets, in everything we do.

The YA leader agreed, stating that 'You're expected to look at the way that you spend money through those values'. Next, how the norms are reinforced during the budgeting process is examined.

Valuing people – For four of the interviewees, valuing people involved spending money on looking after those on their team, or on volunteer leaders and other volunteers in their area. FS relies heavily on volunteers to meet the needs of the congregation. To show their gratitude to the volunteers, FS staff host an annual dinner for volunteers. At this dinner, the staff prepare and serve the meal.

According to Youth Worker 2 (YW2), 'There's 400 people invited and out of [FS']
budget, we've had to budget in we're going to feed you all'.

The *we value people* norm extended to supportive working relationships among
staff. Those in the Families' team spoke of supportive working relationships. The
Tots and Kids' leader described her working relationships as 'close' and 'supportive'. The Intermediate leader spoke of 'easy-going' working relationships,
while Youth Worker 1 (YW1) believed the work environment was 'family-like'. In
the context of budgeting, the supportive working relationships were seen in what
YW1 referred to as a 'pastoral care element' to the budgeting process:

> I remember last year thinking of the three different areas that I was working, and then having to
> submit budgets. So, I worked for [a Christian camp] for part of my job. And then I was working
> here, and I worked at [another Christian organisation], and so, for instance at [the Christian
> camp], you would submit your budget and you almost felt like you were fighting for your budget
> there and to the point where we were like 'I don't want to fight about it. I just want you to say yes
> or no and if you say no to it, then that's fine'. But here [at FS], even if they did say 'No' to it, it
> was never like 'Justify that'. It's almost like really pastoral care in its own ... If they were to cut
> anything here, it is like 'Here are the reasons why and we're really sorry about that'.

The Leadership Team viewed their working relationships with other members
of the team as being open, friendly, respectful, caring and close. ITM2 related
how openness and respect among team members affected his wife, ITM1:

> There's a real openness [in financial issues], and I'm an accountant, so I tend to understand
> perhaps a lot more than [ITM1], because she doesn't like figures and such. But if there's some-
> thing she doesn't understand, she's totally free to ask in that meeting. And without being made
> to feel stupid.

Valuing people and supportive working relationships helped to lay a foundation and set the tone for the Leadership Team to function as a team. For four of
the Leadership Team, the team spirit at FS was viewed as making budgeting decisions that were in the best interest of the organisation. According to the People
Care team leader, 'We're working for the bigger need, family, not just for what I
want'. SL2 commented that decisions were often made on the basis of 'What's
best for [FS]?' She also pointed out that people were brought onto the Leadership
Team who worked well in a team environment. Similarly, the Dream team leader
indicated that 'we are in this together. That we are working for the same goals.
That we are trying to do this because we love [FS], we love God'. In a similar vein,
in the opinion of the FA,

> Everyone works for each other, rather than against each other, which is obviously what you
> often find in a secular environment ...That people compete for finance and budget, whereas I
> don't think we have that at all.

The Relational Dimension

The relational dimension covers trust, norms and identification.

Trust – Trustworthiness was referred to by interviewees as being part of the
budgeting process. Staff were entrusted to prepare budgets that were reasonable
and be honest in the way they managed the finances. The Dream Team Leader

commented on trust in the context of budgeting as follows: 'Because people do have a lot of freedom to spend, but there's trust that people will be doing that the right way'. The Finance Administrator expected those with budgeting responsibilities not to spend money at the end of the year, because money was left in their budget.

In the opinion of the Dream team leader, the integrity is vital to the budgeting process:

> I think integrity is probably the one that affects the budgeting process the most, because we really do expect people to be honest with the way they deal with finance. There's a lot of trust, I think. Because people do have a lot of freedom to spend, but there's trust that people will be doing that the right way.

The norm of honesty is related to integrity. Honesty in budget preparation is clearly the expectation of the FA. 'I expect they're going to give me accurate figures. I don't expect that they're going to go: "Oh, I'd just like to add another $2,000 in"'. There is also an expectation that area leaders will not add in new expenses without permission. According to the Tots and Kids' leader:

> If there's something that isn't in your budget, but you think it would be a really cool thing to do, make sure that you ask permission. You just don't go ahead and do it, you suss it out.

In the opinion of SL1, transparency was related to the norm of integrity. '[Transparency is] almost, a spin-off of integrity. If you're doing it honestly, there's nothing to hide'. Staff were free to ask for information on FS' finances. However, some information, for example, staff salaries, was kept confidential. There was an informal rule that the FA's door was always open to staff, so they could approach him at any time to request an update on their budget, or to ask questions regarding financial matters. The church believed they had nothing to hide (transparency) and believed that their decision regarding providing people with information if they asked was the right thing to do (integrity). The church was liberal with spending, especially if it had to do with staff development. Area leaders shared financial information with their volunteers on a need-to-know basis. The FA stated that the finances of the church were open, but that many of the staff were not interested:

> I think it's very open, but my qualifier to that is most people don't want to know. They're actually not that interested ... So those who need to know come and ask. Those who want to know come and ask. Those who aren't interested, which is the majority, don't come and ask.

The view that many of the staff were not interested in budgeting was reiterated by YW1:

> I think that if anyone came and asked about the budget, I'm sure that [the FA] would be happy to tell them. It's like in my head I'm like, 'Who'd want to ask about that? It just seems so boring!'

While there was little financial information communicated to the staff at staff meetings, at Leadership Team level, financial information was disseminated in a transparent and open manner. According to the Families' team leader, 'Everything's open ... everything from missions to what we're spending, to debt'. Leadership Team members were free to ask the FA for more financial information to be supplied if required.

The norm of trust, an element of the relational dimension of social capital, is also related to integrity. Staff were trusted to prepare budgets that were reasonable and be honest in the way they managed the finances of their area. The YA leader spoke about the trust and autonomy given to her when preparing her budget. 'I have never felt like there's been a look over my shoulder to see "How am I doing? How's it going? Why are you allocating that there?"' The FA expected those with budgeting responsibilities not to spend money at the end of the year, simply because there was money left in their budget.

> We trust you not to spend money on things that don't need money spent on, and if you've got money left over, that's fabulous, but we hope that the budget you've given us is accurate.

Trust in financial matters also extended to the use of an organisational credit card. The Tots and Kids' leader related her approach to the use of the credit card:

> So, I've got to be trustworthy in terms of what I use that credit card for. I make sure I've got the records of what I spend it on and that's sent in and gets coded properly, and so that it is what it is.

Despite the widespread trust reported by interviewees, there were isolated instances where staff would include funds in the budget for situations that may arise during the budgeting year. According to the Dream team leader,

> There's a few people that push the boundaries of the budget sometimes, but [the FA's] on top of that I think, so there's again a lot of trust that [the FA] monitors that.

According to ITM3, the Leadership Team had a 'pretty good handle on all the costs'. Due to the transparent nature of the budgeting process, any extra spending 'would get pulled into line pretty quick'. It appeared this was the case with the People Care team leader's desire to have funds available for staff development.

Norms – The norms of cooperation were particularly evident in the budgeting process. The Teams worked cooperatively together to achieve budgeting targets.

According to SL1, the cooperative, team spirit occurred in the budgeting process 'In the things that they don't do', such as empire building or leaders promoting own area to the detriment of other areas. In the context of budgeting, interviewees referred to making decisions that were in the best interest of FS. In the opinion of the FA:

> Everyone realises that there's a limited pool of money and there's no like 'Oh, my ministry's more important than yours. My [area's] more important than yours. I should have that money'. That's just something we don't have. So, I think in terms of the team thing, everyone works for each other, rather than against each other.

Likewise, the Tots and Kids' leader was aware of the needs of others when preparing her budget:

> I guess it's a sense that you're part of a team, so you can't be overboard and silly about your budget because there's only one pie and everyone is needing a slice of that pie, and so I guess it keeps you realistic and open that if you are cut back, there are good reasons for that. Your budget is only a submission, and so you would be prepared to tweak and pull things back if that's what's needed for everyone to get a fair share of the pie.

The People Care team leader related how a team approach and a cooperative spirit influenced her when the FA reduced her budget:

[The FA is] shaving money off my budget, but we still do it in a light-hearted cooperative manner. There's a real sense of, you know what? We're both working for the same purpose here. You're not my enemy. I'm not getting what I want, but we're working for the same goal, and that's fine … We're working for the bigger need, family, not just for what I want.

Likewise, the Dream team leader considered that the cooperative spirit influenced the way those with budgeting responsibilities approached budgeting:

People are passionate about their own areas, but at the same time, again, people are here because they love [FS] as a whole, and I think that comes through in the way that people are really reasonable about budgeting. They realise they can't have all the money because there's other really valuable stuff going on in other departments and I think that's again probably part of the community spirit of knowing each other, then you're going to be really reasonable in your requests.

She continued by saying that while people were passionate about their areas, 'I don't think there's anyone trying to build their kingdom at the expense of other people'. SL1 commented that he could not remember a Leadership Team member behaving in a selfish manner:

I think it shows up in the way that you don't see them fighting for portions of the pie. You don't see them sort of parochial, pushing their little barrow at the expense of others. They all come to the table wanting the best across the board, and, and I've never, ever been in a discussion where I've felt like 'That was selfish. You're really pushing for your team in a way that's illicit. In a way that's really meaning that other people are going to get stuck because you've pushed your agenda.   •

The FA was also of the opinion that the notion of the 'bigger picture' acted against people building empires. ITM2 believed that the servant approach to leadership seen at FS negated any tendency towards empire building:

I think there's a high level of servanthood, with the servant leadership type thing. At all the levels of people, the leaders seek to serve the people that they're responsible for. So, it's not trying to build their own little hierarchy.

The People Care team leader mentioned that she had not seen any competition between Leadership Team members for resources:

I don't see [areas] competing at all. Yes different [areas] have different amounts of budget, because they have different requirements … At a Leadership Team level, we all lead a[n] [area], or most of us lead a[n] [area]. We would look at each other's budget and think 'Well go for it. That's what you need'.

In contrast to empire building, two interviewees spoke of making sacrifices in their budget:

There's definitely times where's it's like, no, you can't have that because we don't have the money for it. But I think when you take a position on the staff at a church you expect that there will be sacrifices somewhere. You can't have everything all the time, because it's a church. It's not a business. (YA leader)

Likewise, in the context of capital budgeting, the People Care team leader referred to a sacrificial attitude that led to a focus on the common good:

I think in all honesty, it's sacrificial in as much as we all are thinking about the greater good. The good of people who come to [FS]. Not our own good, or our own departmental good or our own kingdom.

In the opinion of SL1, people were the primary focus of FS: 'Our bottom-line is not profit. Our bottom-line is people'. Interviewees were in agreement that the main goal of FS was spiritual, involving people. According to SL1, the purpose of FS was:

To see God's Kingdom established in the earth. We want to see God glorified. We want to see people come to Christ. We want to see families healed and lives touched, and people changed, and we want to see the gospel.

Accordingly, money (and budgeting for that money) played a secondary, supportive role:

[Money is] secondary. It's a by-product. It's a by-product of what we do ... I think once finance becomes the key issue of a church's life, something has been perverted. Ministry is the key issue. Yes, ministry costs money. But our, our belief is that if it's valid and if God's in it, He'll supply. So that's how we function.

While the people employed are paid less than the market rate, the leadership believed that employees are happy to work for the church because they place service to God ahead of money. However, an alternative interpretation is that while the church claims to value people, the value the church claim to put on their staff is not reflected in the salary paid to staff. The Leadership Team could be out of touch with their staff and staff could be disgruntled with the low pay rate. However, this did not seem to be the case. The church is also a charitable organisation and so providing social services is important for the leaders rather than working for money.

The FA explained the relationship between the primary and secondary goals at FS as follows: '[Money] is very secondary. It's a means to an end. In the end, it's what allows us to operate, but it's not what causes us to operate'. The Families' team leader believed that whilst money (and budgeting for that money) was not a primary focus, FS' finances were still managed well:

It's such a bizarre balance ... from my eyes is [money is] not the primary focus, but also in my opinion, that doesn't mean it's not well looked after. It doesn't mean it's haphazard. I just think it's not the primary focus.

Generosity – A further norm influencing the budgeting process at FS is the norm of generosity. SL1 stated: 'I want us to be generous, because that's what God's like. And we must be like Him'. The People Care team leader shared how, whenever possible, the staff aim to 'Always operate with generous open hands'. Interviewees believed the funding given to their areas was generous. The Tots and Kids' leader commented: 'They've always been incredibly generous, and they will pretty much give us what we need to do to get the job done'. YW1 related how she has never 'pushed back' on funding given to the youth, because, when compared to other places she has worked, she feels 'They're really generous here at [FS], anyway with what we need'.

Generosity included providing funds in the budget for staff in special circumstances and paying visiting speakers well. 'We pay speakers who come very generously, plus meet all of their accommodation costs and transport and costs and all that sort of stuff' (People Care team leader). She contrasted FS' generosity in paying visiting speakers with the situation facing a colleague at another church who was 'asked to go from Wellington to Auckland to speak at a church and he was given $50 ... and he had to pay for his airfares, return airfares'.

The People Care team leader spoke about how money was set aside in the budget to fund those in need. 'So, there's a budget there for helps [sic.] budget. There's a budget for any number of situations where people need help or finances or something like that'. Similarly, YW2 believed:

> [FS] is probably one of the most generous workplaces or churches that I know of. They will, with no expense spared, try and help other people ... I've never had a time where I've had someone who's needed a food parcel or anything where I've been told 'You can't spend the money because we don't have it'.

ITM3, an accountant, expressed FS' view on generosity in financial terms, saying: 'We'd rather be generous ... and have less cash in the bank ... Than being tight and having more cash in the bank'. SL1 also expressed his preference for FS to be generous rather than accumulate money:

> Where we can and where we are able, without throwing the whole budgeting process into chaos because we're just being reckless, we really try to be generous. That's why over the years, we haven't had surpluses. We're not aiming for surplus. We're trying to bless people, so if we've got surplus and there's a need, I wouldn't bank it. I'd give it to the need.

The People Care team leader reiterated the opinion of SL1 that their desire was to balance being generous with wise financial management. In her opinion, FS is 'Wise and careful, not frivolous or silly, but [with] a real value on generosity as well'. These were examples provided by interviewees about the generosity of the church to people in the congregation and those who do not attend the church. The church was not so much focussed on surpluses, but rather to donate money to the needy in the community. Interviewees spoke about how the values have been internalised and incorporated into their area of responsibility. According to the YA leader, 'We all have chosen to live our lives by those values, and to lead through those values, so we treat each other through those values as well'. SL1 pointed out that the values are 'Not just a plaque we put on the wall'. For him, the values are 'What calls us forth, and it is what drives our organisation'.

By adopting FS' values as their own personal values, interviewees have internalised (Coleman, 1990) the values, and have identified with the values. Identification is an element of the relational dimension of social capital. Interviewees were also displaying what Leana and Van Buren (1999) term associability, as they have laid down their personal values and adopted the values of the collective, in this case, FS. Associability and identification were also seen in the budgeting process where interviewees laid down individual goals and worked cooperatively towards FS' goals.

DISCUSSION

The purpose of this chapter is to examine the budgeting process in a local church from a social capital perspective. At FS, budgeting was a social process as much as a technical process. The social norms evident permeated the budgeting process. The presence of norms agrees with the social capital literature stance that norms are an important feature of social capital (Cohen & Prusak, 2001; Nahapiet & Ghoshal, 1998).

The study supports the literature that budgets are management tools most pervasively utilised in organisations for resource allocation decisions (Bower, 2017; Davila & Wouters, 2005). Organisations that choose initial MCS better suited to their strategy tend to perform better (Nath & Sharma, 2014; Sharma et al., 2014; Soobaroyen et al., 2019).

An aspect of budgeting at FS was the interviewees' participation and explanation by subordinates led to improved performance. In the budget-setting process, members were able to negotiate their way through the budgeting process, which enhances social capital (Hauriasi et al., 2016).

Merchant (1985) notes that the propensities to create budgetary slack are lower when managers participate actively in budgeting. The pressure to meet financial targets can shape manipulation of short-term performance measures and encouragement of a myopic, short-term orientation. The study supports Irvine's (2005) and Lightbody's (2000) views that the budgeting process is an enabling and liberating contributor to a church's fulfilment of its spiritual vision. The budget is used as a control device (Lyne, 1988).

It was evident from the interview data that the norms and values present at FS brought interviewees together to achieve the commonly understood organisational goal. Supportive working relationships among those involved in budgeting, similar to social capital, were also reported by Hauriasi et al. (2016) in their study of budgeting in the Anglican Church of Melanesia. It appears that the relaxed nature of the budgeting process, consultation, decision-making by consensus and the nurturing of empathy and agreement reflected 'traditional ethnic identities' (p. 1305) in the Solomon Islands culture.

However, 'strong norms and mutual identification' may also limit a group's 'openness to information and to alternative ways of doing things, producing forms of collective blindness that sometimes have disastrous consequences' (Nahapiet & Ghoshal, 1998, p. 245). Cohen and Prusak (2001) suggest a solution to a tendency towards groupthink is 'to let more people and information enter in from outside the group' (p. 71). Adler and Kwon (2002) and Nahapiet and Ghoshal (1998) note that problems may occur in a group with strong social norms and beliefs, if access to sources of ideas and information becomes restricted. FS' Leadership Team recognised that insularity could be a problem, and with this end in mind, in 2012, they brought in three independent team members who attended FS, but were not on the staff, into the Leadership Team.

Clear evidence of sacrificial behaviour was found at FS in the context of budgeting. Interviewees spoke of being prepared to make sacrifices in the budget for their area to accommodate the needs of others. Such behaviour was not recorded by Irvine (2005) in the study of budgeting practices in a local church. Nor was it mentioned by Kluvers (2001) in his exploratory study of budgeting in churches in Melbourne, Australia.

The shared spiritual goal of extending the Kingdom of God was born out of a Christian worldview and represented a 'shared vision and purpose' (Pearson et al., 2008, p. 957) among staff. In the social capital literature, a shared view is often referred to as a shared vision, purpose, understanding or goal among those in the organisation (Carr, Cole, Ring, & Blettner, 2011; Chow & Chan, 2008; Inkpen & Tsang, 2005). Nahapiet and Ghoshal (1998) use the term 'shared systems of meaning' (p. 244) to refer to the same phenomenon. Likewise, the secondary focus on money (and budgeting for that money) represents a 'shared understanding of the business' (Huppi & Seemann, 2001, p. 36), as those involved in budgeting all agree on the secondary importance of money to the running of FS. The agreement among interviewees on the primary and secondary goals contributed to the social nature of the budgeting process and could be loosely seen as a further norm operating in the budgeting process.

Whilst the shared understanding of the common goal of FS is spiritual in nature, money (and budgeting for that money) is required to achieve the common goal of extending the Kingdom of God. Those with budgeting responsibilities were conscious of the common good and worked cooperatively to ensure budgeting decisions were made in FS' best interests. By doing so, those with budgeting responsibilities were identifying with FS, and seeing themselves 'as part of the collective' (Pearson et al., 2008, p. 959). The social process of working cooperatively towards the shared spiritual goal was also seen in the way managers did not seek to build their area into an empire and also in a sacrificial attitude towards budgeting. The dominance of a spiritual goal in the budgeting process was also seen at a local church in Sydney, Australia (Irvine, 2005). In a similar way to FS, the spiritual vision for the church was expressed through the budget. As in the case of FS, 'the budget was never to take over as an end in itself, but always to be subservient to the vision' (Irvine, 2005, p. 225).

CONCLUSION

This study has examined the budgeting in a local church from a social capital perspective. The social capital provides novel insights into the construction of budgets and its social aspects. The main finding of this present study is that at FS, budgeting was a social process that can be explained by social capital theory. This social process was evident in the way the budgeting process reinforced social norms and trust, and in the way, interviewees identified with organisational norms and goals. The presence of commonly understood goals also contributed to the social nature of the budgeting process. These shared goals were underpinned by the shared Christian worldview held by interviewees. The reality of resource allocation through budgets is a complex process involving technical, organisational, cultural and interpersonal forces that are fundamentally related (Bower, 2017).

The study makes a specific contribution to the literature on budgeting in a church. It addresses Hopwood's (1983) call for understanding accounting, in this case budgeting, in the social context in which it operates. This social context entails relationships that are not merely technical. This study begins to fill a gap in the budgeting and social capital literature, as it examines how social aspects influence the budgeting process. In doing so, this study provides a new insight into an aspect of budgeting that has not previously been studied. Budgeting was found to foster, strengthen and reinforce social capital among those involved in the process. The budgeting process achieved these ends through people coming together and working cooperatively towards a shared understanding of the common goal.

Chenhall et al. (2010, 2012) and Vieira et al. (2013) were the only studies located in the literature that referred to social capital in the context of budgeting. In contrast to Chenhall et al. (2010, 2012) and Vieira et al. (2013), this study focusses entirely on the budgeting *process*, and the importance of social capital within the budgeting process. This study has adapted Nahapiet and Ghoshal (1998) social capital framework to examine budgeting practices at FS. In doing so, Nahapiet and Ghoshal (1998) framework of social capital has been adapted and applied to a context not previously studied, i.e., the budgeting process. The study will be useful to a broader-not-for-profit/charity or even a public sector that can get an insight that budgeting is social process. The presence of commonly understood goals in these organisations will contribute to the social nature of budgeting process. This study will be of interest to practitioners involved in budgeting, as well as those involved in setting budgeting policy in an organisation, as it highlights the social side of budgeting. The study raises awareness among practitioners on how social aspects influence the budgeting process of the organisation.

Whilst this study proposes a social capital interpretation of budgeting by drawing on social capital theory, there are a number of limitations. There may be an element of self-selection, as the church agreed to participate in the study and chose to allow a researcher to examine social aspects of its budgeting process. This study has drawn on Nahapiet and Ghoshal (1998) framework of social capital. It is possible that a different model of social capital may provide differing results or add more insight to the topic. This study has relied on interviews to collect data. However, interviews may not provide the depth of information that can be obtained from a longitudinal case study, where observations are made over an extended time period.

The social capital interpretation of budgeting presented in this study opens the door to a number of research opportunities. The approach taken in this study could be extended to an organisation in the public sector or extended to differing types of not-for-profit organisations. This study could be extended internationally in countries with different histories or cultures.

This study contributes to the literature in relation to the natural or social processes of budgeting. Boland and Pondy (1983) view accounting, and by implication budgeting, as a union of natural and rational processes. The importance of the rational aspects of the budgeting process is not negated in this study. Rather, this study focusses on the natural aspects, providing evidence that at FS, budgeting is a social process, one that can be explained by social capital theory.

NOTES

1. Fountain Springs (FS) is a pseudonym used to protect the identity of the organisation.
2. Management and budgetary control is a process for managers to set financial and operational objectives with budgets to compare actual results and adjust performance accordingly.
3. www.charities.govt.nz
4. www.charities.govt.nz
5. Pseudonyms have been used for team names to protect the identity of the organisation.
6. The four teams are the Families' Team, the People Care Team, the Dream Team and the Administration Team. Each team has a team leader. Within the Families' Team, there are four areas – Tots and Kids, intermediate, Youth and Young Adults. The person in charge of each area is an Area Leader. Each Area Leader has staff and volunteers that they lead and oversee. For example, the Youth Leader has two paid Youth Workers, as well as other volunteer leaders.

ACKNOWLEDGMENTS

An earlier version of the chapter was presented at the Australasian Performance Measurement Conference in Queenstown, New Zealand and at the Accounting and Finance Association of Australia and New Zealand Annual Conference. The chapter was also presented as part of seminar series at La Trobe University in Australia. The authors would like to thank Ralph Adler and Lachlan MacDonald-Kerr for their valuable comments on the earlier versions of the chapter. The authors also would like to thank the reviewers and participants of the Australasian Performance Measurement Conference and Accounting and Finance Association of Australia and New Zealand for their comments which helped to improve the chapter.

REFERENCES

Adler, P. S., & Kwon, S. W. (2002). Social capital: Prospects for a new concept. *Academy of Management Review, 27*(1), 17–40.
Barry, D. (2015). *Water under the bridge: Loads of other stuff too: A journey into values-shaped.* Hamilton: Author.
Bazeley, P. (2013). *Qualitative data analysis: Practical strategies.* London: Sage.
Boland Jr, R. J., & Pondy, L. R. (1983). Accounting in organizations: A union of natural and rational perspectives. *Accounting, Organizations and Society, 8*(2–3), 223–234.
Booth, P. (1993). Accounting in churches: A research framework and agenda. *Accounting, Auditing & Accountability Journal, 6*(4), 37–67.
Bourdieu, P. (1986). The forms of capital. In J. G. Richardson (Ed.), *Handbook of theory and research for the sociology of education* (pp. 241–258). New York, NY: Greenwood Press.
Bower, J. L. (2017). Managing resource allocation: Personal reflections from a managerial perspective. *Journal of Management, 43*(8), 2421–2429.
Carmona, S., & Ezzamel, M. (2006). Accounting and religion: A historical perspective. *Accounting History, 11*(2), 117–127.
Carr, J. C., Cole, M. S., Ring, J. K., & Blettner, D. P. (2011). A measure of variations in internal social capital among family firms. *Entrepreneurship Theory and Practice, 35*(6), 1207–1227.
Chenhall, R. H., Hall, M., & Smith, D. (2010). Social capital and management control systems: A study of a non-government organization. *Accounting, Organizations and Society, 35*(8), 737–756.

Chenhall, R. H., Hall, M., & Smith, D. (2012). *Performance measurement and management control in non-profit organisations: CGMA Report*. London: Chartered Institute of Management Accountants. Retrieved from http://www.lse.ac.uk/accounting/pdf/Social_Capital_Performance_Measurement.pdf

Chenhall, R. H., & Morris, D. (1995). Organic decision and communication processes and management accounting systems in entrepreneurial and conservative business organizations. *Omega International Journal of Management Science, 23*(5), 485–497.

Chow, W. S., & Chan, L. S. (2008). Social network, social trust and shared goals in organizational knowledge sharing. *Information & Management, 45*(7), 458–465.

Chua, W. F. (1986). Radical developments in accounting thought. *The Accounting Review, 61*(4), 601–632.

Cohen, D., & Prusak, L. (2001). *In good company: How social capital makes organizations work.* Boston, MA: Harvard Business School Press.

Coleman, J. S. (1987). Norms as social capital. In G. Radnitzky & P. Bernholz (Eds.), *Economic Imperialism: The economic approach applied outside the field of economics* (pp. 133–155). New York, NY: Paragon House.

Coleman, J. S. (1988). Social capital in the creation of human capital. *American Journal of Sociology, 94*, S95–S120.

Coleman, J. S. (1990). *Foundations of social theory.* Cambridge, MA: Belknap Press of Harvard University Press.

Corbin Dwyer, S., & Buckle, J. L. (2009). The space between: On being an insider-outsider in qualitative research. *International Journal of Qualitative Methods, 8*(1), 54–63.

Cordery, C. (2015). Accounting history and religion: A review of studies and a research agenda. *Accounting History, 20*(4), 430–463.

Covaleski, M. A., Evans, J. H., Luft, J. L., & Shields, M. D. (2003). Budgeting research: Three theoretical perspectives and criteria for selective integration. *Journal of Management Accounting Research, 15*(1), 3–49.

Davila, T., & Wouters, M. (2005). Managing budgets emphasis through the explicit design of conditional budgetary slack. *Accounting, Organizations and Society, 30*(7–8), 587–608.

Fuller, T., & Tian, Y. (2006). Social and symbolic capital and responsible entrepreneurship: An empirical investigation of SME narratives. *Journal of Business Ethics, 67*(3), 287–304.

Gibb, A., & Scott, M. (1985). Strategic awareness, personal commitment and the process of planning in the small business. *Journal of Management Studies, 22*(6), 597–631.

Hatzakis, T., Lycett, M., Macredie, R. D., & Martin, V. A. (2005). Towards the development of a social capital approach to evaluating change management interventions. *European Journal of Information Systems, 14*(1), 60–74.

Hauriasi, A., Van-Peursem, K., & Davey, H. (2016). Budget processes in the Anglican Church of Melanesia: An emergent ethnic identity. *Accounting, Auditing & Accountability Journal, 29*(8), 1294–1319.

Hope, J., & Fraser, R. (2003). New ways of setting rewards: The beyond budgeting model. *California Management Review, 45*(4), 104–119.

Hopper, T., & Powell, A. (1985). Making sense of research into the organizational and social aspects of management accounting: A review of its underlying assumptions. *Journal of Management Studies, 22*(5), 429–465.

Hopwood, A. G. (1983). On trying to understand accounting in the contexts in which it operates. *Accounting, Organizations and Society, 8*(2/3), 287–305.

Huppi, R., & Seemann, P. (2001). *Social capital: Securing competitive advantage in the new economy.* Harlow: Pearson Education.

Inkpen, A. C., & Tsang, E. W. K. (2005). Social capital, networks, and knowledge transfer. *The Academy of Management Review, 30*(1), 146–165.

International Integrated Reporting Council. (2013). Consultation draft of the international <IR> framework. Retrieved from http://integratedreporting.org/wp-content/uploads/2013/12/13-12-08-THE-INTERNATIONAL-IR-FRAMEWORK-2-1.pdf

Irvine, H. (2005). Balancing money and mission in a local church budget. *Accounting, Auditing & Accountability Journal, 18*(2), 211–237.

Jacobs, K. (2005). The sacred and the secular: Examining the role of accounting in the religious context. *Accounting, Auditing & Accountability Journal, 18*(2), 189–210.

Kenno, S. A., Lau, M. C., & Sainty, B. J. (2018). In search of a theory of budgeting: A literature review. *Accounting Perspectives, 17*(4), 507–553.

Kluvers, R. (2001). Budgeting in Catholic parishes: An exploratory study. *Financial Accountability & Management, 17*(1), 41–58.

Knoke, D. (2009). Playing well together: Creating corporate social capital in strategic alliance networks. *American Behavioral Scientist, 52*(12), 1690–1708.

Kramer, S., & Hartmann, F. (2014). How do top-down and bottom-up budgeting affect budget slack and performance through social and economic exchange. *Abacus, 50*(3), 314–340.

Kurt, A. C., & Feng, N. C. (2019). Firm performance implications of using qualitative criteria in CEO bonus contracts. *Advances in Management Accounting, 31*, 55–89.

Kuruppu, C., Adhikari, P., Gunarathna, V., Ambalangodage, D., Perera, P., & Karunarathna, C. (2016). Participatory budgeting in a Sri Lankan urban council: A practice of power and domination. *Critical Perspectives on Accounting, 41*, 1–17.

Laughlin, R. C. (1990). A model of financial accountability and the Church of England. *Financial Accountability & Management, 6*(2), 93–114.

Laughlin, R. (1995). Empirical research in accounting: Alternative approaches and a case for "middle-range" thinking. *Accounting, Auditing & Accountability Journal, 8*(1), 63–87.

Laughlin, R. C. (1988). Accounting in its social context: An analysis of the accounting systems of the Church of England. *Accounting, Auditing & Accountability Journal, 1*(2), 19–42.

Lawrence, S., & Sharma, U. (2002). Commodification of education and academic labour- using the balanced scorecard in a university setting. *Critical Perspectives on Accounting, 13*, 661–677.

Leana, C. R., & Van Buren, H. J. (1999). Organizational social capital and employment practices. *Academy of Management Review, 24*(3), 538–555.

Libby, T. (1999). The influence of voice and explanation on performance in a participative budgeting setting. *Accounting, Organizations and Society, 24*, 125–137.

Lightbody, M. (2000). Storing and shielding: Financial management behaviour in a church organization. *Accounting, Auditing & Accountability Journal, 13*(2), 156–174.

Lightbody, M. (2003). On being a financial manager in a church organisation: Understanding the experience. *Financial Accountability & Management, 19*(2), 117–139.

Lyne, S. R. (1988). The role of the budget in medium and large UK companies and the relationship with budget pressure and participation. *Accounting and Business Research, 18*(71), 195–212.

Mani, Y., & Lakhal, L. (2015). Exploring the family effect on firm performance. *International Journal of Entrepreneurial Behavior & Research, 21*(6), 898–917.

McPhail, K., & Cordery, C. J. (2019). Theological perspectives on accounting: Worldviews don't change overnight. *Accounting, Auditing and Accountability Journal, 32*(8), 2330–2352.

McPhail, K., Gorringe, T., & Gray, R. (2004). Accounting and theology: Initiating a dialogue between immediacy and eternity. *Accounting, Auditing and Accountability Journal, 17*(3), 320–326.

Merchant, K. A. (1985). Budgeting and the propensity to create budgetary slack. *Accounting, Organizations and Society, 10*(1), 201–210.

Merchant, K. A. (1990). The effects of financial controls on data manipulation and management myopia. *Accounting, Organizations and Society, 15*(4), 297–313.

Meyers, R. T. (1996). Is there a key to the normative budgeting lock? *Policy Sciences, 29*(3), 171–188.

Nahapiet, J., & Ghoshal, S. (1998). Social capital, intellectual capital, and the organizational advantage. *Academy of Management Review, 23*(2), 242–266.

Nath, N., & Sharma, U. (2014). Performance management systems in the public housing sector: Dissemination to diffusion. *Australian Accounting Review, 24*(1), 2–20.

O'Grady, W., Akroyd, C., & Scott, I. (2017). Beyond budgeting: Distinguishing modes of adaptive performance management. *Advances in Management Accounting, 29*, 33–53.

Parker, R. J., & Kyj, L. (2006). Vertical information sharing in the budgeting process. *Accounting, Organizations and Society, 31*(1), 27–45.

Parker, L. D., & Northcott, D. (2016). Qualitative generalising in accounting research: Concepts and strategies. *Accounting, Auditing & Accountability Journal, 29*(6), 1100–1131.

Pearson, A. W., Carr, J. C., & Shaw, J. C. (2008). Toward a theory of familiness: A social capital perspective. *Entrepreneurship Theory and Practice, 32*(6), 949–969.

Putnam, R. D. (1993). The prosperous community: Social capital and public life. *The American Prospect, 13*, 35–42.

Putnam, R. D. (1995a). Bowling alone: America's declining social capital. *Journal of Democracy, 6*(1), 65–78.

Putnam, R. D. (1995b). Tuning in, tuning out: The strange disappearance of social capital in America. *PS: Political Science & Politics, 28*(4), 664–683.

Putnam, R. D. (2000). *Bowling alone: The collapse and revival of American Community*. New York, NY: Simon & Schuster.

Robison, L. J., Shmidt, A. A., & Siles, M. E. (2002). Is social capital really capital? *Review of Social Economy, 60*, 1–24.]

Saldana, J. (2013). *The coding manual for qualitative researchers.* Los Angeles, CA: Sage.

Scapens, R. W. (1990). Researching management accounting practice: The role of case study methods. *British Accounting Review, 22*(3), 259–281.

Sharma, U., & Frost, D. (2020). Social capital and the budgeting process: A study of three organisations. *Accounting Forum, 44*(4), 379–397.

Sharma, U., Lawrence, S., & Lowe, A. (2010). Institutional contradiction and management control innovation: A field study of total quality management practices in a privatised telecommunications company. *Management Accounting Research, 21*(4), 251–264.

Sharma, U., Lawrence, S., & Lowe, A. (2014). Accountants as institutional entrepreneurs: Changing routines in a telecommunications company. *Qualitative Research in Accounting and Management, 11*(3), 190–214.

Simons, R. (1995). *Levers of control: How managers use innovative control systems to drive strategic renewal.* Boston, MA: Harvard Business School Press.

Soobaroyen, T., Ntim, C. G., Broad, M. J., Agrizzi, D., & Vithana, K. (2019). Exploring the oversight of risk management in UK higher education institutions: The case of audit committees. *Accounting Forum, 43*(4), 404–425.

Subramaniam, N., Stewart, J., Ng, C., & Shulman, A. (2013). Understanding corporate governance in the Australian public sector: A social capital approach. *Accounting, Auditing & Accountability Journal, 26*(6), 946–977.

Vieira, R., Ha, T. T. L., & O'Dwyer, B. (2013). Interplay of management control systems and social enterprises: A case study of a social enterprise in Vietnam. Paper presented at the Seventh Asia Pacific Interdisciplinary Research in Accounting Conference (APIRA), 26–28 July, Kobe, Japan. Retrieved from http://www.apira2013.org/proceedings/pdfs/K278.pdf

HOW CONTEXTUALLY DEPENDENT, NON-MONETARY PREFERENCES INFLUENCE COST REPORTING MISREPRESENTATIONS

Timothy C. Miller, Sean A. Peffer and Dan N. Stone

ABSTRACT

This study contributes to the participative budgeting and budget misrepresentation literature by exploring: (1) whether managers' judgments of fair behaviors are malleable and context-dependent and (2) if these judgments of fair behavior impact cost reporting misrepresentations. Two experiments investigate these questions. Experiment 1 (n = 42) tests whether the behavior that managers judge to be "fair" differs based on the decision context (i.e., initial economic position [IEP]). Experiment 2 (n = 130) investigates: (1) how managers' deployment of fairness beliefs influences their reporting misrepresentations and (2) how decision aids that reduce task complexity impact managers' deployment of fairness beliefs in their misreporting decisions. The study found that managers deploy fairness beliefs (i.e., honesty or equality) consistent with maximizing their context-relevant income. Hence, fairness beliefs constrain misrepresentations in predictable ways. In addition, we find more accounting information is not always beneficial. The presence of decision aids actually increases misrepresentations when managers are initially advantaged (i.e., start with more resources than others). The implications from these findings are relevant to the honesty and budgeting literature and provide novel findings of how managers' preferences for fairness constrain managers from maximizing their income. The chapter demonstrates that contextual factors can influence the deployment of managers' fairness beliefs which, in turn,

Advances in Management Accounting, Volume 35, 73–98
ISSN: 1474-7871/doi:10.1108/S1474-787120230000035004

differentially impact their reporting misrepresentation. Another contribution is that providing decision aids, which reduce task complexity, may not always benefit companies, since such aids may increase misrepresentation under certain conditions.

Keywords: Participative budgeting; budgetary slack; managers' moral incentives; honesty; misrepresentation; experiment

INTRODUCTION

Managers often use private information to misreport costs and consume excess resources. However, research indicates that: (a) managers typically do not evidence economically rational decisions by fully misrepresenting and maximizing their incomes and (b) these results obtain due to managers' non-monetary or non-pecuniary preferences.[1] One of these preferences is a concern for "fairness." Managers want to be "fair." However, what constitutes "fair" may depend upon the decisions and contexts. We predict and test: (1) whether managers' determinations of fairness are partially determined by how defining fairness maximizes their context-dependent income, (2) whether these determinations of fairness predictively impact managers' misreporting behaviors, and (3) whether decision aids, which reduce task complexity, influence managers' fairness determinations and misreporting behaviors.

Two multiperiod experiments test our predictions. In our first experiment, we test whether managers' definitions of fairness are situational by manipulating a contextual variable that we refer to as IEP. IEP is defined as the managers' income compared with others who have invested equivalent effort. Managers who receive more (less) than comparison others who have invested the same effort are labeled "advantaged" ("disadvantaged"). We choose this contextual variable for its importance and ubiquity in organizations where information about peer employees' income is often available. For instance, about 25% of firms directly inform executives of peer income through relative performance schemes (Gong, Li, & Shin, 2011). In addition, all US government employee salaries are publicly available; thus, government employees can access their peers' incomes.

We also choose IEP because the definition of "fairness" that maximizes managers' incomes differs depending upon managers' IEP. Fairness is a subjective determination of what is right or wrong in a specific situation. We propose that managers prefer acting fairly. However, the realm of fair actions can be looked at in many ways. We propose that managers will choose a perspective or definition regarding fairness that allows them to maximize their incomes depending upon their decision contexts. Specifically, in the framework of our first experiment, disadvantaged managers will define fair actions as reporting to achieve equality and advantaged managers will define fair actions as reporting honestly.

In our second experiment, we use the same task with a separate subject pool and do not measure fairness beliefs to avoid demand effects. We then test if the differential judgments about what is "fair" from the first experiment predictably impact reporting decisions. So, while our first experiment measures managers' *beliefs* about what is fair to implement, our second experiment measures whether managers' *actions* (i.e., misreporting) are consistent with those beliefs. In addition, we introduce decision aids that greatly reduce task complexity. We then test whether using decision aids affects the extent to which managers' fairness beliefs constrain their misreporting behavior.

Our findings are consistent with our predictions. We find that managers choose their beliefs about what is fair (e.g., honesty or equality) consistent with the definition that maximizes their incomes given their context (IEP). We also find that managers' misreporting behavior is consistent with their chosen fairness belief along with their monetary self-interest. Additionally, we find that employing decision aids that decrease task complexity actually increases misrepresentation in the case of disadvantaged managers.

This study contributes in three ways. First, it supports research that shows that managers' actions are a joint product of monetary incentives and non-monetary preferences (e.g., fairness). Second, it advances this research by showing that the non-monetary preference managers believe to be fair differs by context consistent with definitional choices that maximize managerial self-interest. Finally, it provides evidence that the effect of decision aids in this context is contingent upon a manager's placement relative to a comparison other; increasing misrepresentation in one instance and having no impact in another.

BACKGROUND AND LITERATURE REVIEW

Participative Budgeting, Budgetary Slack, and Misrepresentation

Misrepresentation in participative budgeting research has over a 30-year history. It originated in Young's (1985) publication in the *Journal of Accounting Research* (see Brown, Evans, & Moser, 2009 and Mahlendorf, Schäffer, & Skiba, 2015 for reviews on different aspects of this research stream). One important goal of this literature has been investigating the relevant antecedents to eliciting employees' private information for better managerial decision-making. The research investigates potential influences on this elicitation over a wide range of variables: e.g., contract structure (Waller, 1988), information asymmetry (Chow, Cooper, & Waller, 1988), reputation (Chong & Loy, 2015), negotiation (Fisher, Frederickson, & Peffer, 2002 and Groen, 2018), participation (Dow, Watson, Greenberg, & Greenberg, 2012), framing (Brown, Fisher, Peffer, & Sprinkle, 2017), and individual desires for fairness, ethics, or other non-monetary preferences (Hobson, Mellon, & Stevens, 2011).

This study further investigates the effect of non-monetary preferences on the misrepresentation of private information. Fairness (Cohen, Holder-Webb, Sharp, & Pant, 2007; Zhang, 2008) or ethical (Frederickson & Cloyd, 1998) preferences have previously been found to reduce misrepresentation. For instance, Frederickson and Cloyd found that participants claim personal integrity is the most important factor in failing to maximize income through misrepresentation – implying ethics is essential in the decision. Likewise, Jollineau, Vance, and Webb (2012) find that the perceived ethical nature of a superior's request affects compliance with that request. Similarly, Zhang (2008) and Cohen et al. (2007) find that the perception of the principals' behavior regarding fairness affects misrepresentation.[2]

While non-monetary preferences for fairness or ethics are prevalent in the literature, it is often a subjective question whether a particular action is consistent with these preferences. Typical definitions of fairness or ethics found in the literature are based on perceptions, considerations, or beliefs. For instance, Cohen et al. (2007, pp. 1119–1120) define fairness "as an attribute of an action or outcome." In other words, the way an individual perceives the fairness of the outcomes associated with a potential behavior may affect an individual's willingness to undertake a particular action. Similarly, Jollineau et al. (2012, p. 2) rely on "beliefs about the ethical nature of providing accounting estimates." Indeed, determining the fairness, morality, or ethics of situations is sometimes so complex that an entire branch of philosophy (moral philosophy) explores this topic, which centers on *right* and *wrong* action. We, therefore, consider the behaviors managers consider to be fair to be subjective judgments.

While determining whether actions are consistent with fairness is subjective, this is not the case for all non-monetary preferences. Behavior consistent with honesty, equality, and equity can be objectively determined. Individuals are either honest or dishonest. They behave either in accordance with equality, equity, or neither. The presence of distinct preferences regarding the distribution of income (such as preferences for equality and equity) has been seen in several studies, including: Evans et al. (2001) regarding the division of income surplus among managers, Kim, Evans and Moser (2005) regarding equity preferences affecting the amount of taxable income individuals choose to report, and Matuszewski (2010) which finds that perceptions about the causes of inequity influence the magnitude of misrepresentation caused by these preferences. Honesty as a non-monetary concern unto itself is also investigated in Evans et al. (2001), Hannan, Rankin, and Towry (2006), and Rankin, Schwartz, and Young (2008). Furthermore, Douthit and Stevens (2015) find that honesty preferences in budgeting appear robust when a superior has rejection authority. These studies find that while there appears to be an independent desire for these behaviors, tradeoffs exist between non-monetary preferences and monetary desires.

Consistent with prior literature, we explore a setting where managers have private information regarding their costs and discretion in cost reporting.[3] Managers can exploit private information to misreport and increase their income at the expense of others. Monetary preferences and non-monetary preferences determine the amount of misrepresentation. Research convincingly demonstrates that individuals have monetary preferences (Alchian & Demsetz, 1972, p. 780; Cohen et al., 2007), and that non-monetary preferences inhibit income-maximizing misrepresentation. We further this research by investigating whether managers' definitions of the non-monetary preference of fairness are contextually dependent, and whether managers' subsequent misrepresentations are consistent with their contextually determined definitions.

EXPERIMENT 1

Experiment 1 investigates what managers subjectively determine to be "fair" behavior regarding misrepresentations in a cost-reporting task where they have private information. The degree of misrepresentation reported partially determines the incomes for both managers. In our study, managers' misreporting increases their own profit, but decreases that of the other manager. Consistent with prior research (e.g., Cohen et al., 2007; Drake, Matuszewski, & Miller, 2014; Frederickson & Cloyd, 1998; Stevens, 2002; Zhang, 2008), we assume that managers prefer ethical or fair behavior. We expect that managers will judge behaviors as "fair" when they are consistent with the non-monetary preferences of honesty, equality, or equity. Furthermore, consistent with theories of moral reasoning (Bucciarelli, Khemlani, & Johnson-Laird, 2008), we expect managers to choose their definition of fairness to maximize their income while still constraining their misrepresentation by their chosen definition of fairness. Simply put, managers' desire to be fair will constrain their misreporting, but they will choose their definition of what constitutes "fair" (i.e., honesty, equality, or equity) to maximize their compensation.

Hypothesis Development

To test our predictions, we create a situation where there are tradeoffs not only between the monetary and non-monetary preferences but also between the deployment of these different non-monetary preferences. To accomplish this, we construct a reporting environment where achieving equality in outcomes, means managers have to behave dishonestly. Likewise, in achieving an honest outcome, they must be willing to sacrifice an equal outcome. In addition, we need to create a situation for our participants where different deployed definitions of fairness maximize income. Finally, once these tradeoffs are established in our experiment, we can test whether the managers predictably profess whether honesty, equity, or equality is fair in each context. To do this, we rely on a contextual factor, IEP, to manipulate whether behavior consistent with a non-monetary preference for honesty, equality, or equity will result in higher income. Specifically, the manipulation of IEP alters the proportional outcomes of an honest report in a dyad (i.e., a two-manager exchange with one active and one passive partner) such that one manager receives more (less) than the comparable manager for equivalent effort. Hence, managers are either "disadvantaged" or "advantaged." Prior research has investigated peer comparisons such as this in budget settings, finding they affect happiness and conflict resolution mode (Lee, 2012). We, therefore, find the use of the comparison manager to be a useful and literature consistent tool to manipulate what is perceived as "fair." We expect that managers will believe that it is "fair" to act consistent with the non-monetary preferences that allow them to maximize income. While other objective non-monetary preferences exist outside the investigated constructs of honesty, equality, and equity, we focus and test our theory with these preferences, as they are prevalent concerns in the literature.

Disadvantaged Managers – Disadvantaged managers receive fewer resources (i.e., less income) than their partner managers if they report honestly. Implementing preferences for equality or equity allows for greater income relative to implementing a preference for honesty. Monetary desires should drive managers to adopt preferences for equality or equity as their definitions of fair.

Non-Monetary Preferences for Equality and Equity

For parsimony, in the present study, preferences for equity and equality result in identical actions. Regarding equity, an equitable distribution allocates earnings proportional to individual work investments. We ensure that there is no differential effort expended by the paired managers in our study. Since the "work investment" is identical across managers, the equitable solution is the same as the equal solution. This allows for a cleaner test of whether the actions of the manager are consistent with preferences for honesty versus equity/equality.

We note two other non-monetary distributional preferences from the literature (Bolton & Ockenfels, 2000; Engelmann & Strobel, 2004; Fehr & Schmidt, 1999) that could be considered "fair" in our setting: preferences for *Utilitarianism*, which states that income should be split to provide the "most happiness for the most people" (Mill, 1997, p. 81), and preferences regarding the *Maximin*, which states that the income should be split to maximize the outcome of the individual obtaining the smallest amount (Kolm, 1996). While we do not seek to differentiate the implementation of these preferences, we do wish to control for them to maximize the power of our inferences. We control for these preferences by limiting the exchange to two managers (maximin) and through the design of the incentive equations (utilitarianism). Implementing a maximin preference entails maximizing the outcomes of the individual obtaining the smallest amount: this occurs when all individuals are paid equally. While this outcome is possible with any size group with enough iteration, the smaller the group, the easier is its achievement. Alternatively, due to our incentive equation design, implementing a utilitarianism preference in this setting involves misrepresenting to decrease personal income, a behavior not expected by our theory.[4] Therefore, an implementation of equality, equity, or maximin preference will result in a manager reporting to obtain 50% of the income. As these preferences allow for higher income than honesty, we expect managers who are disadvantaged to believe that it is "fair" to implement a preference for equality/equity as opposed to honesty. For parsimony's sake, we are going to refer to the equality/equity/maximin preferences as equality for the remainder of the chapter.

Advantaged Managers (Positive Comparison) – An advantaged manager receives more resources (i.e., income) than a comparison manager with an honest report. In this case, implementing a preference for honesty nets more income than implementing a preference for equality. Advantaged managers will therefore choose honesty as their definition of fair, as it allows them to gain more resources.

While both advantaged and disadvantaged managers have monetary incentives to misrepresent, research shows that non-monetary preferences inhibit income-maximizing misrepresentation. However, we are first interested in what managers believe to be fair. We predict that managers' choice of what is fair will be consistent with quantifiable non-monetary preferences, and that the preferences they select will be the ones that maximize their income given their IEPs.

H1. Managers' relative *beliefs* pertaining to whether it is fair to report honestly *or* in accordance with equality depend upon their contextual situation such that:

H1a. Managers that receive *less* than a comparison other due to IEP will believe it is more "fair" to behave in accordance with equality.

H1b. Managers that receive *more* than a comparison other will believe that it is more "fair" to behave in accordance with honesty.

Method

The experiment (loosely based on Hannan et al., 2006) assigns each participant to the role of a manager (manager A) and requests that they report known raw material costs to another manager present in the room (manager B). The cost reporting repeats, with rotating dyads and different costs, for eight periods. Manager A has the option each period of increasing their income, through misrepresentation of costs, and, by doing so, reallocating income from manager B to themselves. Participants, in the role of manager B, do not interact with manager A outside of accepting payment at the conclusion of the experiment.[5] These same general procedures are used for both studies.

The focus of experiment 1 is on what managers' report as "fair." This information is gathered from managers before they make their reporting decisions (the focus of experiment 2). When making their reporting decisions, managers receive instantaneous feedback, similar to the feedback of the decision aid condition in experiment 2, consisting of the actual cost, their reported cost, and the resulting incomes (gross and percentage) of both managers. This feedback enables participants to revise their reports and see the impact of their decision on both themselves and their paired manager. We describe the entirety of the procedure for both studies here, although the second part of the procedure concerns the hypotheses for experiment 2.

Overview

Five equations define the relations among production, budget, sales price, cost, and profit. A production budget (equation 1) models inefficiencies in resource allocation introduced by managers' misrepresentations. For instance, if managers bias budgetary reports, the resource allocations for firms may be suboptimal and thus reduce firm income. The production budget is a decreasing function of reported cost. Setting production according to equation 1, divisional profit (equation 2) decreases as a direct result of misrepresentation. The unit sale price is set at 100 lira,[6] while actual cost varied by period between 57 and 73 lira.[7] Managers could report any cost that (1) varied between 55 and 78 lira and (2) did not result in negative income for either manager.[8]

$$\text{Production Budget}_{(\text{Units Made})} = 500 + 50 * (\text{Unit Sale Price}_{(\text{in lira})} -$$
$$\text{Reported Cost}_{(\text{in lira})}) \qquad (1)$$

$$\text{Divisional Profit} = \text{Production Budget} * (\text{Unit Sale Price} - \text{Reported Cost}) \quad (2)$$

Manager A's compensation consists of three items per period (equation 3): salary, profit sharing, and misrepresented income (if any). Salary is 30,000 lira with profit sharing at 10% of divisional profits. Misrepresented income (equation 4) equals the difference between the reported and actual cost, multiplied by production. The final equation (equation 5) defines the share of income received by manager B, i.e., residual divisional profit less manager A's salary.

$$\text{Income}_{\text{manager A}} = \text{Salary} + 10\% (\text{Divisional Profit}) + \text{Misrepresented Income} \quad (3)$$

$$\text{Misrepresented Income} = \text{Production Budget} * (\text{Reported Cost} - \text{Actual Cost}) \quad (4)$$

$$\text{Income}_{\text{manager B}} = 90\% (\text{Divisional Profit}) - \text{Salary} \qquad (5)$$

Procedures
The experimental protocol consists of the following steps:

1. Participants enter the experimental lab, are seated, and draw a random participant number that assigned them to an IEP condition, either *advantaged* or *disadvantaged*.[9]
2. Participants learn that: (a) they are to play the role of manager A, (b) they are paired with another participant in the room who plays the role of manager B, (c) their choices affect both their own pay and manager B's pay, and (d) they and their partner managers are paid for one randomly selected period.
3. Participants correctly answer four questions to evaluate understanding and reinforce some of the major points of the forthcoming reporting task. These questions ensure that participants correctly identify that:
   o they play the role of manager A,
   o they are anonymous to manager B,
   o they are randomly paired with a different manager B each period, and,
   o their choices affect their ultimate payment and the payment of their paired manager.
4. Participants receive and read the five compensation equations as well as five simulations of actual and reported costs with the resulting experimental

outcomes.[10] Participants then review these simulations and answer questions regarding the outcomes of these simulations. Participants must answer all questions correctly before continuing to ensure they understood the task.

5. Participants in the advantaged (disadvantaged) conditions are told that, because of economic conditions, reporting their actual cost causes them to receive more (less) of the income than manager B. Before continuing, participants must correctly answer questions ensuring they understood their IEP.

6. This step is only present in experiment 1 (not experiment 2). Participants are asked to report what they believe to be "fair" actions. Before entering the reporting segment of this section, participants verify that they understand that their income is not be affected by this section of the experiment, that they are only reporting on what they believe to be fair; and that the section of the experiment where their pay is to be determined comes after this point.

   o Participants receive eight costs, one at a time, with one set of costs for each of the IEP condition.[11] The cost sets are static within the IEP conditions, i.e., each experimental participant in the advantaged (disadvantaged) group receives the same costs as every other participant in the advantaged (disadvantaged) group. The costs are also randomly ordered across trials 1 through 8 between participants. The disadvantaged managers' cost range between 57 and 65 lira – resulting in manager A receiving between 36% (57 Lira) and 48% (65 Lira) of the income, absent misrepresentation. The advantaged managers' costs range from 66.5 to 73 lira – resulting in between 51% (66.5 Lira) and 70% (73 lira) of income, again absent misrepresentation. Regardless of their IEP, if managers choose to maximize their income through misrepresentation, they increase their income share to approximately 97%.[12]

   o For each of the eight trials, the instrument displays the actual cost, and requests that managers input the reported cost. The screen displays and updates in real time the incomes (both in Lira and as a %) of manager A and manager B.[13] When satisfied, participants submit their cost reports and moved to the next trial. At the end of eight periods of reporting what they believed to be "fair," they move to the cost reporting section.

7. Both studies then continue with this "cost-reporting" step. The cost-reporting section consists of eight periods, with the same cost sets, as described in the prior step (6). The operative difference between this step and step 6 above is that participants are paid based on their choices in this section of the study. The procedure is as follows:

   o Similar to the process to collect "fairness beliefs," participants are randomly assigned to dyads of two managers.[14] As manager A, participants receive private cost information and choose how much to report. They are aware that they are paired with another study participant, manager B, and that their decisions affect the amount they earn, the amount manager B earns, and the overall amount earned by the two managers. The manager B role is passive and has no role to play aside from receiving income.

o Each period, manager A receives an actual cost *(actual cost)* from their assigned IEP cost set and chooses a cost to report *(reported cost)* for that period. Cost reports are verified through a feedback mechanism and managers are asked if they wish to revise their submissions.
o This step is repeated for eight periods.

8. To conclude, participants answer demographic and other post-experimental questions and are thanked for their participation.[15]

Results

H1 predicts that contextual variables, i.e., IEP, affect which non-monetary preferences managers will report as "fair." We predict that disadvantaged managers will believe that reporting to achieve equality is fair, while advantaged managers will believe that reporting honestly is fair. Forty-two undergraduate students participate in experiment 1. We use two dependent variables to evaluate this hypothesis: (1) gross misrepresentation and (2) distributional equality. Remember that these are what the managers reported would be "fair" to report and not their subsequent actual reporting actions that determined their experiment pay.

The degree of gross misrepresentation[16] equals what the managers reported would be fair to report less the actual cost. By this measure, the results indicate that advantaged managers are less likely to believe that it is fair to misrepresent costs. Advantaged managers state it is fair to misrepresent 0.11 lira, on average, while disadvantaged managers state it is fair to misrepresent 3.07 lira [17] (Table 1, Panels A and B, $p < 0.01$). These results are consistent with IEP influencing the degree to which managers believe it is fair to misrepresent.

We next compare their beliefs of what would be fair to report with benchmarks that represent reporting for either honesty or equality. *H1a* and *H1b* predict that disadvantaged managers will define fairness as equality while advantaged managers will define fairness as honesty. We compare participant's submitted beliefs[18] with benchmarks of zero misrepresentation (i.e., reporting honestly) in the advantaged condition, and, reporting to obtain a 50% distribution of income (i.e., reporting to achieve equality) in the disadvantaged condition.

In the advantaged condition, participants do not profess to believe it is fair to misrepresent. There is not a significant difference between the amount believed fair to report in the advantaged condition and an honest report (Table 1, Panel A, $p = 0.83$). This is consistent with an income-maximizing preference for honesty in this condition. In contrast, disadvantaged participants do believe that it is fair to misrepresent. The amount they believe is fair to misrepresent differs from an honest report (Table 1, Panel A, $p < 0.01$). Furthermore, consistent with deploying a preference for equality in the disadvantaged condition, participants believe it is fair to misrepresent to create distributions that do not differ from equality (Table 1, Panel A, $p = 0.88$). However, participants do vary from an equal distribution in the advantaged condition (Table 1, Panel A, $p < 0.01$).

Overall, the reported results support *H1* – that the contextual factor, IEP, does indeed affect which non-monetary preferences participants believe to be

Table 1. Experiment 1: Amount Believed Fair to Report
(i.e., Submitted Beliefs) by IEP.

Panel A. Actions Reported as "Fair" by Condition Versus Test Values.

	IEP[c]	N	Mean (Std. Err)	Test Value	t-test	p
Equality[a]	Advantaged	23	0.58 (0.02)	0.50	3.55	< 0.01
	Disadvantaged	19	0.50 (0.02)	0.50	0.15	0.88
Honesty[b]	Advantaged	23	0.11 (0.53)	0.00	0.21	0.83
	Disadvantaged	19	3.07 (0.59)	0.00	5.24	<0.01

Panel B. Repeated Measures ANOVA Results Predicting Gross Misrepresentation.

Between Participants				
Source	**df**	**Mean Square**	**F**	**p**
Intercept	1	844.54	16.16	0.00
IEP	1	727.73	13.92	0.00
Error	40	52.27		

Within Participants				
Source	**df**	**Mean Square**	**F**	**p**
Period	7.00	9.21	2.90	0.01
Period * IEP	7.00	4.66	1.47	0.18
Error	280.00	3.18		

Notes: [a]Difference from equality measures how far a manager believed it is *fair* to report away from equality. The reported mean is the overall percentage of income participants think it is fair to obtain through their reporting behavior (e.g., 0.50 means they think it is fair to take 50% of income).
[b]This measure assesses how much misrepresentation is included in the cost reports participants report as *fair*. The formula to compute this variable is (Cost Reported as Fair − Actual Cost Provided). Therefore, an honest report scored a difference of zero.
[c]IEP has two possible values: (1) Advantaged and (2) Disadvantaged. Advantaged participants receive actual costs that result in obtaining *more* than one-half of total income given an honest reported cost. Disadvantaged obtain *less* than one-half of total income given an honest reported cost. Regardless of condition, participants can obtain approximately 97% of income given full misrepresentation.

fair and that the non-monetary preference chosen is consistent with the one that maximizes their income. This finding builds on earlier cited research in a novel way that shows participants do define fairness differently in different contexts, and their chosen definitions are consistent with the non-monetary preference that aligns with wealth maximization. Experiment 2 tests whether these different beliefs affect the actual misreporting behavior of experimental participants.

EXPERIMENT 2

Experiment 2 builds upon the results from experiment 1 with a new subject pool. Experiment 1 measures what participants believe is fair given different IEP manipulations. Experiment 2 excludes measuring what participants believe is fair to avoid priming. Instead, it investigates whether actual reporting behavior when there is income on the line is consistent with the reportedly deployed beliefs from experiment 1. The two studies are designed to complement each other and are near replications.

We replicate the IEP manipulation from experiment 1 and examine whether managers' actions (i.e., the cost they actually report) reflect the differential professed fairness beliefs found in experiment 1. Managers' actions will be driven by monetary desires constrained by their preferences for what is "fair." Monetary desires should increase misrepresentation in both the advantaged and disadvantaged contexts. However, the preferences for honesty and equality found in experiment 1 will bound this misrepresentation and lead to detectable differences in the managers' actual reporting choices between IEP conditions.[19]

H2. IEP will affect managers reporting decisions such that:

H2a. Disadvantaged managers will misrepresent more than advantaged managers.

H2b. Disadvantaged managers will report to attain closer to an equal distribution of income than advantaged managers.

Decision Aid – In addition to the IEP manipulation, Experiment 2 also manipulates the presence of a decision aid. The decision aid is designed to reduce task complexity in deploying fairness beliefs. However, the presence of the decision aid also increases the saliency of the fairness beliefs. Task complexity has been shown to have a large effect on the effectiveness of monetary incentives (cf. Bonner & Sprinkle, 2002). Namely, the effect of incentives decreases as task complexity increases since participants do not have the requisite skill set to complete the task, even with increases in effort. We expect this observed relation regarding monetary incentives to persist with non-monetary preferences.

We believe that managers will have a non-monetary preference for equality when they are disadvantaged. However, task complexity may inhibit the implementation of this preference as it is cognitively effortful to determine the amount to report to achieve equality in our task. By employing decision aids in our disadvantaged IEP condition, we can see what impact complexity has on the deployment of this preference.

Alternatively, we believe managers will have a non-monetary preference for honesty when they are advantaged. Being honest in this setting is not cognitively effortful. Therefore, we believe that the primary effect of decision aids in the advantaged condition will not be a change in reporting due to a reduction of complexity, but rather a priming effect that will make the outcomes of the participants' reporting choice more salient.

All information needed to calculate the economic consequences of reporting is available in our setting; however, computing these values requires cognitively effortful calculations.[20] Decision aids, while not increasing total information available, reduce the complexity of calculations. It also increases the saliency of the consequences of managers' reporting decisions by automatically calculating and displaying the outcomes of the manager's reports. One possible effect of increasing outcome saliency (Mullen, Brown, & Smith, 1992) is increasing the impact of moral intentions on actions. For example, real-time roadside displays showing motorists' driving speed reduce speeding by focusing driver attention on the current speed even in the absence of legal or economic consequences (Wrapson, Harré, & Murrell, 2006). Drolet, Larrick, and Morris (1998) propose a similar effect that increasing the saliency of the other's perspective (i.e., what they will receive given the reporting decision) in a dyad increases the fairness of actions and reduces self-serving biases. Inferring from this work to the present setting, providing decision aids that increase the saliency of the effect of the managers' misrepresentation on the income distribution should increase the impact of the fairness belief on the amount of misrepresentation.

These decision aids, by reducing complexity and increasing saliency, have differential predictions depending on managers' IEP.

Advantaged Managers (Positive Comparison)

Advantaged managers' reporting decisions are a tradeoff between monetary desires and a preference for honesty. Decision aids are not expected to simplify the decision as there should be little complexity in implementing a preference for honesty. Therefore, the remaining effect of decision aids is to increase the saliency of the effect of the reporting decision on the other managers, thus, increasing the effect of the preference for honesty. Consistent with Wrapson et al. (2006) and Drolet et al. (1998) cited above, we can predict:

H3. Providing decision aids to advantaged managers will decrease misrepresentation relative to advantaged managers without decision aids.

Disadvantaged Managers (Negative Comparison)

Disadvantaged managers' actions are tradeoff between monetary desires and a preference for equality. Without decision aids, managers must exert cognitive effort to determine what to report to achieve their desired outcome. Due to effort aversion and the complexity of the task, they are unlikely to fully calculate the consequences of their reporting decisions. If they then desire to implement preferences for equality, without fully calculating the consequences, their reports must be estimated. Assuming managers estimate to determine their desired cost report, it is unclear whether reports will show a stronger effect from their preference for equality (50% distribution) or their monetary desires (>50% distribution) when ambiguity is higher in the absence of decision aids.

Decision aids reduce the cognitive effort of calculating the outcome of managers' reporting choices. As such, they allow managers to more easily report to achieve their desired outcomes. At the same time, decision aids should increase the outcome saliency (Mullen et al., 1992) which increases the impact of moral intentions on actions. In the case of disadvantaged managers, this means managers' desire for equality increases when given decision aids.

In summary, providing decision aids should increase disadvantaged managers' preferences for equality versus monetary gain. Simultaneously, decision aids should remove the need to estimate the outcome of the reporting decisions. What is not known, however, is the effect of the disadvantaged managers' estimations in the absence decision aids. Will managers use the ambiguity resulting from their estimations to more heavily implement their monetary preference or their preference for equality? As we have found no theory to support a prediction here, we ask the following research question:

RQ. Will decision aids increase, decrease, or have no effect on disadvantaged managers' misrepresentations?

Method

Experiment 2 evaluates whether managers' misrepresentations are consistent with the expressed fairness beliefs of the participants from experiment 1. One hundred thirty undergraduate students participate in a computer-based laboratory experiment for research credit and financial compensation. IEP (two levels) and the presence of decision aids (two levels) are manipulated between participants. Participants are randomly assigned to one of the resulting four conditions: (1) advantaged economic condition/no decision aid, (2) advantaged economic condition/decision aid, (3) disadvantaged economic condition/no decision aid, and (4) disadvantaged economic condition/decision aid.

Procedure Differences Versus Experiment 1

Students are recruited from a college-wide pool of individuals enrolled in introductory business courses.[21] The procedures for experiment 2 are identical to experiment 1 except for removing the assessment of what is "fair" to report and adding a decision aid manipulation to the cost reporting section of the experiment. The assessment of "fairness" is removed to avoid priming the subsequent misreporting decision.

Decision aids (i.e., "a tool that aids judgment in a straightforward algorithmic manner" Messier, 1992, p. 214) calculate the income consequences of the reporting choice. Before finalizing their cost report, participants in the decision aid condition receive feedback as follows:

> Your income at this report is X1 lira (P1%). Manager B's income at this report is X2 lira (P2%). Would you like to accept this report and continue to the next period?[22]

Alternatively, participants not in the decision aid condition read, "You have submitted a reported cost of C lira to manager B; are you satisfied with this report?" Participants in both conditions then revise or accept their report before continuing to the next period.[23, 24]

Dependent Measures

Our first dependent variable is misrepresentation (reported cost − actual cost). This is also our primary measure of honesty. Although giving away income (i.e., reporting less than the actual cost) is *inconsistent* with our theory that managers implement income-maximizing non-monetary preferences, there are conditions when it is *consistent* with implementing a non-monetary preference that does not maximize income. For instance, a manager choosing to implement a preference for equality when advantaged would be required to give away income to behave in a fashion consistent with that preference. Therefore, as previously mentioned, while this is unexpected, we allow this behavior to have a more robust, i.e., realistic, experiment.

Our second dependent variable is the percentage of the total income claimed by manager A (where a value of 50% is an equal split and a value of 90% means that manager A has 90% while manager B has 10%). This is our measure used for evaluating whether the reporting is consistent with a preference for equality.

We also use a supplemental dependent variable in experiment 2, which measures misrepresentation as a proportion of the available misrepresentation opportunity (Evans et al. 2001). We do not use this as the main honesty dependent variable in the present investigation for multiple reasons. First, actual costs varied due to the IEP; therefore, a proportional measure of misrepresentation contains denominator effects. In other words, because of the varying denominator between IEP conditions in this case, between-condition effects could result from either different behavior or varying denominator ranges between conditions. Second, counter to prior research and noted above, costs can be misrepresented downward. This design choice, which allows for implementing non-income maximizing non-monetary preferences, causes issues with the denominator that are not present in other research. To reduce the impact of these factors, we alter the denominator used in prior research to instead be either (1) given positive misrepresentation – the difference between actual cost and the cost ceiling of 78 lira (consistent with prior research) or (2) given negative misrepresentation – the difference between the cost floor of 55 lira (or the lowest cost which does not result in negative income) and the actual cost. Thus, this supplemental proportional measure ranges from -100% to $+100\%$, dependent on the actual cost, where 0% is an accurate cost report. The proportional measure in prior research has a range of 0% to 100%. Correlation between this supplemental measure and gross misrepresentation averaged across six periods are highly significant ($p < 0.01$; Spearman's Rho $= 0.95$; Pearson $= 0.90$).

While we present the supplemental and main DV results concurrently, we believe gross misrepresentation, versus proportional misrepresentation, gives a more accurate view of the participant's intentions for the aforementioned reasons.

Results

H2a predicts that disadvantaged managers misrepresent more than advantaged managers. On average, disadvantaged managers misrepresent 3.68 while advantaged managers misrepresent 1.89 ($p < 0.01$; Table 2, Panels A & B). However, there is a significant interaction with the presence of decision aids suggesting caution in the interpretation of the main effect. Therefore, we present planned comparisons for the decision aid conditions separately for both the presence and absence of decision aids. The results indicate that, in the presence of decision aids, disadvantaged managers misrepresent 4.69 Lira, significantly more than advantaged managers, 1.72 Lira (Table 2, Panel A; $p < 0.01$, untabulated). There is no significant difference ($p = 0.43$, untabulated) in the absence of decision aids. Thus, *H2a* is supported, but appears to be driven by the condition where decision aids are present.

H2b predicts that disadvantaged managers should report to attain a final distribution closer to equality than advantaged managers. Three direct comparisons in Table 3 support this inference. First, there is a main effect for IEP in the repeated measures ANOVA ($p < 0.01$, Table 3, Panel B) showing advantaged managers on average obtain 67.57% of the final distribution while disadvantaged managers obtain 52.49%. Due to the interaction, we again present planned comparisons with and without decision aids. In the presence of decision aids, disadvantaged managers obtain 55.49% of the distribution and advantaged managers obtain 66.76% ($p < 0.01$, untabulated). In the absence of decision aids, advantaged managers obtain 68.32% versus 49.49% for the disadvantaged managers ($p < 0.01$, untabulated). These results support *H2b*.

H3 states that providing decision aids should decrease misrepresentation for advantaged managers. However, we find no evidence to support *H3*. Our theory is that, by providing decision aids, the saliency of the outcome will be increased, thus changing the tradeoff calculation between income and honesty in favor of honesty. The difference in misrepresentation for advantaged managers with decision aids (1.72, Table 2) and without decision aids (2.05, Table 2) is not significant ($p > 0.61$, untabulated). A possible explanation for this finding is that the tradeoff between honesty and income was already weighted heavily enough toward honesty that the increased saliency had no detectable effect, however, this is merely conjecture.

RQ 1 asks whether disadvantaged managers misrepresent differently with and without decision aids. We phrase this as a research question due to the ambiguity of expected behavior when managers are in a complex task. Namely, how will managers use the ambiguity of not having decision aids to tradeoff their monetary preference and their preference for equality? The means in Table 3 indicate that managers with decision aids, as they are driven by both monetary preferences and are predicted to implement more of a preference for equality, do obtain at least 50% of the final distribution (55.59% is significantly different than 50%, $p < 0.01$ untabulated). While disadvantaged managers with decision aids misrepresent to obtain significantly more than one-half of income, those without decision aids do not obtain an amount different from 50% (i.e., 49.49% does not differ from 50%, $p = 0.80$ two-tailed, untabulated).

Particularly interesting is the evidence for the implementation of non-monetary preferences for disadvantaged managers in the absence of decision aids. Both monetary desires and desires for equality appear to influence managerial behavior. We therefore predict that, by reducing the complexity of the task through decision aids, managers will more truly represent their desired tradeoffs between both monetary and non-monetary preferences and will misrepresent to obtain more than 50% of the income. This occurs as managers take 55.49%. More interesting though is the percentage of the income taken by managers without decision aids, which is significantly less than the percentage taken in the presence of decision aids: 55.49% versus 49.49% ($p < 0.01$ two-tailed, untabulated). If we

Table 2.   Experiment 2: Effects of IEP and Decision Aid on Gross Misrepresentation.[a]

Panel A. Between Participants Descriptive Statistics.

IEP[b]	Decision Aid[c] Presence		
	Mean (SEM) Sample Size		
	Yes	**No**	**Overall**
Advantaged	1.72	2.05	1.89
	(0.59)	(0.54)	(0.40)
	$N = 29$	$N = 35$	$N = 64$
Disadvantaged	4.69	2.68	3.68
	(0.54)	(0.55)	(0.38)
	$N = 34$	$N = 32$	$N = 66$
Overall	3.21	2.367	2.79
	(0.40)	(0.04)	(0.28)
	$N = 63$	$N = 67$	$N = 130$

Panel B. Repeated Measures ANOVA Results.

Between Participants

Source	df	Mean Square	F	p
Intercept	1	8029.50	100.38	<0.01
Decision Aid	1	181.61	10.40	0.13
IEP	1	832.42	2.26	<0.01
Decision Aid * IEP	1	355.96	4.48	0.04
Error		80.025		

Within Participants

Source	df	Mean Square	F	p
Period	7	18.81	1.82	0.08
Period * Decision Aid	7	7.33	0.71	0.66
Period * IEP	7	5.94	0.58	0.78
Period * Decision Aid * IEP	7	10.42	1.01	0.423
Error	882			

Notes: [a]This measure assesses how much misrepresentation is included in the cost reports. The formula to compute this variable is (Reported Cost – Actual Cost Provided). Therefore, an honest report scores a difference of zero.
[b]IEP has two possible values: (1) Advantaged and (2) Disadvantaged. Advantaged participants receive actual costs that result in obtaining *more* than one-half of total income given an honest reported cost. Disadvantaged obtain *less* than one-half of total income given an honest reported cost. Regardless of condition, participants can obtain approximately 97% of income given full misrepresentation.
[c]This manipulation provides (or not) decision aids that calculate the effect that the reported cost has on personal and partner gross income and relative income.

assume that actions in the presence of decision aids represent the intentions of managers seeking to balance monetary desires and fairness, then one explanation for this finding is that, in the presence of ambiguity, managers are *more concerned with violating their non-monetary or fairness preference* than with failing to maximize their income. While this finding is not the stated goal of the research, we feel it is a particularly interesting and hopeful insight into human nature.

Table 3.   Experiment 2: Effects of IEP and Decision Aid on Equality.[a]

Panel A. Between Participants Descriptive Statistics.

Decision Aid[c] Presence

IEP[b]	Mean (SEM) Sample Size		
	Yes	No	Overall
Advantaged	66.76%	68.32%	67.57%
	(0.02)	(0.02)	(0.01)
	$N = 29$	$N = 35$	$N = 64$
Disadvantaged	55.49%	49.49%	52.49%
	(0.02)	(0.02)	(0.01)
	$N = 34$	$N = 32$	$N = 66$
Overall	58.91%	61.12%	60.02%
	(0.01)	(0.02)	(0.01)
	$N = 63$	$N = 67$	$N = 130$

Panel B. Repeated Measures ANOVA Results.

Between Participants

Source	df	Mean square	F	p
Intercept	1	372.68	3518.03	<0.01
Decision Aid	1	0.13	1.20	0.28
IEP	1	5.85	55.25	<0.01
Decision Aid * IEP	1	0.37	3.49	0.06
Error				

Within Participants

Source	df	Mean square	F	p
Period	7	0.02	1.26	0.26
Period * Decision Aid	7	0.01	1.00	0.43
Period * IEP	7	0.01	0.42	0.89
Period * Decision Aid * IEP	7	0.01	0.76	0.62
Error	882	0.01		

Notes: [a]Equality is the overall percentage of income participants reported to obtain (e.g., 50% means they are paid half the total income, while 30% means they obtain 30% while their passive partner receives 70%).
[b]IEP has two possible values: (1) Advantaged and (2) Disadvantaged. Advantaged participants receive actual costs that result in obtaining *more* than one-half of total income given an honest reported cost. Disadvantaged obtain *less* than one-half of total income given an honest reported cost. Regardless of condition, participants can obtain approximately 97% of income given full misrepresentation.
[c]This manipulation provides (or not) decision aids that calculate the effect that the reported cost has on personal and partner gross income and relative income.

In summary, *H2* is supported. Managers' actions appear to be consistent with their contextually influenced definitions of fairness, consistent with the findings of experiment 1. With decision aids, advantaged managers do not misrepresent differentially than without them, failing to support *H3*. As expected, monetary desires and a preference for equality do cause disadvantaged managers to misrepresent to obtain more than 50% of the final distribution in the presence of decision aids; however, disadvantaged managers misrepresent significantly less without decision aids, than with them.

Table 4. Experiment 2: Effects of IEP and Decision Aid on Proportional Misrepresentation.

Panel A. Between Participants Descriptive Statistics.

	Decision Aid[c] Presence		
IEP[b]	**Mean (SEM) Sample Size**		
	Yes	**No**	**Overall**
Advantaged	22.59%	25.03%	23.81%
	(0.05)	(0.05)	(0.03)
	N = 29	N = 35	N = 64
Disadvantaged	25.89%	12.15%	19.02%
	(0.05)	(0.05)	(0.03)
	N = 34	N = 32	N = 66
Overall	24.24%	18.59%	21.41%
	(0.03)	(0.03)	(0.02)
	N = 63	N = 67	N = 130

Panel B. Repeated Measures ANOVA Results.

Between Participants				
Source	**df**	**Mean Square**	**F**	**p**
Intercept	1	47.44	84.20	<0.01
Decision Aid	1	0.83	1.47	0.23
IEP	1	0.59	1.05	0.31
Decision Aid * IEP	1	1.69	3.00	0.09
Error				

Within Participants				
Source	**df**	**Mean Square**	**F**	**p**
Period	7	0.01	1.65	0.12
Period * Decision Aid	7	0.07	1.11	0.35
Period * IEP	7	0.25	0.41	0.90
Period * Decision Aid * IEP	7	0.05	0.80	0.59
Error	882	0.06		

Notes: [a]This measure assesses how much misrepresentation is included in the cost reports as a proportion of the available amount. The formula to compute this variable is (Reported Cost – Actual Cost)/(available misrepresentation). The denominator (available misrepresentation) varies depending on: (1) positive misrepresentation – the difference between actual cost and the cost ceiling of 78 Lira (consistent with prior research) or (2) given negative misrepresentation, the difference between the cost floor of 55 Lira (or the lowest cost which does not result in negative income) and the actual cost. Thus, this proportional measure ranges from −100% to +100% dependent on the actual cost – where 0% is an accurate cost report.
[b]IEP has two possible values: (1) Advantaged and (2) Disadvantaged. Advantaged participants receive actual costs that result in obtaining *more* than one-half of total income given an honest reported cost. Disadvantaged obtain *less* than one-half of total income given an honest reported cost. Regardless of condition, participants can obtain approximately 97% of income given full misrepresentation.
[c]This manipulation provides (or not) decision aids that calculate the effect that the reported cost has on personal and partner gross income and relative income.

Differences from Misrepresentation Rates in Prior Research

The average misrepresentation in experiment 2 per the proportional dependent variable of approximately 21.41% (Table 4, panel A) is lower than that found in some prior research (e.g., Evans et al. reported approximately 50% misrepresentation for a similar contract) for two likely reasons. First, the lower average misrepresentation may be due to the quadratic nature of our experimental equations. Namely, while misrepresentation increases manager A's income, it simultaneously decreases not only manager B's income but also the joint income of both participants. Without a thorough understanding of these mechanisms by managers, it is possible that they would report overly conservative (i.e., low) costs to avoid decreasing their own income by decreasing overall income. The quadratic structure of the experimental equations is a departure from prior research, but necessary so that the various distributional preferences (i.e., equity, equality, and maximin) collapsed into one distinct, measurable action (i.e., reporting to achieve 50%). It is possible this conservative reporting caused less misrepresentation[25] in the current experiment than has been seen in prior experiments.

In addition, Evans et al. (2001) truncate their sample for any cost reports that give away income as such reports are inconsistent with a utility function that values wealth and honesty. As discussed earlier, we allow negative cost reports to test our theory of differentially implemented non-monetary preferences. In total, we have 93 negative cost reports out of 1,040 ($n = 130*8$ reports per participants) total cost reports for an approximately 9% average negative rate. This also lowers our overall rate.

SUMMARY AND CONCLUSIONS

Managers' misrepresentations are a joint function of monetary desires *and* non-monetary preferences. We predict and test: (1) whether managers' determinations of what is fair is determined by what definition of fair maximizes their income in a particular context, (2) whether this predictively impacts managers' misreporting behaviors, and (3) whether decision aids, which reduce task complexity, impact how managers' fairness determinations impact misreporting behaviors. We manipulate a contextual factor, IEP, and investigate these contentions in two experiments. Experiment 1 investigates managers' beliefs about what is fair, and experiment 2 investigates manager's subsequent reporting behavior. Furthermore, we provide simple accounting decision aids in experiment 2 so that we can investigate this relationship in tasks of varying complexity (i.e., decision aids reduce the effort needed to deploy a belief for equality into a cost report). The primary contribution of this chapter is to demonstrate that contextual factors predictably affect manager's beliefs of what constitutes fair outcomes, which, in turn, predictably and differentially influence cost reporting decisions and misrepresentation.

The results from our laboratory experiments are largely consistent with predictions. Experiment 1's results provide evidence that managers believe different non-monetary preferences (i.e., honesty or equality) are "fair" in different contexts and that which one they believe to be "fair" is determined by their economic self-interest. Experiment 2 results build on these results and show that the contextually dependent, non-monetary preferences for honesty or equality found in experiment 1 constrain monetary preferences on misreporting. In addition, while there is no difference in misreporting in the advantaged condition with and without decision aids, disadvantaged managers misreport significantly more with decision aids than without.

This research contributes to the overall literature in three ways. First, our study supports research findings that managers' actions are influenced by self-interest *and* conditional non-monetary preferences, consistent with findings in the misrepresentation literature largely started with Evans et al. (2001). Second, managers appear to bound self-interest with moral incentives such as a belief in what is "fair," contributing to the altruism findings found in the economic game literature (e.g., Cox & Sadiraj, 2012; Fehr & Schmidt, 1999). By manipulating IEP, and thus the income-maximizing non-monetary preference, we investigate and show an antecedent to this self-interest bounding in a simplified managerial task.

More importantly, our study bridges these literatures and supports the idea that non-monetary preferences for honesty and distributional preferences may be related by predictably suppressing monetary desires in a manner that managers believe to be ethical or "fair." In fact, managers implement a non-monetary preference dependent on what will allow them more income. We support our conjecture with philosophy and economic research and further support it with a series of two experiments showing that managers do alter what they believe to be fair based on IEP. Furthermore, we find that managers' actions, even in the presence of monetary incentives, are consistent with the differential implementation of these non-monetary preferences. We believe this to be the first study that investigates the differential deployment of these non-monetary preferences into reports dependent on a contextual factor.

Finally, our study provides evidence that more accounting information does not uniformly improve organizational outcomes. Providing decision aids, thereby increasing outcome clarity, increased misreporting among disadvantaged managers who, if they reported honestly, would receive less than a comparison other. This same manipulation proved not to have a detectable effect for advantaged managers. Thus, providing accounting information actually increased misrepresentation contingent on the contextual IEP variable.

Parsimony guides the study's experimental design. We collapse four conceptual distributional preferences (i.e., equity, equality, maximin, and utilitarianism) into one operational distribution – equality – to which we can compare preferences for honesty. This design enables the experimental test of whether managers' actions are consistent with the implementation of differential non-monetary preferences. Consequently, the studies investigate only a subset of the many possible non-monetary preferences managers may choose. For example, even among distributional preferences, our data do not distinguish which of the four discussed preferences (or a combination) are chosen and enacted by participants outside of the experimental setting. Thus, we are unable to distinguish, for example, whether participants are acting based upon "equality," "equity," or a "maximin" preference. This does not, however, lessen the validity of our situation-deployed non-monetary preference theory.

Parsimony also drives the choice of a simplified context and laboratory experiment. The power of experiments is their ability to isolate causal variables.

However, their weakness is their omission of many potentially relevant factors that are not present in the current study but may affect managers' perceptions of fairness. This includes past resource allocations, the personal and professional characteristics of other managers, comparisons of ability among managers, potential affect drivers, and so on. Through random assignment to conditions (success partially demonstrated by insignificant demographic differences among conditions), these factors are controlled in our experiment.

A limitation of this research is a possible inadvertent framing effect in the manipulation of the IEP. The manipulation for advantaged managers constrains the phrase "*you will earn more money*" while the disadvantaged manipulation states, "*your partner (manager 'B') will earn more money.*" The likely result of this framing effect would be a focus on the self (other) for advantaged (disadvantaged) managers. A focus on the self (other) is likely to cause less (more) concern for other participants. If these framing effects are driving our results, we would expect greater misrepresentation in the self-focus, advantaged condition. Our results show the opposite trend that managers assigned to the advantaged manipulation misrepresent less than those assigned the disadvantaged manipulation. While we believe this potential framing effect works against our results, future research may wish to avoid this wording and seek a "cleaner" manipulation.

These discoveries about the situational fluidity and adaptability of non-monetary preferences have important implications for accountants. For instance, providing an outcome decision aids to managers, thus reducing the complexity of a choice, may actually increase misrepresentation. These findings challenge the common assumption that greater transparency in accounting information is invariably beneficial. These findings suggest pathways through which misrepresentation in reporting may be limited, thereby increasing the effectiveness of budgeting, planning, and resource allocation, which, consequently, may generate greater organizational gains. More generally, our finding that, given ambiguity, participants tended more toward the "fair" or "ethical" behavior consistent with an implemented distributional preference, as opposed to self-interest is, to us, a particularly encouraging insight into human nature.

NOTES

1. Research has been conducted on non-monetary preferences such as honesty and equality (e.g., Evans III, Hannan, Krishnan, & Moser, 2001; Hannan et al., 2006), equity (e.g., Matuszewski, 2010), pay dispersion (Guo, Libby, & Liu, 2017) and, more generally, ethics or fairness (Frederickson & Cloyd, 1998; Jollineau et al., 2012).

2. Rankin et al. (2008) impose limits on these findings. Specifically, they find that allowing a principal to deny reports reduces the relevance of ethics by moving the decision closer to the realm of negotiation. However, Douthit and Stevens (2015) find honesty effects persist even in this context.

3. Dictator games are a commonly used experimental economic setup where one participant decides how much money of a limited set to send to another individual (Google searches are certainly not reliable for accurate numbers of papers, they are likely useful to get an idea of the magnitude of literature available. In that vein, a Google scholar search for dictator games yielded over 12,000 papers). We use a version of the dictator game to investigate the tradeoff between these monetary and non-monetary preferences. While non-monetary distributional preferences for equality, equity, maximin, and efficiency have been

investigated (e.g., Cox & Sadiraj, 2012) as well as non-monetary preferences for honesty (e.g., Thielmann & Hilbig, 2018); we know of no research that directly tests the conditional deployment of these preferences in these type settings.

4. The incentive equations in the study are constructed such that a manager would have to misreport costs in a negative fashion to increase the total earnings of the matched dyad. As we posit that managers choose to implement the non-monetary preference that maximizes their income, a preference for utilitarianism should not be implemented in our study as it reduces personal income. While we do not expect this behavior, we do allow for it.

5. Participants are assigned both the role of manager A and manager B simultaneously. This choice was made to maximize sample size while avoiding deception. Participants are told they are manager A (this is true) and that another participant in the room is assigned as their manager B and will bear the consequences of their choices (this is also true). We are silent regarding their own role as manager B for another participant until the payment period at the conclusion of the experiment. By doing this, we avoid lying to participants, maximize sample size, and increase participants' payments as they are paid for their roles as managers A and B.

6. At the end of the experiment, the experimental denomination, "lira" converted to dollars at an exchange rate of 3,750 lira to $1.

7. Cost parameters allowed for the manipulation of IEPs and avoided an equal split of income.

8. Due to ethical and practical limitations, we avoid conditions that allow participants to incur debt (i.e., owe the experimenter income). Hence, cost reporting is limited such that the manager's income cannot become negative.

9. They are also assigned to a "decision aid" condition for the actual cost reporting section – this manipulation is explained more fully in experiment 2 and is irrelevant to the current hypothesis test.

10. The actual four questions on this screen reference the answers to these solved equations. The first question, for example, is "If the actual cost is 65.95 lira and manager 'A' reports a cost of 65.95, then will manager A make less than or more than manager B?" The solution to this question is reflected in one of the five given solutions to the equations.

11. Instructions indicate that the actual cost for manager A participants vary due to economic conditions. This implies that income relative to manager B is also due to economic conditions and thus not any differences in skill, education, effort, or any other factors that may vary an equitable distribution from an equal distribution.

12. At the lowest (highest) actual cost draw of 57 (73) Lira, a participant who maximally misrepresents obtains 96.1% (97.6%) of total income. The results from maximizing misrepresentation on other cost draws vary between these extremes.

13. This feedback given here is identical to the feedback given to the participants in the experiment 2 cost reporting decision aid condition.

14. Participants are told, and did, experience a single period of interaction without any opportunity for negotiation in order to help remove any concerns regarding reputation or any other potential iterative effects. The paired managers do not know the cost distribution of the reporting managers.

15. Participants are paid an average of $19.55 for their combined roles at the conclusion of all experimental sessions. Payments are made at the conclusion of the experimental sessions to avoid earlier participants from describing procedures to later ones. Participants are also debriefed at this time and given the opportunity to ask the administrator any questions.

16. We use both the phrase honesty (reporting the cost equal to the actual cost) and misrepresentation (reported cost-actual cost) throughout. This is to allow a benchmark measure for honest behavior as well as a measure of the degree of misrepresentation in accordance with prior research. However, the operationalization of this measurement is all based on the same reported costs gathered from participants over eight periods.

17. As a percentage (misrepresentation / available misrepresentation), advantaged (disadvantaged) managers believe it is fair to misrepresent 1% (18%) of the total available range.

18. Submitted beliefs are the cost reports made in each of eight rounds that participants believed to be fair considering the actual cost given to them. There is a marginal effect of period within-subjects as seen in Table 1. This would show that the magnitude of available misrepresentation due to varying actual costs had a potentially small impact on what they believed to be fair. However, the lack of interaction with the terms of interest gives us some comfort this does not significantly affect our results.

19. We do examine differences from benchmarks of an honest report and an equal report in the results section as well as comparing results across conditions.

20. Managers in all conditions are given paper, pencil, and calculator at their workstations to use to calculate decision outcomes.

21. While different samples are used in experiments 1 and 2, an analysis of the demographic variables of age ($p > 0.446$), gender ($p > 0.189$), and GPA ($p > 0.512$) finds no differences in the samples used.

22. The decision aid condition and the study 1 feedback for submitting fairness beliefs are very similar. The only difference being study 1 feedback was presented on the in real time prior to submitting reports. Study 2 used a pop-up box on submitting a report to provide feedback. At that point Study 2 participants could accept or revise their report.

23. Participants with the decision aid revise reports approximately 6.5 times on average over the 8 periods, while participants without the decision aid revise only approximately 0.25 times. As expected, increasing the accessibility of information causes an increase in revisions.

24. Outcomes are not displayed after the acceptance of the cost report for the non-decision aid condition. Having done so would have weakened the decision aid manipulation by providing a result similar to the decision aid condition for subsequent period results, thereby weakening the power of the manipulation comparison between cells.

25. Some prior research has described individuals who always report the truth or always lie to maximize personal income. In our study, 18 participants told the truth while none of the participants lied to maximize income.

ACKNOWLEDGMENTS

Thanks to Robert Ramsay and Richard Smith for detailed comments on earlier versions of this chapter. Thanks also to participants at workshops at the University of Kentucky, Kent State University, the 2017 AAA Annual Meeting of the AAA, the 2010 and 2011 Management Accounting Section and 2011 AAA Ohio Region Research Conferences for comments and suggestions, and, to the Von Allmen School of Accounting and the Institute of Management Accountants for generous financial support.

REFERENCES

Alchian, A. A., & Demsetz, H. (1972). Production, information costs and economic organization. *The American Economic Review*, 62(5), 777–795.

Bolton, G. E., & Ockenfels, A. (2000). ERC: A theory of equity, reciprocity, and competition. *The American Economic Review*, 90(1), 166–193.

Bonner, S. E., & Sprinkle, G. B. (2002). The effects of monetary incentives on effort and task performance: Theories, evidence, and a framework for research. *Accounting, Organizations, and Society*, 27, 303–345.

Brown, J. L., Evans, J. H., & Moser, D. V. (2009). Agency theory and participative budgeting experiments. *Journal of Management Accounting Research*, 21(1), 317–345.

Brown, J. L., Fisher, J. G., Peffer, S. A., & Sprinkle, G. B. (2017). The effect of budget framing and budget-setting process on managerial reporting. *Journal of Management Accounting Research*, 29(1), 31–44.

Bucciarelli, M., Khemlani, S., & Johnson-Laird, P. N. (2008). The psychology of moral reasoning. *Judgment and Decision Making, 3*(2), 121–139.

Chong, V. K., & Loy, C. Y. (2015). The effect of a leader's reputation on budgetary slack. *Advances in Management Accounting, 25*, 49–102.

Chow, C. W., Cooper, J. C., & Waller, W. S. (1988). Participative budgeting: Effects of a truth-inducing pay scheme and information asymmetry on slack and performance. *The Accounting Review, 63*(1), 111–122.

Cohen, J. R., Holder-Webb, L., Sharp, D. J., & Pant, L. W. (2007). The effects of perceived fairness on opportunistic behavior. *Contemporary Accounting Research, 24*(4), 1119–1138.

Cox, J. C., & Sadiraj, V. (2012). Direct tests of individual preferences for efficiency and equity. *Economic Inquiry, 50*(4), 920–931.

Douthit, J. D., & Stevens, D. E. (2015). The robustness of honesty effects on budget proposals when the superior has rejection authority. *The Accounting Review, 90*(2), 467–493.

Dow, K. E., Watson, M. W., Greenberg, P. S., & Greenberg, R. H. (2012). Understanding participation: Situational participation, intrinsic involvement, and influence. *Advances in Management Accounting, 21*, 25–47.

Drake, A. R., Matuszewski, L. J., & Miller, F. (2014). The effect of personality traits and fairness on honesty in managerial reporting. *Advances in Management Accounting, 22*, 43–69.

Drolet, A., Larrick, R., & Morris, M. W. (1998). Thinking of others: How perspective taking changes negotiators' aspirations and fairness perceptions as a function of negotiator relationships. *Basic and Applied Social Psychology, 20*(1), 23–31.

Engelmann, D., & Strobel, M. (2004). Inequality aversion, efficiency, and maximin preferences in simple distribution experiments. *American Economic Review, 94*(4), 857–869.

Evans III, J. H., Hannan, R. L., Krishnan, R., & Moser, D. V. (2001). Honesty in managerial reporting. *The Accounting Review, 76*(4), 537–559.

Fehr, E., & Schmidt, K. M. (1999). A theory of fairness, competition, and cooperation. *The Quarterly Journal of Economics, 114*(3), 817–868.

Fisher, J., Frederickson, J. R., & Peffer, S. A. (2002). The effect of information asymmetry on negotiated budgets: An empirical investigation. *Accounting, Organizations and Society, 27*(1–2), 27–43.

Frederickson, J. R., & Cloyd, C. B. (1998). The effects of performance cues, subordinate susceptibility to social influences, and the nature of the subordinate's private information on budgetary slack. *Advances in Accounting, 16*(1), 89–115.

Gong, G., Li, L. Y., & Shin, J. Y. (2011). Relative performance evaluation and related peer groups in executive compensation contracts. *The Accounting Review, 86*(3), 1007–1043.

Groen, B. A. (2018). A survey study into participation in goal setting, fairness, and goal commitment: Effects of including multiple types of fairness. *Journal of Management Accounting Research, 30*(2), 207–240.

Guo, L., Libby, T., & Liu, X. (2017). The effects of vertical pay dispersion: Experimental evidence in a budget setting. *Contemporary Accounting Research, 34*(1), 555–576.

Hannan, R. L., Rankin, F. W., & Towry, K. L. (2006). The effect of information systems on honesty in managerial reporting: A behavioral perspective. *Contemporary Accounting Research, 23*(4), 885–918.

Hobson, J. L., Mellon, M. J., & Stevens, D. E. (2011). Determinants of moral judgments regarding budgetary slack: An experimental examination of pay scheme and personal values. *Behavioral Research in Accounting, 23*(1), 87–107.

Jollineau, S. J., Vance, T. W., & Webb, A. (2012). Subordinates as the first line of defense against biased financial reporting. *Journal of Management Accounting Research, 24*(1), 1–24.

Kim, C. K., Evans III, J. H., & Moser, D. V. (2005). Economic and equity effects on tax reporting decisions. *Accounting, Organizations and Society, 30*(7–8), 609–625.

Kolm, S.-C. (1996). *Modern theories of justice.* Cambridge, MA: The MIT Press.

Lee, J. Y. (2012). Relative hedonic utility and budgetary conflict resolution. *Advances in Managerial Accounting, 21*, 77–86.

Mahlendorf, M. D., Schäffer, U., & Skiba, O. (2015). Antecedents of participative budgeting – A review of empirical evidence. *Advances in Management Accounting, 25*, 1–27.

Matuszewski, L. J. (2010). Honesty in managerial reporting: Is it affected by perceptions of horizontal equity? *Journal of Management Accounting Research, 22*(1), 233–250.

Messier, W. F. (1992). Research in and development of audit decision aids. In R. H. Ashton & A. H. Ashton (Eds.), *Judgment and decision-making research in accounting and auditing* (pp. 207–230). Cambridge: Cambridge University Press.

Mill, J. S. (1997). Utilitarianism. In D. Fouke (Ed.), *Safe as milk: An introduction to philosophy* (pp. 81–96). New York, NY: American Heritage.

Mullen, B., Brown, R., & Smith, C. (1992). Ingroup bias as a function of salience, relevance, and status: An integration. *European Journal of Social Psychology, 22*(2), 103–122.

Rankin, F. W., Schwartz, S. T., & Young, R. A. (2008). The effect of honesty and superior authority on budget proposals. *The Accounting Review, 83*(4), 1083–1099.

Stevens, D. E. (2002). The effects of reputation and ethics on budgetary slack. *Journal of Management Accounting Research, 14*(1), 153–171.

Thielmann, I., & Hilbig, B. E. (2018). Is it all about the money? A re-analysis of the link between honesty-humility and dictator game giving. *Journal of Research in Personality, 76,* 1–5.

Waller, W. S. (1988). Slack in participative budgeting: The joint effect of a truth-inducing pay scheme and risk preferences. *Accounting, Organizations and Society, 13*(1), 87–98.

Wrapson, W., Harré, N., & Murrell, P. (2006). Reductions in driver speed using posted feedback of speeding information: Social comparison or implied surveillance? *Accident Analysis & Prevention, 38*(6), 1119–1126.

Young, S. M. (1985). Participative budgeting: The effects of risk aversion and asymmetric information on budgetary slack. *Journal of Accounting Research, 23*(2), 829–842.

Zhang, Y. (2008). The effects of perceived fairness and communication on honesty and collusion in a multi-agent setting. *The Accounting Review, 83*(4), 1125–1146.

ADVERSE EFFECTS OF CONFIDENCE IN COMPLEX COST SYSTEMS AMID COMPETITION

Ella Mae Matsumura, Tyler Thomas and Dimitri Yatsenko

ABSTRACT

Organizations desire more accurate cost systems as competition increases, and consequently increase cost system complexity, as cost systems with greater complexity are potentially more accurate than simpler systems. However, even complex systems are prone to impactful inaccuracies, for example, due to design or calculation issues, that can adversely affect decision-making and firm performance. The authors investigate whether and the extent to which cost system complexity and competition decrease managers' attribution of cost-system-driven adverse firm effects to the cost system. The authors find greater cost system complexity (by inspiring greater confidence in the cost system) and higher competition (by providing a plausible external cause) decrease managers' attribution of cost-system-driven adverse firm effects to the cost system. With both greater cost system complexity and higher competition, managers observing signals of material cost inaccuracies are potentially the least likely to attribute cost-system-driven adverse firm effects to the cost system.

Keywords: Cost system; complexity; competition; confidence; attribution; experiment

Advances in Management Accounting, Volume 35, 99–127
Copyright © 2023 by Emerald Publishing Limited
ISSN: 1474-7871/doi:10.1108/S1474-787120230000035005

INTRODUCTION

Cost accounting systems provide critical information for managers' decision-making, planning, and control throughout the organization. Cost systems can vary in complexity from simple (e.g., plantwide overhead rates) to very complex (e.g., activity-based costing), and it is often maintained that more complex cost systems have the *potential* to provide more accurate costs than less complex cost systems (Atkinson, Kaplan, Matsumura, & Young, 2012; Blocher, Stout, Juras, & Cokins, 2012; Horngren, Datar, & Rajan, 2014). However, complex cost systems might still contain material inaccuracies that adversely affect organizational decision-making and performance. For example, firm profitability could suffer if managers set product prices based on materially inaccurate product cost information. Irrespective of cost system complexity, recognizing signals that adverse firm effects could be due to material inaccuracies in the cost system is necessary in order to mitigate these adverse effects.

Practitioner literature argues greater competition necessitates greater cost system complexity due to the presumed greater accuracy, and prior research finds managers *believe* greater complexity (and presumed greater accuracy) is beneficial when faced with increased competition. However, prior studies have shown inconsistencies in how market competition affects the desire for greater cost system complexity (Geiger & Ittner, 1996; Hansen, 1998; Libby & Waterhouse, 1996; Player & Lacerda, 1999). Krishnan, Luft, and Shields (2002) provide a step forward in reconciling these inconsistencies by documenting that expected changes in competition affect the level of costing accuracy that individuals deem necessary. We take a different approach to examining market competition and cost system complexity and argue that stable levels of higher competition (as opposed to an expected increase in competition) inhibit managers from attending to the cost system and potential inaccuracies therein. Specifically, we evaluate how cost system complexity and competition affect managers' attribution of cost-system-driven adverse firm outcomes to the cost system.

Impactful and material inaccuracies can exist in systems of varied complexity due to issues in implementation, data aggregation, and data capture, and such inaccuracies can lead to subsequent adverse effects, such as low or declining profitability (Datar & Gupta, 1994). A necessary step in addressing cost system inaccuracies is realizing there might be an issue with the cost system, i.e., attributing cost-system-driven firm adverse effects to the cost system. Cooper (1989) identifies several signals of an inaccurate cost system, such as high reported margins on complex products absent premium pricing, surprising outcomes of submitted bids, and lack of customers' reaction to price increases. These signals coupled with declining profitability raise concerns that the cost system contains material inaccuracies. In the presence of these signals, managers would benefit from correctly attributing cost-system-driven adverse firm effects to the cost system and correcting the cost system inaccuracies causing the adverse effects.

We contend more complex cost systems engender higher manager confidence in the system than simpler cost systems, causing managers to be more complacent (i.e., to accept the cost information at face value and be less likely to attribute cost-system-driven adverse firm effects to the cost system). We posit that two factors can lead to increased confidence in more complex systems. First, managers might rely on the belief that more complexity *necessarily* leads to more accuracy, leading to more confidence in the information provided by a more complex system. Second, increases in available information can lead to greater confidence in the information and the corresponding decisions (Hall, Ariss, & Todorov, 2007; Zacharakis & Shepherd, 2001). We argue that as increases in cost system complexity provide a greater amount of information, manager confidence in the system increases. Consequently, we predict greater cost system complexity will invoke greater confidence in the system, rendering managers less likely to attribute cost-system-driven adverse firm effects to the cost system.

We further argue that higher market competition decreases managers' attribution of cost-system-driven adverse firm effects to the cost system, by providing a plausible external cause for these effects. Managers can be biased by motivated reasoning to attribute adverse organizational effects to factors external to the firm, as attributing adverse organization effects to factors internal to the firm could reflect poorly on them as managers. Motivated reasoning can lead individuals to evaluate and interpret information in a manner consistent with their preferences (Ditto & Lopez, 1992; Kunda, 1990; Lundgren & Prislin, 1998). Thus, we predict that with higher competition, compared to lower competition, external influence is more plausible, and managers will be less likely to attribute cost-system-driven adverse firm outcomes to the cost system. Lastly, we evaluate whether the combined effect of cost system complexity and market competition inhibits managers' attribution of cost-system-driven adverse firm effects to the cost system more than either cost system complexity or competition alone.

We test our predictions in an experiment. Participants act as plant managers tasked with investigating the cause(s) of declining profitability of their manufacturing firm in which impactful cost system inaccuracies exist. Participants are not explicitly informed of cost system inaccuracies, but can infer that inaccuracies exist based on cues or signals seeded in the experimental materials. We use a 2×2 design, manipulating the complexity of the organization's cost system (a single plantwide overhead rate vs five departmental overhead rates) and the level of market competition (one vs four competitors) between participants. We evaluate the extent to which participants attribute the cause of the firm's declining profitability to the cost system.

Consistent with our predictions, we find greater cost system complexity leads to more confidence in the system, which reduces the extent to which managers attribute cost-system-driven adverse firm effects to the cost system. We further find higher competition impedes managers' attribution of adverse firm effects to the cost system and inaccuracies therein. Lastly, our findings are consistent with an additive effect of complexity and competition on managers' attribution of adverse firm outcomes to the cost system. Thus, managers with more complex cost systems and higher competition are the least likely to attribute cost-system-driven adverse firm effects to the cost system.

Our study makes several contributions to the accounting literature. First, we add to research on cost systems and their refinement, by showing that even a small increase in cost system complexity increases confidence in the cost system and the information it generates. However, this confidence can lead to complacency, as managers who have high confidence in the system are less likely to attribute cost-system-driven adverse firm effects to the cost system. Second, we add to prior literature on inconsistencies in the relationship between cost system information and competition by demonstrating that managers attribute cost-system-driven adverse firm outcomes to the cost system to a lesser extent in the presence of higher competition. Lastly, we find managers experiencing greater cost system complexity and higher competition attribute the cause of adverse organizational effects externally and overlook the cost system as an explanation, potentially more so than either greater cost system complexity or higher competition alone. Managers of firms with more complex cost systems operating in a higher competition environment not only attribute cost-system-driven adverse firm effects to the cost system to a lesser extent, but also display more consensus (or agreement) in this assessment that the cost system is not to blame for the firm's adverse effects.

Our findings are highly relevant to practitioners involved in implementing, monitoring, or using information from a cost system. Firms using refined cost systems have greater confidence in the information generated by the cost system, which may lead firms to discount signals of cost system inaccuracy, and firms in competitive markets may be similarly inclined to overlook these inaccuracy signals by attributing these signals to the competitive environment. Thus, firms using complex cost accounting systems while in a competitive market may be least likely to attribute cost-system-driven adverse firm effects to the cost system, allowing cost system inaccuracies to persist and further adversely affect firm performance.

THEORY DEVELOPMENT AND HYPOTHESES

Cost System Complexity

Cost systems provide critical information for decisions throughout the firm, including product mix, pricing, and capital investment decisions. These systems vary in both complexity and structure, ranging from straightforward traditional allocation systems to very complex activity-based costing systems. The simplest manufacturing overhead allocation system is a plantwide rate system using one cost pool for all manufacturing overhead.[1] More accurate allocations of overhead costs are anticipated from departmental cost pools and associated departmental overhead rates, relative to plantwide rates, as different allocation bases (proportional to units produced) can be used across departments. Activity-based costing is designed to provide even more accurate cost assignments by accumulating costs by activities and using cost drivers associated not only with units produced, but also batches and distinct products. Researchers of management accounting practice stress the need to improve cost system accuracy through refinement and added complexity to improve measurement and information for decision makers (e.g., Anderson, Hesford, & Young, 2002; Cooper & Kaplan, 1992). However, regardless of the type of cost system, managers need to be wary of impactful cost system inaccuracies, due to design, calculation, or other issues, as refined or complex cost systems can still contain material inaccuracies, and at times the process of refinement can lead to costing issues (Cardinaels & Labro, 2008; Datar & Gupta, 1994; Labro, 2019).

Prior literature identifies detrimental effects of inaccuracies in costing systems and has evaluated some mechanisms to overcome them (Dearman & Shields, 2001; Heitger, 2007). We evaluate the effect of cost system complexity and the level of market competition on managers' attribution of cost-system-driven adverse firm effects to the cost system. Cooper (1989) outlines several signals indicative of material cost system inaccuracies, such as: complex and difficult-to-manufacture products are reported to be very profitable, products with high reported margins have no competition in the market, competitors' high-volume products are priced at levels lower than the cost reported by the internal cost system, and products with low reported margins are sold by competitors for low prices. When managers observe these signals, they should question whether the cost system is providing sufficiently accurate information to avoid adversely affecting the firm's decision-making (Cooper, 1989).[2]

Cost System Complexity and Manager Confidence

Despite academic research finding refined or complex cost systems can contain material inaccuracies (Cardinaels & Labro, 2008; Datar & Gupta, 1994; Labro, 2019), there is a widespread understanding (or implicit assumption) that more complex cost systems are designed with the *intent* to provide more accurate costing information than simple systems (e.g., those using plantwide overhead rates). Managers may, therefore, believe that more complex systems are *necessarily* more accurate, and place more confidence in cost system information from a more complex system. Increased confidence in more complex cost systems might be viewed as a rational response because more complex systems are *expected* to provide more accurate costing information (Cooper & Kaplan, 1992; Kaplan & Anderson, 2004). However, if increased confidence in more complex systems impedes the attribution of cost-system-driven adverse firm effects to the cost system, then this response can be detrimental to the firm's decision-making and profitability.

Relative to simpler cost systems, more complex cost systems provide and use more pieces of information about the allocation of an organization's costs, which can lead to higher expectations of system accuracy and increased confidence in the information the system provides. Prior research demonstrates increases in available information enhance confidence in decision-making, leading to decision-making biases (Fleisig, 2011; Hall et al., 2007; Smith, 2010; Zacharakis & Shepherd, 2001). We expect that the greater amount of available information in more complex cost systems increases confidence in the cost system, the information it provides, and decisions based on that information. Therefore, we posit that more complex cost systems inspire greater confidence, relative to simpler systems, not only by an impression of greater accuracy, but also by providing more information about the cost allocation process.[3]

Increased confidence in the firm's cost system can foster complacency, which leads management to accept the information at face value and expend fewer resources to monitor the system for impactful cost inaccuracies. Such inaccuracies can persist to adversely affect the organization, as neglecting to adjust the relationships in the cost system to keep them aligned with manufacturing realities results in distorted cost estimates and misinformed management decisions (Cooper, 1989). For example, setting prices based on inaccurate cost information could adversely affect firm profitability. Thus, we predict greater cost system complexity will increase managers' confidence in the system, and in turn, reduce the likelihood that managers attribute cost-system-driven adverse firm effects to the cost system, as illustrated in Fig. 1.

H1. **Greater cost system complexity increases the confidence managers have in the system, which inhibits their attribution of cost-system-driven adverse firm effects to the cost system.**

Market Competition

Several applied studies supporting the use of more complex cost systems argue increases in competition require greater cost system complexity due to presumed greater accuracy (Cooper, 1989; Player & Lacerda, 1999). Furthermore, analytical literature shows that as competition increases in non-monopolistic markets, the relative benefit of cost system refinement increases until it stabilizes at a medium level (Hansen, 1998). However, prior archival and survey studies provide mixed support for this analytical prediction. Khandwalla (1972) and Libby and Waterhouse (1996) do not find an association between cost system refinement and price competition, while Geiger and Ittner (1996) and Anderson et al. (2002) find an association between more refined cost systems and increased competition. A survey of Australian manufacturing firms finds cost system refinement relates to competition via a U-shaped curve, indicating cost allocation refinement is lowest at an intermediate level of competition (Wallace, 2013).

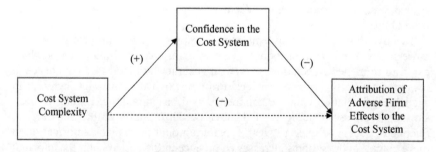

Fig. 1   H1: Mediation.
H1 predicts that greater cost system complexity increases the confidence managers have in the system, which inhibits their attribution of cost-system-driven adverse firm effects to the cost system.

Krishnan et al. (2002) note the inconsistent findings from prior studies evaluating the relationship between cost system accuracy and competition could be due to several factors: measurement of the sophistication of the cost system, increasing costing accuracy with increased competition might not be optimal, and differences in how costing systems change with a change in competition. The authors document that expected changes in competition affect the level of costing accuracy individuals deem necessary, thus changing the relationship between cost system accuracy and competition. Specifically, individuals in a non-monopolistic environment react to an upcoming increase (decrease) in competition by collecting more (less) cost information, which increases (decreases) the accuracy of the system, as there is a direct correlation between the quantity of cost information and increased accuracy in the study. The authors argue individuals use an internal theory similar to the heuristic that greater cost accuracy is needed when competition increases, and this theory guides their decisions as to the level of accuracy of the cost information required prior to operating in a more competitive market.

We add insight into the relationship between cost system accuracy and competition by evaluating another factor that influences this relationship. Specifically, we argue that higher competition inhibits managers from attributing cost-system-driven adverse firm effects to the cost system. Rather than asking managers to choose to acquire more, or more accurate information in anticipation of an increase in competition, as in Krishnan et al. (2002), we evaluate managers' reactions to adverse organizational outcomes when operating in a more competitive market, with more or less complex cost systems. Participants in Krishnan et al. (2002) desire more accurate cost information *in anticipation* of an increase in competition, and thus, it seems reasonable that in a higher competition setting, individuals will seek more accurate cost information to remain competitive. Such behavior would support their internal theory that greater competition requires greater cost accuracy.

Extending Krishnan et al. (2002), we argue that managers operating in higher competition with a given cost system will attribute cost-system-driven adverse firm effects to the cost system to a lesser extent relative to managers facing lower competition. This is because adverse organizational outcomes can (indirectly) reflect poorly on managers, which can bias them through motivated reasoning to attribute adverse organizational outcomes to causes external to themselves and the firm, such that these adverse effects do not reflect poorly on them as managers. Motivated reasoning influences how individuals evaluate information to support a desired conclusion, affecting how they search, process, and weigh information in their decision process to come to the conclusion they desire (Ditto & Lopez, 1992; Ditto, Scepansky, Munro, Apanovitch, & Lockhart, 1998; Kunda, 1990; Lundgren & Prislin, 1998), and has been shown in prior accounting research in various contexts (e.g., Bloomfield & Luft, 2006; Cloyd & Spilker, 1999; Kadous, Kennedy, & Peecher, 2003; Tayler, 2010). Thus, amid higher competition, we argue managers will be biased to attribute adverse firm outcomes to market competition, and not to the firm's internal cost system, so as not to reflect poorly on themselves. Furthermore, this bias will be stronger amid higher compared to lower competition, as higher competition provides a more plausible cause for adverse firm outcomes.

In sum, prior findings show managers believe preparing for a change to higher competition warrants greater cost system accuracy. We argue, however, that managers who experience operating in higher competition will focus less on the cost system and be less likely to attribute cost-system-driven adverse firm effects to the cost system, relative to managers operating in lower competition. This is because higher competition provides managers a more plausible external explanation for declining profitability compared to lower competition, leading to our second hypothesis.

H2. **Greater market competition inhibits managers' attribution of cost-system-driven adverse firm effects to the cost system.**

Greater Cost System Complexity and Higher Market Competition

We evaluate whether the combination of a more complex cost system and higher market competition has a greater effect on managers' attribution of cost-system-driven adverse firm effects to the cost system, than either factor alone. This analysis adds further insight into the relationship between cost system information and competition and how these factors potentially combine to affect managers' decisions concerning cost system accuracy. Managers who receive information from a more complex cost system have higher confidence in the system, and thus, are less likely to attribute adverse firm effects to cost system inaccuracies compared to managers who receive cost information from a simpler system. Furthermore, when operating amid higher competition, managers are motivated to attribute declining profitability to this external factor and not to cost system inaccuracies. Consequently, when faced with greater cost system complexity simultaneous with higher market competition, managers might be least likely to attribute adverse organizational effects to cost system inaccuracies, due to the combined effects of increased confidence in the cost system and the presence of additional plausible causes of the adverse firm outcomes.

Alternatively, either greater cost system complexity or higher market competition might have a sufficient effect on managers' attribution of cost-system-driven adverse firm effects to the cost system to render the other incrementally inconsequential. Both factors motivate managers away from attributing cost-system-driven adverse firm effects to the cost system, either due to increased confidence in the cost system or by providing a plausible external cause. As noted above, motivated reasoning can affect how managers evaluate available information to reach a desired conclusion (Ditto et al., 1998; Ditto & Lopez, 1992; Kunda, 1990; Lundgren & Prislin, 1998). This bias can reduce the amount of information needed to support a conclusion (Dawson, Savitsky, & Dunning, 2006; Lord, Ross, & Lepper, 1979). In our context, managers could view either greater cost system complexity or higher market competition as sufficient to justify attributing blame away from the cost system.

In sum, it is an empirical question as to how cost system complexity and the level of market competition combine to inhibit managers' attribution of cost-system-driven adverse firm effects to the cost system. Therefore, we evaluate the combined effect of greater cost system complexity and higher competition as a research question.

RQ. **Does greater cost system complexity amid higher competition inhibit managers' attribution of cost-system-driven adverse firm effects to the cost system more than either greater cost system complexity or higher competition alone?**

METHODOLOGY

Participants and Design

A total of 170 business students recruited from a participant pool at a large Midwestern University participated in the study. Prior studies show students are appropriate participants for tasks not requiring experience (e.g., Libby, Bloomfield, & Nelson, 2002). Our task only requires general business and cost system knowledge, and the participating students have the relevant expertise to perform the task successfully. The available participant-recruiting tool does not allow filtering by specific classes, so we recruit business students, most of whom should have taken the introductory managerial accounting course early in their coursework. However, we believe knowledge of management accounting is required to make informed decisions during the study, so the following analysis only uses data from the 136 participants who have completed or are currently enrolled in a management accounting course.[4] The use of students with managerial accounting coursework biases against our findings, as such students learned cost accounting relatively recently, which increases the likelihood of correctly attributing cost-system-driven adverse firm effects to the cost system across all conditions. The study took place after the point in the semester when each managerial accounting course/section had covered the costing topics pertinent to the study. Thus, students enrolled in a managerial accounting course had the requisite managerial accounting knowledge regarding cost systems.

The mean age of these participants is about 21 years, ranging from 18 to 32, and 61% are female.[5] Participants have taken (or are currently enrolled in) an average of 3.88 accounting courses, including an average of 1.38 management accounting courses. Participants completed the study at their own pace without a time limit. The pay per participant is $9.53 for less than 30 minutes, on average.

We use a 2 × 2 between-participant experimental design, in which we manipulate the complexity of the cost system and the level of market competition. To operationalize cost system complexity (*Cost_System_Complexity*), we keep the type of system constant (traditional) while varying the complexity by increasing the number of cost allocation pools. Specifically, the cost system uses either a single plantwide overhead rate or five departmental overhead rates (Less Complex vs More Complex). We chose not to use an activity-based costing system as the more complex type of cost system, in order to prevent students from using a potentially learned heuristic from their managerial accounting courses that activity-based costing provides much greater accuracy than traditional cost systems. Our design choice results in a weaker manipulation of cost system complexity, such that finding an effect with this choice is more difficult than finding an effect of an activity-based costing system over a plantwide system. We would expect even stronger results if activity-based costing and plantwide systems were compared.

The cost systems in our study are designed to report identical product costs for a given product. Furthermore, the accuracy of the cost information is held constant across the two systems and all conditions, as both systems contain the same impactful inaccuracy stemming from the design choice to use budgeted (estimated) instead of practical capacity levels for overhead allocation bases. Using budgeted levels of bases can lead to fluctuating overhead rates that do not accurately reflect the cost of overhead resources used, potentially influencing subsequent decisions (Atkinson et al., 2012; Balakrishnan & Sprinkle, 2002; Labro & Vanhoucke, 2007). Notably, management accounting courses at the institution where the study took place emphasize capacity issues in product costing, providing training relevant to the material cost inaccuracy present in our experimental instrument, and thus, the consequences of a firm using budgeted instead of practical capacity levels as cost bases to allocate manufacturing overhead should be familiar to our participants. We made this decision to control for the costing inaccuracy, and accuracy overall, between the costing systems, as our focus is on manipulating and analyzing differences in cost system complexity directly and not differences in resultant accuracy.

We manipulate the level of competition (*Competition*) by varying the number of competitors in the market; in the Lower competition condition the firm has a single competitor, and in the Higher competition condition the firm has four competitors.[6] We select these levels of market competition to be in line with the Hansen (1998) model of cost system complexity and competition and with Krishnan et al. (2002).

Task and Procedure

Participants are provided with information about a fictitious manufacturing company and are asked to assume the role of a plant manager, with the directive of investigating the declining profitability of the firm.[7] The experimental materials describe a scenario with several plausible explanations for declining firm profitability, including industry decline, competition, and cost system issues. Participants are told that although demand is growing in some segments of its customer base, evidence of robust industry revenue growth following the recession has not yet materialized (see Appendix 1). We also allow participants to consider and provide their own explanations not directly mentioned in the materials. The order of information presented has a natural flow from general to specific, as information on industry background is followed by information on market competition and information on the cost system. All participants view the information in the same order.

In all conditions, the firm manufactures two products. The first is a longstanding high-volume product, and the second is a newer, more complex, and low-volume product. Sales of the first product have decreased steadily and sales of the second product have increased steadily. Participants are given their firm's products' gross margin as a percentage of sales, along with industry sales growth compared to that of their firm. Industry sales growth has declined, and the firm's sales growth has declined even more. They are also informed that their firm either faces a single competitor or four competitors, and are provided information concerning the competing firm(s).

After reviewing the market competition information, participants read information about the firm's cost system, with manufacturing overhead costs allocated either using a single plantwide rate or five departmental rates. Participants review the entire overhead allocation process, starting with the calculation of overhead rate(s) and ending with the allocation of the costs to products, using the calculated overhead rate(s). The overhead cost allocation calculations are designed such that reported overhead costs for a given product are the same across all conditions, to control for cost system accuracy. Nevertheless, as described earlier, the cost system contains an impactful inaccuracy (described but not labeled as an inaccuracy), common across all conditions, stemming from the design choice of using estimated instead of practical capacity levels for overhead allocation bases.

After reviewing the information on industry background, market competition, and the cost system, participants respond to a quiz to verify their understanding of the information. They must answer all of the questions correctly before proceeding. Participants then learn their task is to investigate the cause of their firm's steadily decreasing profit over the past five years, and to report on the likely cause(s) of the declining profitability. Participants are informed that in addition to their $5 show-up fee, they can earn a bonus that is dependent on the quality of their report as to the likely cause(s) of the declining profitability.

Next, participants are given the opportunity to obtain additional information to help in this investigation process. As a material cost system inaccuracy is driving the declining profitability for the organization, we operationalize higher quality of the report as greater attribution of the declining profitability to the cost system. Much of the additional information participants can choose to view is linked to signals of impactful cost system inaccuracies, as identified in Cooper (1989). Appendix 2 shows the additional information available for participants to search.

The additional information pertains to either the cost system or market competition, with four attributes (or pieces of information) within each of these options. However, each piece is informative in identifying the distorted cost system as the cause of declining profitability. The four pieces of information about the cost system reveal idle capacity in the plant and higher reported gross margins on the complex product. The information about market competition informs participants their competition charges more for a complex product and less for a simple product and realizes higher sales of the simple product and lower sales of the complex product. This information suggests undercosting of the complex product and overcosting of the simple product. The information cues are intermixed, and participants are not shown the choices divided between the cost system and market competition. Participants can obtain the information with no cost, one piece at a time and in any order, but the information requires time and effort to review.[8]

Once participants complete their information search they are asked to indicate their belief as to the cause(s) of the firm's cost-system-driven declining profitability by allocating 100 points to four potential causes: industry decline, market competition, cost system, or other with an explanation (see Appendix 3).[9] Participants are told that their bonus depends on their allocation, reinforcing the earlier information that their bonus is dependent on the quality of their report as to the cause(s) of the declining profitability. Our dependent variable, *System_ Attribution*, is the number of points allocated to the cost system, as a measure of managers' attribution of cost-system-driven adverse firm effects to the cost system. We then ask participants to describe how they arrived at and what they considered in their attribution decision. Participants complete the exercise by answering post-experiment questions to capture demographics and potential insights into participant judgments.

The last screen informs participants of their earned bonus. The bonus is a function of points allocated to the cost system, as follows: Participants receive a $1 bonus if they allocate 0 to 9 points to the cost system, $2 if they allocate 10 to 19 points, etc. The maximum bonus of $10 is achieved if participants allocate at least 90 points to the cost system. This bonus is in addition to a $5 show-up fee.

RESULTS AND DISCUSSION

We first test whether participants perceive the cost system with five departmental cost drivers (More Complex) as more complex than the system with one plantwide cost driver (Less Complex) using a post-experimental question. The question asked, "How complex is [*your firm's*] cost system?" with answers on a seven-point Likert scale with endpoints of 1 = Not at all Complex and 7 = Extremely Complex. The mean rating for participants in the Less Complex system condition is significantly less than that for participants in the More Complex system condition (untabulated, $2.45 < 3.45$, $p < 0.01$, two-tailed). It is important to note the cost systems used in the experiment are both traditional cost systems that are not overly complex. Nevertheless, participants identify the minor difference in cost system complexity between these systems, even without comparison.

To identify whether participants believe that the number of competitors impacts a firm's profitability, the following post-experimental question is included: "If [*your firm*] had one or four competitor(s) [based on the competition condition], how likely is it that [*your firm's*] profitability would have been higher?" The responses are on a seven-point Likert scale with endpoints of 1 = Extremely Unlikely and 7 = Extremely Likely. Participants in the Lower competition condition rated the likelihood of higher profitability if the firm had four competitors as 2.42, and participants in the Higher competition condition rated the likelihood of higher profitability if the firm had one competitor as 5.18. This difference is statistically significant, indicating participants believe profitability is inversely related to competition intensity (untabulated, $p < 0.01$, two-tailed).[10]

To assess participants' familiarity with cost systems and the overhead alloca-tion process, as well as capacity issues, we evaluate responses to two post-experi-mental questions rated on seven-point Likert scales (endpoints of 1 = Extremely Unfamiliar and 7 = Extremely Familiar, with a midpoint of 4). First, participants respond to the question, "How familiar are you with product costing systems in a classroom setting?" the mean rating for this question is 5.32, which is significantly higher than the midpoint of the scale (untabulated, $p < 0.01$, two-tailed). This question provides some evidence participants believe they are familiar with cost systems and can address the system issues described in our experiment.[11] Second, participants respond to the question, "How familiar are you with overhead cost allocation and capacity costs in a classroom setting?" The mean response is 5.38 which is significantly higher than the midpoint (untabulated, $p < 0.01$, two-tailed). There are no differences in mean response by condition. Notably, only 19 participants answered this question as a 4 or below, with the majority of participants answering "5 = Somewhat familiar," and "6 = Familiar." This is not surprising, as capacity issues in overhead allocation are emphasized in the intro-ductory managerial accounting course.

Main Analyses

Our primary dependent variable is managers' attribution of cost-system-driven adverse firm effects to the cost system (*System_Attribution*). As noted earlier, *System_Attribution* is the number of points allocated to the cost system as one of four potential causes of declining profitability. Our independent variables are *Complexity* (Less Complex or More Complex system) and *Competition* (Lower or Higher). We develop a measure of our mediator, confidence in the cost system (*Confidence*), using a questionnaire consisting of seven post-experiment questions on seven-point Likert scales concerning aspects of confidence in the cost sys-tem and its corresponding information (see Appendix 4). We create a confidence score that is the sum of the responses to the seven questions. These responses have a Cronbach's Alpha of 0.88, indicating good internal consistency, and each question loads on one factor with an eigenvalue of 3.71.[12] Table 1 outlines the descriptive statistics, by condition, for factors to which participants attribute the firm's declining profitability,[13] as well as *Confidence*. The descriptive statistics are consistent with our hypotheses, such that managers with greater cost system complexity or more competition are less likely to attribute cost-system-driven adverse firm effects to the cost system. Furthermore, managers with both greater cost system complexity and more competition are the least likely to attribute cost-system-driven adverse firm effects to the cost system. We statistically evalu-ate our hypotheses and research question below.

Cost System Complexity

We predict greater cost system complexity will increase the confidence manag-ers place in the cost system and in turn decrease the likelihood managers will attribute cost-system-driven adverse firm effects to the cost system (*H1*; see Fig. 1). Table 2 presents the results of the *H1* tests. As an initial test of the

Table 1. Cell Means (Standard Deviations) of Attributed Cause(s) of Declining Profitability and Confidence Scores.

		Less Complex Cost System	More Complex Cost System	Total
Lower Competition	Observations	38	31	69
	Industry Decline	17.63 (13.64)	22.16 (15.96)	19.67 (14.79)
	Market Competition	28.50 (16.61)	27.35 (14.28)	27.98 (15.50)
	System_Attribution	**44.50 (22.78)**	**34.03 (25.87)**	**39.80 (24.60)**
	Other	9.36 (12.00)	16.45 (17.85)	12.55 (15.21)
	Confidence	**17.89 (7.53)**	**23.58 (7.78)**	**20.50 (8.10)**
Higher Competition	Observations	33	34	67
	Industry Decline	15.85 (9.22)	22.06 (16.70)	19.00 (13.80)
	Market Competition	32.94 (16.12)	29.26 (14.04)	31.07 (15.10)
	System_Attribution	**37.12 (20.95)**	**29.56 (19.94)**	**33.28 (20.64)**
	Other	14.09 (16.22)	19.12 (20.39)	16.64 (18.49)
	Confidence	**18.79 (6.57)**	**23.24 (6.54)**	**21.04 (6.88)**
Total	Observations	71	65	136
	Industry Decline	16.80 (11.75)	22.11 (16.23)	19.34 (14.26)
	Market Competition	30.56 (16.42)	28.35 (14.08)	29.51 (15.33)
	System_Attribution	**41.07 (22.11)**	**31.69 (22.88)**	**36.59 (22.89)**
	Other	11.56 (14.21)	17.84 (19.12)	14.57 (16.97)
	Confidence	**18.31 (7.07)**	**23.40 (7.10)**	**20.74 (7.50)**

Notes: We use the variables *System_Attribution* and *Confidence* to test our hypotheses and research question and show these variables and the corresponding results in boldface. The table shows average allocations of 100 points to 4 possible causes of declining profitability: Industry Decline, Market Competition, Cost System, and Other (along with an explanation). *System_Attribution* is the number of points participants allocate to the cost system as the probable cause of declining firm profitability, and *Confidence* is a composite score consisting of the sum of the scores on seven questions designed to capture confidence in the cost system (see Appendix 4).

mediation effect, we follow the Baron and Kenny (1986) approach presented in Table 2a. First, consistent with the difference in means in Table 1 (31.69 < 41.07), *System_Attribution* is lower for participants in the More Complex system condition (using departmental rates) than for those in the Less Complex system condition (using a plantwide rate) ($b_1 = -9.38$, $p = 0.01$, one-tailed). Therefore, we find cost system complexity decreases managers' attribution of cost-system-driven adverse firm effects to the cost system. Second, *Cost_System_Complexity* leads to higher confidence in the system ($b_1 = 5.09$, $p = 0.01$, one-tailed). Finally, when *Confidence* is included in the model evaluating the effect of *Cost_System_Complexity* on *System_Attribution*, then *Cost_System_Complexity* is no longer significant ($b_1 = -0.93$, $p = 0.39$, one-tailed) and *Confidence* is significant ($b_1 = -1.66$, $p = 0.01$, one-tailed). These results support the predicted mediation in *H1*.[14]

To provide further support for the mediation model, we use a bootstrapped test of the indirect effect following Preacher and Hayes (2004, 2008) and a Sobel-Goodman mediation test of the indirect effect of the model, shown in Table 2b. The bootstrapped test of the indirect effect is significant, as evidenced by the 95% confidence interval that does not include zero and the non-bootstrapped

Table 2. *H1* Mediation Test: Effect of *Cost_System_Complexity* on *Confidence* and *System_Attribution.*

Table 2a. Traditional Test for Mediation (Baron & Kenny, 1986).

Step 1: *System_Attribution* Regressed on *Cost_System_Complexity*

Step 2: *Confidence* Regressed on *Cost_System_Complexity*

Step 3: *System_Attribution* Regressed on *Cost_System_Complexity* and *Confidence*

	Step 1 DV: *System_Attribution*	Step 2 DV: *Confidence*	Step 3 DV: *System_Attribution*
Intercept	41.07	18.31	71.48
t-statistic	15.39	21.78	14.69
p-value	0.01	0.01	0.01
Cost_System_Complexity	−9.38	5.09	−0.93
t-statistic	(−2.43)	(4.19)	(−0.26)
p-value	**0.01**	**0.01**	**0.39**
Confidence			−1.66
t-statistic			(−7.08)
p-value			**0.01**
N	136	136	136
Residual Degrees of freedom	134	134	133
Adj_R^2	0.035	0.11	0.29

Note: Bolded *p*-values are one-tailed.

Table 2b. Bootstrapped Test of the Indirect Effect Based on Preacher and Hayes (2004, 2008).[a]

	Coefficient	Bias	Bootstrap Std. Error	95% Confidence Interval	
Indirect effect	−8.45	−0.021	2.29	−13.24	−4.23

Notes: $N = 136$; Replications $= 10,000$.

System_Attribution is the dependent variable, measured as the number of points participants allocate to the cost system as the probable cause of declining firm profitability.

Confidence is a composite score consisting of the sum of the scores on seven questions (five-point Likert scales) designed to capture confidence in the cost system (see Appendix 4).

Cost_System_Complexity is an indicator variable, coded as 1 for the more complex cost system (five overhead allocation rates), and 0 for the less complex cost system (one overhead allocation rate).

[a]The non-bootstrapped Sobel-Goodman test of indirect effect is also significant ($p < 0.01$).

Sobel-Goodman test shows a significant indirect effect of *Cost_System_Complexity* on *System_Attribution* through *Confidence* ($p < 0.01$, one-tailed). Thus, we find support for *H1* and conclude that confidence mediates the negative relationship between cost system complexity and attribution of cost-system-driven adverse firm effects to the cost system, such that cost system complexity increases confidence in the system, reducing the likelihood that managers attribute cost-system-driven adverse firm effects to the cost system.

Market Competition

We argue that with more competition, managers will attribute cost-system-driven declining profitability to the cost system to a lesser extent than with less competition (*H2*). Table 3 presents the results of the tests of *H2*. Consistent with our prediction and the difference in means in Table 1 (33.28 < 39.80), *System_Attribution* is lower for participants in the Higher competition condition than for those in the Lower competition conditions, and this difference is significant ($b_1 = -6.51$, $p = 0.05$, one-tailed). Our findings are consistent with greater market competition reducing managers' attribution of cost-system-driven adverse firm effects to the cost system, by providing a plausible external cause of declining profitability.

Cost System Complexity and Market Competition

We also evaluate the combined effects of cost system complexity and market competition to address our research question: Does having greater cost system complexity amid higher competition inhibit managers' attribution of cost-system-driven adverse firm effects to the cost system more so than either greater cost system complexity or higher competition alone? To examine our research question, we run an ANOVA, shown in Table 4, with *System_Attribution* as the dependent variable and *Cost_System_Complexity* and *Competition* as the independent variables, including *Confidence* in the model, consistent with our mediation model for *H1*.[15] We find the effect of *Cost_System_Complexity* through *Confidence* is significant ($p < 0.01$, two-tailed) and the effect of *Competition* is marginally significant ($p = 0.10$, two-tailed), but their interaction is not significant ($p = 0.90$, two-tailed). These results are consistent with greater cost system complexity and higher market competition combined having a potentially greater effect in inhibiting managers' attribution of cost-system-driven adverse firm effects to the cost system than either factor alone. Fig. 2 depicts these results.

Table 3. *H2* General Linear Model: Effect of *Competition* on *System_ Attribution*.

	Prediction	DV: *System_Attribution*
Intercept		39.80
t-statistic		14.54
p-value		0.01
Competition	–	−6.51
t-statistic		(−1.67)
p-value		**0.05**
N		136
Residual Degrees of freedom		134
Adj_*R*²		0.01

Notes: Bolded *p*-values are one-tailed.
System_Attribution is the dependent variable, measured as the number of points participants allocate to the cost system as the probable cause of declining firm profitability.
Competition is an indicator variable, coded as 1 for higher competition (four competitors), and 0 for lower competition (1 competitor).

Table 4. Research Question ANOVA: Effect of *Cost_System_Complexity* and *Competition* on *System_Attribution*.

Source	df	Mean Square	F	Sig.
Model	4	5,636	15.33	0.00
Cost_System_Complexity[a]	1	13	0.03	0.85
Competition	1	1,013	2.75	0.10
Interaction	1	6	0.02	0.90
Confidence[a]	1	18,278	49.70	0.00
Error	131	368		

Notes: *System_Attribution* is the dependent variable, measured as the number of points participants allocate to the cost system as the probable cause of declining firm profitability.
Cost_System_Complexity is an indicator variable, coded as 1 for the more complex cost system (five overhead allocation rates), and 0 for the less complex cost system (one overhead allocation rate).
Competition is an indicator variable, coded as 1 for higher competition (four competitors), and 0 for lower competition (one competitor).
[a]We include *Confidence* because as predicted, it mediates the effect of *Cost_System_Complexity* on *System_Attribution*.

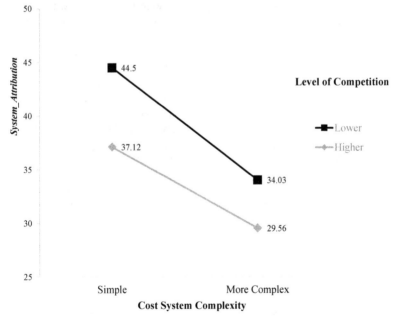

Fig. 2 Effect of *Cost_System_Complexity* and *Competition* on *System_Attribution*. *System_Attribution* is the dependent variable, measured as the number of points participants allocate to the cost system as the probable cause of declining firm profitability. *Cost_System_Complexity* is an indicator variable, coded as 1 for the more complex cost system (five overhead allocation rates), and 0 for the less complex cost system (one overhead allocation rate). *Competition* is an indicator variable, coded as 1 for higher competition (four competitors), and 0 for lower competition (one competitor).

Supplemental Analyses

We offer two supplemental findings to support our theoretical arguments. First, we evaluate the relationship between managers' identification with the firm and their attribution of adverse firm effects to the cost system, as identification with the firm can leave a manager more susceptible to motivated reasoning bias following adverse firm outcomes. A negative relationship would suggest managers who identify with the firm are biased to attribute adverse organizational outcomes to factors external to the firm, and not to factors internal to the firm, which could reflect poorly on them as a manager. Using an adapted version of a validated questionnaire from Mael and Ashforth (1992), see Appendix 5, we find a significant negative correlation between participants' identification with the firm and *System_Attribution* (untabulated, $p = 0.03$, two-tailed, $n = 61$).[16] With greater identification, participants are less likely to attribute adverse effects to the cost system, which is internal to the firm. Therefore, when managers identify with the firm, they prefer to attribute blame to external factors, to avoid reflecting poorly on themselves.[17]

Second, we examine whether greater market competition can increase managers' consensus that the cost system is not the cause of the adverse effects. We argue greater competition offers managers a plausible external factor to which they can attribute adverse firm effects, and provide results that with greater competition, managers are less likely to attribute cost-system-driven adverse firm effects to the cost system. The failure to attribute cost-system-driven adverse firm effects to the cost system can be of further concern, however, if there is greater agreement (or consensus) that the cost system is not at the heart of the issue. To examine this issue, we define consensus as the level of variance around *System_Attribution* within a condition, as a measure of participant agreement within a condition. We analyze the variance in *System_Attribution* between the Higher and Lower competition conditions to determine if consensus is higher with participants operating amid higher competition. Using Levene's test of difference in variance, we find the variance in the attribution of cost-system-driven declining profitability to the cost system is lower for participants in the Higher competition conditions (untabulated, $p = 0.05$, two-tailed). That is, with higher competition there is a greater level of agreement that the cost system is less to blame for the adverse organizational effects, compared with lower competition.

This finding, in conjunction with managers' increased confidence with greater cost system complexity, suggests managers with more complex cost systems amid higher competition will be more confident in the system and be in more agreement that the cost system is not to blame for poor outcomes. This view could lead to a reduced likelihood that material cost system inaccuracies are discovered, allowing the perpetuation of these inaccuracies and the corresponding adverse effects to the firm.

CONCLUSION

Understanding and accurately measuring costs and cost behavior are critical for organizational decision-making and success. However, material inaccuracies can arise within cost systems and adversely affect the firm, and if managers are complacent, these inaccuracies can persist, leading to continued negative effects on the organization. It is vital for managers to attend to the signals of problematic issues within the cost system and make necessary adjustments to address any material inaccuracies that exist. Cooper (1989) notes several signals to which managers need to attend to and monitor to help ensure cost system accuracy, with several of these identified in the final column of Appendix 2. Accordingly, our study examines factors that can inhibit managers' attribution of cost-system-driven adverse firm effects to the cost system.

We find greater cost system complexity increases managers' confidence in the cost system, but that this confidence has an adverse effect as it decreases the likelihood that managers will attribute cost-system-driven adverse firm effects to the cost system. We also find greater market competition inhibits managers' attribution of cost-system-driven adverse firm effects to the cost system. Finally, we demonstrate greater cost system complexity coupled with higher market competition potentially inhibits managers' attribution of cost-system-driven adverse firm effects to the cost system more than either factor alone.

Our study makes several contributions to the accounting literature. First, we expand the existing measure of confidence that exists in the literature and use the measure to demonstrate that a small increase in cost system complexity significantly increases confidence in the cost system, which leads managers to underestimate the likelihood that the cost system contains impactful inaccuracies and is the cause of adverse firm effects. We show that even a relatively minor increase in system complexity increases managers' confidence in the system, which in turn reduces the attribution of cost-system-driven adverse firm effects to the cost system. If such inaccuracies are not attended to, then they can perpetuate and continue to adversely affect the firm. Notably, we illustrate this effect with a minor increase in system complexity. As firms increase the complexity of their cost systems, this effect could increase substantially.

Second, we add to the literature examining the interplay between cost systems and competition. Prior research findings are mixed, but provide some evidence managers believe upcoming increased competition requires more attention to the cost system and more accurate cost information. We demonstrate higher competition reduces managers' attribution of cost-system-driven adverse firm effects to the cost system, allowing for persistence of reduced cost accuracy and adverse firm effects. Our findings also highlight a further issue as managers' decisions are misinformed to the extent that relationships in the cost system are not aligned with manufacturing or nonmanufacturing realities (Cooper, 1989).

Third, we demonstrate greater cost complexity and higher competition combined potentially inhibit managers' attribution of cost-system-driven adverse firm effects to the cost system more than either of these factors alone. Thus, as system complexity increases and competition is higher, managers are potentially the least likely to attribute cost-system-driven adverse firm effects to the cost system, allowing the inaccuracies to perpetuate and continue to adversely affect profitability.

Our study is subject to several limitations and opportunities for future research. The limitations include those commonly associated with experimental studies, such as the extent of generalizability to real-world situations. Our simplified hypothetical scenario could be enhanced to include the influence of other key information components, such as marketing strategies or key strategic initiatives, to address our research question. Furthermore, although prior studies show students are appropriate for tasks such as ours that do not require experience, professionals could be used as participants, especially in a more complex experimental setting. We also evaluate two traditional costing systems in our study and participants are not involved in developing or refining the cost system. Future studies can compare the use of a traditional cost system to an activity-based cost system and/or examine how participation in revising the cost system interacts with system complexity and confidence. Lastly, we evaluate one aspect of competition, i.e., number of competitors, but different types of competition can affect firms differently (Khandwalla, 1972). Future research can analyze how various types of competition differentially affect managers' attribution of cost-system-driven adverse firm effects to the cost system.

NOTES

1. We focus on manufacturing overhead allocation because manufacturing overhead costs often constitute a large proportion of manufacturing costs, and the assignment of direct costs is fairly straightforward. Cost systems can also vary in complexity and structure within service and merchandising companies, and for nonmanufacturing functions within manufacturing firms.

2. Cooper's (1989) signals can arise in cost systems of varying complexity.

3. Prior accounting research shows high confidence in a cost system is associated with "choosing" a cost system, independent of the type of system chosen (Jermias, 2001, 2006). However, we examine whether greater cost system complexity leads to increased confidence in the cost system, without system selection, and we argue this increased confidence from greater cost system complexity can inhibit managers' attribution of cost-system-driven adverse firm effects to the cost system.

4. There are no qualitative differences between the results presented and results using the entire sample. *H2* is marginally significant when tested using the entire sample.

5. Our inferences remain unchanged when we include age and/or gender in the regression.

6. The number of competitors is only one aspect of competition intensity (Khandwalla, 1972), and fierce competition can exist even between a small number of competitors (e.g., Pepsi and Coca-Cola). We use the number of competitors as one salient characteristic to proxy for competition intensity. In the Results section, we confirm participants associate a higher number of competitors with more intense competition and lower firm profitability.

7. The instrument is adapted from Thomas (2016) and approval for the study was obtained from the Institutional Review Board at the institution at which the study was run.

8. We made a design choice not to charge for information, in order to control for information availability. However, this makes finding differences in search patterns more difficult, as participants tend to go through all the materials available. In analyzing participants' "information search," we find most participants tried to view most of the information provided and did so generally in an orderly manner, i.e., across rows of both columns or down columns for each row. Due to the lack of variation in this data, we do not expound on participants' information search in the Results section.

9. Examples of prior accounting studies using a similar allocation approach are Kelly (2010) and Tayler (2010).

10. These results concerning cost system complexity and competition are robust to including all participants.

11. We also ask participants the question, "How familiar are you with product costing in a non-classroom setting (e.g., in a firm)?" with responses on a seven-point Likert scale. The mean response to this question is unsurprisingly lower (2.87), as we use student participants.

12. The eigenvalue on the next factor is only 0.11. All of the questions load strongly on the first factor, except question 3 with a more moderate loading. If we drop question 3 from the *Confidence* measure we find no differences in our results.

13. Common responses in the "Other" category include product quality, pricing of products/product mix, operating below capacity, and marketing.

14. Participants' GPA and the number of accounting courses taken are significant when included as covariates in our models testing the hypotheses, but our inferences remain unchanged.

15. Because we predict and find *Confidence* mediates the effect of *Cost_System_Complexity*, we include *Confidence* in the ANOVA to test our research question to account for this mediation effect.

16. As we conducted the experiment, it came to our attention that support for our theory would be enhanced if we could demonstrate that participants "identify" with their firm in our laboratory setting. Thus, we adapted the identification questionnaire from Mael and Ashforth (1992), added it to the experimental instrument, and collected the information from the remainder of our participants ($n = 61$).

17. We argue identification with the firm leads managers to be susceptible to motivated reasoning bias following adverse firm outcomes, and higher competition provides a more plausible external cause for the attribution of adverse outcomes than lower competition. We do not posit the level of competition affects manager identification with the firm.

ACKNOWLEDGMENTS

We thank the editor (Chris Akroyd) and two anonymous reviewers for their guidance. We would also like to thank Emily Griffith, Rachel Martin, Axel Schulz, Karl Schumacher, Steve Smith, Stuart Smith, Ryan Sommerfeldt, Ivo Tafkov, Todd Thornock, Richard Walstra, Adam Watanabe du Pon, Di Yang, and participants at the Management Accounting Experimental Research Brown Bag, University of Wisconsin-Madison Workshop, 2017 Management Accounting Section Midyear Meeting, 2017 AAA Annual Meeting, 2017 Accounting, Behavior and Organizations Section Meeting, 2017 AAA Midwest Region Meeting, and 2018 BYU Accounting Research Symposium for their helpful comments. We further gratefully acknowledge funding for this project from the BRITE Lab Research Grant and the Department of Accounting and Information Systems of the Wisconsin School of Business.

REFERENCES

Anderson, S. W., Hesford, J. W., & Young, S. M. (2002). Factors influencing the performance of activity based costing teams: A field study of ABC model development time in the automobile industry. *Accounting, Organizations and Society*, *27*(3), 195–211.

Atkinson, A. A., Kaplan, R. S., Matsumura, E. M., & Young, S. M. (2012). *Management accounting: Information for decision making and strategy execution* (6th ed.). Upper Saddle River, NJ: Pearson Prentice Hall.

Balakrishnan, R., & Sprinkle, G. B. (2002). Integrating profit variance analysis and capacity costing to provide better managerial information. *Issues in Accounting Education*, *17*(2), 149–161.

Baron, R. M., & Kenny, D. A. (1986). The moderator-mediator variable distinction in social psycho-
    logical research: Conceptual, strategic, and statistical considerations. *Journal of Personality and
    Social Psychology*, *51*(6), 1173–1182.
Blocher, E., Stout, D., Juras, P., & Cokins, G. (2012). *Cost management: A strategic emphasis* (6th ed.).
    New York, NY: McGraw-Hill/Irwin.
Bloomfield, R. J., & Luft, J. L. (2006). Responsibility for cost management hinders learning to avoid the
    winner's curse. *The Accounting Review*, *81*(1), 29–47.
Cardinaels, E., & Labro, E. (2008). On the determinants of measurement error in time-driven costing.
    The Accounting Review, *83*(3), 735–756.
Cloyd, C. B., & Spilker, B. C. (1999). The influence of client preferences on tax professionals' search
    for judicial precedents, subsequent judgments and recommendations. *The Accounting Review*,
    74(3), 299–322.
Cooper, R. (1989). You need a new cost system when... *Harvard Business Review*, *67*(1), 77–82.
Cooper, R., & Kaplan, R. S. (1992). Activity-based systems: Measuring the costs of resource usage.
    Accounting Horizons, *6*(3), 1–13.
Datar, S., & Gupta, M. (1994). Aggregation, specification and measurement errors in product costing.
    The Accounting Review, *69*(4), 567–591.
Dawson, E., Savitsky, K., & Dunning, D. (2006). "Don't tell me, I don't want to know": Understanding
    people's reluctance to obtain medical diagnostic information. *Journal of Applied Social
    Psychology*, *36*(3), 751–768.
Dearman, D.T. & Shields, M. D. (2001). Cost knowledge and cost-based judgment performance.
    Journal of Management Accounting Research, *13*(1), 1–18.
Ditto, P. H., & Lopez, D. F. (1992). Motivated skepticism: Use of differential decision criteria for
    preferred and nonpreferred conclusions. *Journal of Personality and Social Psychology*, *63*(4),
    568–584.
Ditto, P. H., Scepansky, J. A., Munro, G. D., Apanovitch, A. M., & Lockhart, L. K. (1998). Motivated
    sensitivity to preference-inconsistent information. *Journal of Personality and Social Psychology*,
    75(1), 53–69.
Fleisig, D. (2011). Adding information may increase overconfidence in accuracy of knowledge retrieval.
    Psychological Reports, *108*(2), 379–392.
Geiger, D. R., & Ittner, C. D. (1996). The influence of funding source and legislative requirements on
    government cost accounting practices. *Accounting, Organizations and Society*, *21*(6), 549–567.
Hall, C. C., Ariss, L., & Todorov, A. (2007). The illusion of knowledge: When more information
    reduces accuracy and increases confidence. *Organizational Behavior and Human Decision
    Processes*, *103*(2), 277–290.
Hansen, S. C. (1998). Cost analysis, cost reduction and competition. *Journal of Management Accounting
    Research*, *10*, 181–203.
Heitger, D. L. (2007). Estimating activity costs: How the provision of accurate historical activity
    data from a biased cost system can improve individuals' cost estimation accuracy. *Behavioral
    Research in Accounting*, *19*(1), 133–159.
Horngren, C. T., Datar, S. M., & Rajan, M. V. (2014). *Cost accounting: A managerial emphasis* (15th
    ed.). Upper Saddle River, NJ: Pearson Prentice Hall.
Jermias, J. (2001). Cognitive dissonance and resistance to change: The influence of commitment confir-
    mation and feedback on judgment usefulness of accounting systems. *Accounting, Organizations
    and Society*, *26*(2), 141–160.
Jermias, J. (2006). The influence of accountability on overconfidence and resistance to change: A
    research framework and experimental evidence. *Management Accounting Research*, *17*(4),
    370–388.
Kadous, K., Kennedy, S. J., & Peecher, M. E. (2003). The effect of quality assessment and direc-
    tional goal commitment on auditors' acceptance of client-preferred accounting methods. *The
    Accounting Review*, *78*(3), 759–778.
Kaplan, R. S., & Anderson, S. R. (2004). Time-driven activity-based costing. *Harvard Business Review*,
    82(11), 131–138.
Kelly, K. (2010). The effects of incentives on information exchange and decision quality in groups.
    Behavioral Research in Accounting, *22*(1), 43–65.

Khandwalla, P. N. (1972). The effect of different types of competition on the use of management controls. *Journal of Accounting Research, 10*(2), 275–285.

Krishnan, R., Luft, J. L., & Shields, M. D. (2002). Competition and cost accounting: Adapting to changing markets. *Contemporary Accounting Research, 19*(2), 271–302.

Kunda, Z. (1990). The case for motivated reasoning. *Psychological Bulletin, 108*(3), 480–498.

Labro, E. (2019). Costing systems. *Foundations and Trends in Accounting, 13*(3–4), 267–404.

Labro, E., & Vanhoucke, M. (2007). A simulation analysis of interactions among errors in costing systems. *The Accounting Review, 82*(4), 939–962.

Libby, R., Bloomfield, R., & Nelson, M. W. (2002). Experimental research in financial accounting. *Accounting, Organizations and Society, 27*(8), 775–810.

Libby, T., & Waterhouse, J. H. (1996). Predicting change in management accounting systems. *Journal of Management Accounting Research, 8*, 137–150.

Lord, C. G., Ross, L., & Lepper, M. R. (1979). Biased assimilation and attitude polarization: The effects of prior theories on subsequently considered evidence. *Journal of Personality and Social Psychology, 37*(11), 2098–2109.

Lundgren, S. R., & Prislin, R. (1998). Motivated cognitive processing and attitude change. *Personality and Social Psychology Bulletin, 24*(7), 715–726.

Mael, F., & Ashforth, B. E. (1992). Alumni and their alma mater: A partial test of the reformulated model of organizational identification. *Journal of Organizational Behavior, 13*(2), 103–123.

Player, S., & Lacerda, R. (1999). *Arthur Andersen's global lessons in activity-based management* (2nd ed.). New York, NY: Wiley.

Preacher, K. J., & Hayes, A. F. (2004). SPSS and SAS procedures for estimating indirect effects in simple mediation models. *Behavior Research Methods, Instruments, & Computers, 36*(4), 717–731.

Preacher, K. J., & Hayes, A. F. (2008). Asymptotic and resampling strategies for assessing and comparing indirect effects in multiple mediator models. *Behavior Research Methods, 40*(3), 879–891.

Smith, S. D. (2010). Confidence and trading aggressiveness of naïve investors: Effects of information quantity and consistency. *Review of Accounting Studies, 15*, 295–316.

Tayler, W. B. (2010). The balanced scorecard as a strategy-evaluation tool: The effects of implementation involvement and a causal-chain focus. *The Accounting Review, 85*(3), 1095–1117.

Thomas, T. F. (2016). Motivating revisions of management accounting systems: An examination of organizational goals and accounting feedback. *Accounting, Organizations and Society, 53*, 1–16.

Wallace, S. (2013). *The non-linear relation between price competition and cost allocation refinement.* Working Paper. James Cook University.

Zacharakis, A. L., & Shepherd, D. A. (2001). The nature of information and overconfidence on venture capitalists' decision making. *Journal of Business Venturing, 16*(4), 311–332.

APPENDIX 1

EXPERIMENTAL MATERIALS

Background & Industry Information

You are a plant manager at [Your firm], Inc. ([Your firm]), an industrial firm based in the Midwest. As a plant manager you are responsible for the production process, including personnel, inventory, equipment, and production output.

The industry in which [Your firm] operates produces components used in production of consumer products by its customers. Competing trends have led to aggregate demand volatility over the last five years, but the market has shown resilience. Manufacturers like [Your firm] have faced the challenge of declining prices of industry products, which have prevented the industry from reaching higher revenue growth over the preceding five-year period.

The industry has turned the page on the recession and its lingering impact, although evidence of robust industry revenue growth has yet to materialize. Demand for products has declined in the past five years due to falling purchases of ultimate products among individuals, retailers, and corporate clients. The industry has also contended with rising competition from alternatives offered by companies from related industries. On the upside, industry demand is growing as certain segments of its customers' business expand.

APPENDIX 2

ADDITIONAL INFORMATION AVAILABLE TO PARTICIPANTS

Question	Answer	Cooper's (1989) Signal (Column Not Shown)
	Cost System (Title Not Shown)	
GROSS MARGIN: How does [*your firm's*] reported gross margin of Red compare to [*your firm's*] reported gross margin of White?	[*Your firm's*] reported gross margin for Red is 24% and the reported gross margin for White is 15%.	Products that are difficult to produce are reported to be very profitable even though they are not premium priced.
COST SYSTEM CHANGES: How has [*your firm's*] current cost allocation system changed over the past five years?	The overhead allocation rate is updated every year but no other changes have been made to [*your firm's*] cost allocation system in the last five years.	
OVERHEAD COST CHANGE: How has [*your firm's*] total manufacturing overhead cost changed over the past five years?	[*Your firm's*] total manufacturing overhead costs have steadily increased over the past five years.	Eliminates a general increase in costs as a plausible explanation of declining profitability.
PRODUCTION LEVELS: How do [*your firm's*] production levels of orders compare to the maximum levels the factory can normally produce?	[*Your firm*] can make more of each product, but there are not enough orders to justify production, so the plant is operating below capacity.	Indicates that the factory has idle capacity.

Question	Answer	Cooper's Signal (Column Not Shown)
	Market Competition (Title Not Shown)	
WHITE'S PRICE: How does [*your firm's*] price of White compare to the price charged by [*your firm's*] competitor / competitors?	Your competitor / competitors charge(s) less for White than [*your firm*] does.	1. Products that are difficult to produce are reported to be very profitable, even though they are not premium priced. 2. Profit margins cannot be easily explained. 3. The competition's high-volume products are priced at apparently unrealistically low levels.
RED'S PRICE: How does [*your firm's*] price of Red compare to the price charged by [*your firm's*] competitor / competitors?	Your competitor / competitors charge(s) more for Red than [*your firm*] does.	1. Products that are difficult to produce are reported to be very profitable, even though they are not premium priced. 2. Profit margins cannot be easily explained.
PRODUCT QUALITY: How does [*your firm's*] product quality compare to the product quality of [*your firm's*] competitor / competitors?	Your competitor's / competitors' product quality is similar to [*your firm's*] product quality.	Eliminates a difference in the quality of products as a plausible explanation of declining profitability.
PRODUCT MIX: How does [*your firm's*] product mix compare to that of [*your firm's*] competitor / competitors that make both White and Red?	Your competitor / competitors sell(s) proportionately more Whites than Reds, compared to [*your firm*].	

Participants select an individual question to retrieve the answer.

APPENDIX 3

MAIN DEPENDENT MEASURE SCREEN

You have had the opportunity to review the available information and now top management would like to know what you believe is responsible for Wisconsin's declining profitability.

Please allocate 100 points between the following possible causes of declining profitability to indicate your belief as to the potential cause(s) of this issue. Your answer must add up to 100 points and your bonus depends on your allocation.

Industry decline	0
Market competition	0
Cost system	0
Other (please explain below)	0
Total	0

Other - Explanation

APPENDIX 4

CONFIDENCE QUESTIONNAIRE

1. How satisfied are you with the product cost information provided by [*your firm's*] cost system?
2. How concerned are you about the accuracy of information being provided by the cost system? [reverse coded]
3. How likely is it that [*your firm's*] profit will decrease further if the cost system is not changed? [reverse coded]
4. Do you think the existing cost system will provide accurate product cost information in the future?
5. How likely are you to recommend [*your firm's*] cost system to similar companies?
6. [*Your firm's*] cost system helps [*your firm*] compete by providing managers with accurate product cost information.
7. [*Your firm's*] cost system helps management make good product-related decisions, such as product pricing and product discontinuation.

Questions are on seven-point Likert scales.
Questions 1–3 are adapted from Jermias (2006).

APPENDIX 5

IDENTIFICATION QUESTIONNAIRE

1. When someone criticizes the firm, it feels like a personal insult.
2. I am very interested in what others think about the firm.
3. If I were to talk about the firm, I would normally say "we" rather than "they."
4. The firm's successes are my successes.
5. When someone praises the firm, it feels like a personal compliment.
6. If a story in the media criticized the firm, I would feel embarrassed.

Participants are asked to consider their firm from the exercise when responding with their agreement to the listed statements on five-point Likert scales. The statements are adapted from Mael and Ashforth (1992).

THE ASSOCIATION BETWEEN THE USE OF STRATEGIC MANAGEMENT ACCOUNTING PRACTICES AND COMPETITIVE ADVANTAGE: THE MODERATING ROLE OF ORGANISATIONAL CULTURE

Sophia Su, Kevin Baird and
Nuraddeen Abubakar Nuhu

ABSTRACT

This study examines the association between the use of strategic management accounting (SMA) practices and competitive advantage and the moderating role of four aspects of organisational culture – teamwork orientation, outcome orientation, innovation orientation and attention to detail orientation – on this association. Online survey data were collected from 408 accountants in Australian business organisations, and structural equation modelling (SEM) was used to analyse the data. The results indicate a positive association between the use of SMA practices and competitive advantage with such an association positively moderated by one cultural dimension, teamwork orientation. Specifically, the findings indicate that the positive effect of SMA practices on competitive advantage is dependent upon the fit between the use of SMA practices and teamwork orientation with more (less) teamwork-oriented

Advances in Management Accounting, Volume 35, 129–157
ISSN: 1474-7871/doi:10.1108/S1474-787120230000035006

organisations exhibiting a stronger (weaker) association between the use of SMA practices and competitive advantage.

Keywords: Organisational culture; strategic management accounting practices; competitive advantage; teamwork orientation, innovation orientation; survey

INTRODUCTION

It has been four decades since Simmonds (1981, p. 26) introduced the concept of SMA, referring to it as 'the provision and analysis of management accounting data about a business and its competitors for use in developing and monitoring the business strategy'. SMA practices emphasise a long-term orientation and external focus (Cadez & Guilding, 2012) and include many different practices such as Activity-based Costing/Management (ABC/M), the Balanced Scorecard (BSC), Target Costing (TC), and Value Chain Analysis (VCA). In a literature review of SMA research from 1981 to 2007, Langfield-Smith (2008, p. 221) concluded that the concept of SMA was not well understood by either researchers or practitioners and noted that 'the normative papers extolling the benefits of SMA and early conceptual developments have not led to widespread adoption of SMA'.

A review of the SMA literature by Rashid, Ali, and Hossain (2020) found 150 SMA-related articles published in the top 23 accounting journals during the period from 2008 to 2019. The review covered a wide range of topics including the paradox of SMA, factors affecting the adoption of SMA practices and the influence of the adoption of SMA practices on organisational performance. A large number of these studies focussed on examining the contingency factors (e.g. business strategy, market orientation, institutional pressures, top management team characteristics, management accountants' involvement, organisational culture and national culture)[1] that affect the adoption of SMA practices (e.g. Baird, Hu, & Reeve, 2011; Baird, Su, & Tung, 2018; Cescon, Costantini, & Grassetti, 2019; Hadid & Al-Sayed, 2021; Turner, Way, Hodari, & Witteman, 2017).

Previous studies have also examined the association between the use of SMA practices and organisational performance (e.g. Aksoylu & Aykan, 2013; Alabdullah, 2019; Cadez & Guilding, 2008; Kalkhouran, Nedaei, & Rasid, 2017; Turner et al., 2017).[2] However, Alamri (2019) argues that the relationship between these two factors is ambiguous and needs to be examined further to consider the impact of organisational contextual factors on such an association. In particular, it is suggested that 'an appropriate SMA fit within an organizational context is a determinant of company performance' (Alamri, 2019, p. 229). However, this stream of research is sparse. Notable exceptions include Cadez and Guilding (2012) who employed a configurational approach to examine the relationships between different configurations of strategy and SMA with performance, and Alamri (2019) who investigated the effect of the fit between the use of SMA practices and four organisational context variables (i.e. structure, resources, information and climate proxied by top management's support, attitudes and credibility) on both financial and non-financial performance.

This study aims to extend this stream of literature by examining the effect of the fit between the use of SMA practices and the organisational culture on competitive advantage. Specifically, we examine the fit between the use of SMA practices, operationalised as a package of 12 SMA practices,[3] with four of O'Reilly, Chatman, and Caldwell (1991) Organisational Culture Profile dimensions: teamwork orientation, outcome orientation, innovation orientation, and attention to detail orientation. We focus on organisational culture as a contextual factor which can influence the effect of SMA practices on competitive advantage for several reasons. First, it is generally agreed that business practices that are compatible with the culture of an organisation are more likely to be successful (Schneider, Brief, & Guzzo, 1996; Swain & Bell, 1999). Second, Alamri (2019) argues that an organisational culture which fits the SMA practice(s) in use is an essential requirement to achieve the effectiveness of the practice(s). This is also consistent with Smith (1998) who made references to matching management practices with cultural settings. Third, given organisational culture cannot change easily (Denison, 1990; Hofstede, Neuijen, Ohayv, & Sanders, 1990), the findings will alert organisations and their managers of the suitability of SMA practices based on their organisational culture and/or direct organisations as to how to gradually adjust their culture to facilitate the success of SMA practices (Baird, Harrison, & Reeve, 2007).

Competitive advantage, defined as 'the advantages that a business may have over another that are difficult to imitate' (Langfield-Smith, Smith, Andon, Hilton, & Thorne, 2018, p. 15), is chosen as the study's outcome variable due to the well discussed theoretical link between the use of SMA practices and competitive advantage. For instance, Roslender and Hart (2002, p. 255) suggest that SMA is 'a powerful approach to account for competitive advantage' while Akenbor and Okoye (2012) argue that SMA practices are introduced to provide more relevant and reliable information to achieve sustainable competitive advantage. Similarly, Oyewo and Ajibolade (2019) posit that the nature of SMA practices, specifically their focus on the long-term and future-orientation, can facilitate organisations to continually improve and maintain an above-industry-average level of performance, thereby leading to competitive advantage. However, 'empirical evidence on the outcomes of SMA usage in relation to creating and sustaining competitive advantage is still lacking' (Oyewo & Ajibolade, 2019, p. 64). Therefore, this study aims to provide empirical evidence of the moderating effect of organisational culture (i.e. teamwork orientation, outcome orientation, innovation orientation and attention to detail orientation) on the association between the use of SMA practices and competitive advantage, with the overall model provided in Fig. 1.

Based on a sample of 408 accountants from Australian business organisations, the SEM analysis reveals that a direct, positive association exists between the use of SMA practices and competitive advantage. Furthermore, we find that the association between the use of SMA practices and competitive advantage is positively moderated by the teamwork orientation dimension of organisational culture.

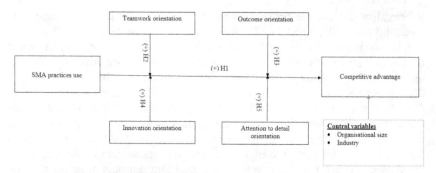

Fig. 1. Conceptual Framework of the Study.

However, contrary to expectations, the other three dimensions of organisational culture (i.e. outcome orientation, innovation orientation and attention to detail orientation) did not significantly moderate the relationship.

The remainder of the chapter is divided into four sections. The next section provides the literature review and develops the hypotheses and is followed by the method section which discusses the research method and data collection process. This is followed by the results section and finally, the discussion and conclusion section.

LITERATURE REVIEW AND HYPOTHESES DEVELOPMENT

SMA Practices

Similar to Simmonds (1981), Bromwich (1990, p. 28) refers to SMA as

> the provision and analysis of financial information on the firm's product markets and competitors' costs and cost structures and the monitoring of the enterprise's strategies and those of its competitors in these markets.

Dixon and Smith (1993, p. 605) define SMA as

> the provision and analysis of information relating to a firm's internal activities, those of its competitors and current and future market trends, in order to assist in the strategy evaluation process.

Following the emergence of SMA practices, a concern was raised as to how to differentiate SMA practices from traditional management accounting practices. Rashid et al. (2020) proposed that SMA practices must: (1) focus on the organisational external environment; (2) focus on both financial and non-financial information; and (3) be long-term and forward-looking oriented. Such criteria are in line with Simmonds (1981) definition of SMA and have been adopted in the present study.

Two main streams of research in the SMA literature consist of studies that examine the factors affecting the use of SMA practices and studies that examine the effect of SMA practices on organisational outcomes. With respect to the first stream, there have been a large number of studies that have examined the contingency factors that affect the adoption of specific SMA practices including business strategy (Cescon et al., 2019; Naranjo-Gil, Maas, & Hartmann, 2009; Turner et al., 2017), market orientation (Cescon et al., 2019; Naranjo-Gil et al., 2009; Turner et al., 2017), institutional pressures (Brandau, Endenich, Trapp, & Hoffjan, 2013; Ma & Tayles, 2009), top management team characteristics (Kalkhouran et al., 2017; Pavlatos & Kostakis, 2018), management accountant involvement (Hadid & Al-Sayed, 2021; Yazdifar, Askarany, Wickramasinghe, Nasseri, & Alam, 2019;), organisational culture (Baird, Harrison, & Reeve, 2004; Baird et al., 2011, 2018) and national culture (Pun, 2001).

The second stream of research consists of studies that have examined the effect of SMA practices on organisational performance. For instance, Cadez and Guilding (2008) identified a positive association between the use of SMA practices and overall organisational performance. Similarly, Aksoylu and Aykan (2013) and Kalkhouran et al. (2017) found that the use of SMA practices exhibited a positive effect on organisational performance. Furthermore, Turner et al. (2017) and Alabdulah (2019) reported a positive association between the use of SMA practices and organisational financial performance.

While a direct association between the use of SMA and organisational performance has been identified in these studies, in line with contingency theory it has been argued that organisational performance is dependent on a fit between the use of SMA practices and organisational contextual factors (Alamri, 2019). For example, Alamri (2019) examined and found that the fit between SMA and four specific contextual factors, including structure, resources, information and climate, can enhance both financial and nonfinancial performance. This study aims to extend this stream of research by providing insight into how the fit between the use of SMA practices and four of O'Reilly et al. (1991) organisational culture dimensions (teamwork orientation, outcome orientation; innovation orientation and attention to detail orientation) affect an organisations competitive advantage. The following section will first develop a hypothesis in relation to the direct association between the use of SMA practices and competitive advantage. This is then followed by the discussion of and the development of hypotheses in regard to the effect of the interaction between the use of SMA practices with each cultural dimension on competitive advantage.

The Association Between the Use of SMA Practices and Competitive Advantage

Based on the Resource-Based View (RBV) theory which argues that 'valuable, costly-to-copy firm resources and capabilities provide the key sources of sustainable competitive advantage' (Hart, 1995, p. 986), we argue that the use of SMA practices, as part of organisational resources and/or capabilities, can enhance competitive advantage. Specifically, the use of SMA practices can assist organisations in developing competitive advantage through identifying, recording and analysing information quickly and accurately (Turner et al., 2017). Similarly, Oboh and Ajibolade (2017) argue that SMA practices facilitate the gathering of information on customers, competitors and the market, which can subsequently contribute to the development of competitive advantage. Furthermore, Aziz (2012) posits that SMA practices operate as unique techniques owned by organisations and can assist organisations in making strategic business decisions that will lead to better competitive advantage over their competitors. Finally, Oyewo and Ajibolade (2019, p. 70) state that the use of SMA practices should 'enable organisations [to] sustain competitive advantage by consistently improving and maintaining an above-industry-average performance not only in the short-run but also in the medium- to long-term'. This strong theoretical link between the use of SMA practices and competitive advantage is supported by Oyewo and Ajibolade (2019) who reported a significant positive association between the use of SMA practices and competitive advantage.

Accordingly, it is hypothesised that:

H1. There will be a positive association between the use of SMA practices and competitive advantage.

The Moderating Effect of Organisational Culture on the Association between the Use of SMA Practices and Competitive Advantage

Organisational culture, which refers to shared values, beliefs and social norms of the collective organisation (Merchant, 1985; Schein, 1990), has drawn increasing attention in the management accounting literature (Akroyd & Kober, 2020; Ax & Greve, 2017; Baird et al., 2004, 2007; Bhimani, 2003; Hadid & Al-Sayed, 2021; Henri, 2006). In particular, a number of empirical studies have provided evidence of the important role of organisational culture in supporting the use/success of management accounting practices. For example, Baird et al. (2004) found a positive association between outcome-oriented culture with the use of ABC. Furthermore, Hadid and Al-Sayed (2021, p. 1) reported a significant positive direct effect between an outcome-oriented culture with the implementation of SMA practices while an innovative culture exhibited 'a significant indirect positive effect on SMA implementation through management accountant networking.' In addition, Henri (2006) found that the extent of a flexible culture was associated with the use of performance measurement systems (PMS) for attention focussing, strategic decision making and legitimisation of actions.

Bhimani (2003) reveals that the alignment between organisational culture and process-based TC enhances the success of this management accounting practice, while Ax and Greve (2017) refer to the importance of compatibility with an existing organisational culture in order to successfully introduce management innovations. Further highlighting the importance of organisational culture, Akroyd and Kober (2020) found that management introduced management controls that were designed to fit their organisational culture, while other authors point to the importance of the organisational culture in supporting the success of management initiatives (Baird et al., 2007; Chia & Koh, 2007). For instance, Chia and Koh (2007, p. 193) state that the success of innovations (such as SMA practices) can be attributed to 'when the level of adoption of an innovation is supported by [a] compatible organisational culture'.

Therefore, in line with this literature which highlights the importance of organisational culture in supporting the use and success of management accounting practices, it is expected that the success of the use of SMA practices, in respect to its effect on competitive advantage, will be influenced (i.e. moderated) by the organisational culture in place. In particular, given that the organisational culture is difficult to change (Denison, 1990; Hofstede et al., 1990), the organisational culture will be either conducive (or not conducive) to the use of SMA practices, thereby enhancing (inhibiting) the effect of the use of SMA practices on competitive advantage. We consider this potential moderating effect through examining the moderating effect of four organisational cultural dimensions (teamwork orientation, outcome orientation, innovation orientation and attention to detail orientation) on the association between the use of SMA practices with a competitive advantage. The nature of these associations is discussed in the following sections.

Teamwork Orientation – An organisational culture which emphasises teamwork orientation focusses on the formation of teams for the purpose of enabling collaboration with others to achieve overall organisational goals (Baird et al., 2018; Windsor & Ashkanasy, 1996). For example, previous studies have documented the importance of a teamwork-oriented culture in enhancing the success of ABM through facilitating cooperation and information sharing amongst employees (Drake, Haka, & Ravenscroft, 2001; Gering, 1999). Similarly, Joyce (1999, p. 54) suggests that 'the key to implementing ABC is to have a cross functional team that included representatives from IT, finance, and the people who own the processes'. We expect this effect to extend to all SMA practices with Langfield-Smith et al. (2018) positing that cooperation amongst employees, an essential trait of teams, is essential for the successful implementation of any organisational system/practice.

Organisations with a higher (lower) teamwork orientation will have greater (less) 'opportunities for synergistic knowledge and information sharing' (Mannix & Neale, 2005, p. 32), thereby enhancing (inhibiting) the ability of SMA practices to facilitate competitive advantage through the provision of information which assists strategic decision-making. Similarly, higher (lower) teamwork orientation will enhance (inhibit) the success of SMA practices due to the more (less) extensive communication of 'potentially complex information in ways that can be easily understood by others on the team' (Janardhanan, Lewis, Reger, & Stevens, 2020, p. 105) and the more (less) frequent distribution of vital information, thereby enhancing (inhibiting) the likelihood that SMA practices are understood and employed effectively (Stephens, Heaphy, Carmeli, Spreitzer, & Dutton, 2013). Furthermore, consistent with the principles of employee empowerment, organisations with a more (less) teamwork-oriented culture are more (less) likely to have empowered responsibility and decision-making authority to lower-level employees, thereby resulting in a greater (lower) sense of appreciation and commitment to successfully implementing SMA practices (Cadez & Guilding, 2012).

Accordingly, in line with Abernethy and Bouwens (2005) who found that the decentralisation of decision-making led to greater success of accounting innovations, it is expected that organisations with a higher (lower) teamwork orientation will introduce SMA practices more (less) effectively due to espousing a stronger (weaker) employee commitment to the success of such practices. Finally, as teams facilitate more interactions, thereby enhancing the cohesion amongst employees by facilitating a shared belief (Mach, Dolan, & Tzafrir, 2010), more (less) teamwork-oriented organisations are more (less) likely to cope with the stress associated with changes (Meneghel, Salanova, & Martínez, 2016), and hence, will be more (less) likely to introduce SMA practices in a way which enhances competitive advantage.

Therefore, a teamwork-oriented culture is expected to facilitate the success of SMA practices through facilitating the exchange of information, empowering employees and minimising employees' resistance to change. Accordingly, we hypothesise that teamwork orientation will positively moderate the association between the use of SMA practices and competitive advantage.

H2. **Teamwork orientation will positively moderate the association between the use of SMA practices and competitive advantage; specifically, the higher (lower) the teamwork orientation, the more (less) effective the use of SMA practices is in influencing competitive advantage.**

Outcome Orientation – Outcome orientation focusses on achieving desired results and having high expectations for performance (O'Reilly et al., 1991). Organisations with a more outcome-oriented culture will be more committed and determined to ensure that adopted business practices are successful, both due to a sense of satisfaction in successfully implementing such practices, and due to their effect on the achievement of desired outcomes and results. Hence, as more outcome-oriented organisations endeavour to be successful in all aspects, including the introduction of new processes, practices and initiatives, they will strive to achieve success in respect to the implementation of SMA practices. Furthermore, given the implementation of SMA practices requires an investment of extensive resources (Langfield-Smith et al., 2018), it is expected that more (less) outcome-oriented organisations will be more (less) likely to have the right mechanisms in place (e.g. employee training, top management support, a detailed change management plan, etc.) to ensure the success of SMA practices. Accordingly, organisations with a higher (lower) outcome orientation will be more (less) likely to introduce SMA practices successfully and in a way which facilitates competitive advantage. In particular, more (less) outcome-oriented organisations will be more (less) focussed on using the information provided to facilitate strategic decision making, thereby enabling them to gain (inhibiting them from gaining) a competitive advantage over their rivals.

Furthermore, given that outcome-oriented organisations focus on the achievement of desired results and leave the processes used to achieve such results to employees themselves (Snell, 1992), Adler and Chen (2011) argue that such a culture enables employees to have a greater level of autonomy and sense of ownership of SMA practices. Accordingly, employees working in a more (less) outcome-oriented culture are less (more) likely to resist SMA practices and more (less) likely to consider SMA practices as their own rather than being imposed by top management. Consequently, employees in more (less) outcome-oriented organisations are more (less) likely to exert greater (less) dedication and commitment to the success of such practices and hence, the use of SMA practices is more (less) likely to influence competitive advantage.

Therefore, an outcome-oriented culture is expected to facilitate the success of SMA practices through fostering the will to succeed and providing employees with the autonomy to drive the success of such practices. Accordingly, we hypothesise that outcome orientation will positively moderate the association between the use of SMA practices and competitive advantage.

H3. Outcome orientation will positively moderate the association between the use of SMA practices and competitive advantage; specifically, the higher (lower) the outcome orientation, the more (less) effective the use of SMA practices is in influencing competitive advantage.

Innovation Orientation – Innovation orientation refers to 'an organisation's receptivity and adaptability to change, and its willingness to experiment' (O'Reilly et al., 1991, p. 505). While a major hurdle in introducing SMA practices is employee resistance to change (Akenbor & Okoye, 2012), Baird et al. (2007) suggest that employees in organisations with more innovative cultures are more willing to accept new techniques, thereby leading to the enhanced success of such techniques. Hence, organisations with a higher (lower) innovation orientation will be more (less) likely to experiment and take the risks required in order for SMA practices to be a success. For example, Pablo, Sitkin, and Jemison (1996) suggest that risk takers (i.e. more innovative individuals) will be more likely to cope with uncertainty and setbacks (i.e. initial failure) and continue to strive towards achieving SMA success, i.e. competitive advantage. In particular, organisations with more (less) innovation-oriented cultures will be more (less) likely to experiment with the use of the information provided by SMA practices to make strategic decisions and develop new strategies in a way which enables the organisation to achieve a competitive advantage over their rivals.

In addition, as innovation and the use of SMA practices are both inherently associated with coping with environmental uncertainties (Hamel & Valikangas, 2003), SMA practices are more likely to be successful in an innovation-oriented culture. In particular, through encouraging experimentation, risk taking and flexible approaches, organisations with more (less) innovation-oriented cultures will be more (less) likely to embrace the use of SMA practices and utilise the information provided in a way which contributes to the development of competitive advantage.

Therefore, an innovation-oriented culture is expected to facilitate the success of SMA practices through encouraging employees to employ and embrace the use of such practices. Accordingly, we hypothesise that innovation orientation will positively moderate the association between the use of SMA practices and competitive advantage.

H4. Innovation orientation will positively moderate the association between the use of SMA practices and competitive advantage; specifically, the higher (lower) the innovation orientation, the more (less) effective the use of SMA practices is in influencing competitive advantage.

Attention to Detail Orientation – The cultural dimension attention to detail orientation involves being precise, careful, rule-oriented and complying with rules and procedures (O'Reilly et al., 1991). Organisations with a higher (lower) attention to detail orientation will be more (less) likely to successfully implement SMA practices, given such practices are more complex than traditional management accounting practices and require more detailed recording and analysis of both financial and non-financial information (Langfield-Smith et al., 2018). Specifically, as the influence of the use of SMA practices on competitive advantage is likely to be dependent upon the accuracy and depth of the information used to facilitate strategic decision making, a higher (lower) attention to detail orientation will enhance (inhibit) the ability of SMA practices to facilitate competitive advantage through the provision of information which assists strategic decision-making, i.e. information which emphasises detail, rules, and accuracy.

In addition, it is expected that organisations which focus on providing employees with specific rules and procedures (i.e. attention to detail) are more likely to construct a comprehensive change management plan during the implementation of SMA practices, thereby overcoming employees' resistance to change and making it more likely that their SMA practices are successfully implemented. Finally, organisations with higher (lower) attention to detail orientation are more (less) likely to value and use the information produced by the various SMA practices for strategic decision-making purposes as such information is up-to-date, future-oriented and includes both financial and non-financial data. Therefore, organisations with a higher (lower) attention to detail orientation are more (less) likely to use SMA practices to facilitate decision-making in a way which effectively develops their strategy, and hence, attains competitive advantage.

Therefore, the attention to detail orientation culture is expected to facilitate the success of SMA practices through emphasising a working environment that is compatible with the use of SMA practices, encouraging change management and appreciating the value and usefulness of the information produced. Accordingly, we hypothesise that attention to detail orientation will positively moderate the association between the use of SMA practices and competitive advantage.

H5. **Attention to detail orientation will positively moderate the association between the use of SMA practices and competitive advantage; specifically, the higher (lower) the attention to detail orientation, the more (less) effective the use of SMA practices is in influencing competitive advantage.**

METHOD

A reputable Australian-based company, Online Research Unit (ORU), was appointed to recruit potential participants and collect data for the study.[4] An online survey questionnaire was sent out to accountants in Australian business organisations. Accountants[5] were chosen as they play an important role in the adoption and operation of SMA practices (Langfield-Smith, 2008; Shank, 2007) and hence, were considered to be appropriate to assess the adoption and success of their organisation's SMA practices. Furthermore, given that large organisations are more likely to have SMA practices in place and to ensure that potential participants have a good understanding of their organisation's culture and SMA practices, only those accountants who worked in organisations with more than 50 employees and had worked for their organisation for more than two years were deemed eligible to participate in the survey.

Accordingly, an online survey questionnaire was sent out to 2,836 accountants in Australian business organisations who met the above criteria, with two reminders sent to those who had not completed the questionnaire. A total of 414 complete survey questionnaires were received, achieving a response rate of 14.6%. To enhance the quality of the data collected, speeder and attention checks were implemented to identify respondents who finished the questionnaire too fast[6] or who provided low-effort responses.[7] As a result, six respondents were removed from the study, leaving 408 usable questionnaires. However, non-response bias tests were unable to be performed due to the anonymity of the survey links sent to respondents, which made it impossible to detect the duration between when the initial requests were made to complete the survey and the time when the survey was completed.

Table 1 reveals the demographic information of the final 408 participants. The majority of the participants (75%) held an undergraduate degree or above and 62.5% of the participants were aged between 31 and 50. The participants worked in a wide range of industries with the most prominent being the Financial and Insurance Services (30.1%) sector and Other Business Services sector (20.1%) (see Table 1 for more details).

Common Method Bias

A number of strategies were implemented to reduce the problem of common method bias. First, based on Jordan and Troth (2020) recommendation, an information coversheet was provided to respondents outlining the purpose of the study. Clear instructions were also provided for each section of the questionnaire to ensure that respondents understood how to answer each question. Secondly, the questions were presented in a random order so that respondents could not easily identify the independent and dependent variables of the study. Thirdly, while ORU rewards participants for completing the questionnaires with gift cards, the cards were mailed to Australian residential addresses for the purpose of identifying panel duplication and minimising panellist fraud, thereby enhancing the quality of the data collected. Finally, as mentioned, attention and speeder checks were put in place to improve the accuracy of the data collected.

The success of these strategies was supported by the results of two technical analyses. First, Harman's (1967) test was conducted with the results showing that the highest total variance explained by a single factor was 39.90%. This was below the 50% threshold, thereby indicating that common method bias is a not an issue (Podsakoff, MacKenzie, Lee, & Podsakoff, 2003). Second, the Common Latent Factor (CLF) test indicated that the difference in the standardised weights between the model with the CLF and the model without the CLF was less than 0.20 across all of the measurement items of each variable (Eichhorn, 2014), thereby indicating that common method bias is unlikely to be a concern.

Table 1.   Profile of Respondents.

Age ($N = 408$)	No. of Responses (Percentage)
21–30 (81)	48 (11.8%)
31–40 (192)	153 (37.5%)
41–50 (125)	102 (25%)
51–60 (76)	63 (15.4%)
60 or over (41)	42 (10.3%)
Education level ($N = 408$)	
School certificate	6 (1.5%)
Higher certificate or equivalent	35 (8.6%)
Diploma or equivalent	61 (15 %)
Undergraduate degree	181 (44.4%)
Postgraduate degree	125 (30.6%)
Organisational size[a] ($N = 408$)	
Between 50 and 99	61 (15%)
Between 100 and 199	122 (29.9%)
Between 200 and 299	56 (13.7%)
More than 300	169 (41.4%)
Industry ($N = 408$)	
1. Extractive sector (e.g. agriculture, forestry, fishing, mining)	18 (4.4%)
2. Manufacturing (including construction)	46 (11.3%)
3. Utilities sector (e.g. electricity, gas, water, waste services)	20 (4.9%)
4. Financial and Insurance Services	123 (30.1%)
5. Other Business Services (e.g. Rental; Hiring & Real Estate Services; Professional, Scientific & Technical Services; Administrative & Support Services)	82 (20.1%)
6. Distribution Services (e.g. Wholesale Trade; Retail Trade; Transport, Postal & Warehousing; Information, Media & Telecommunications)	45 (11%)
7. Social Services (e.g. Public Administration & Safety; Health Care & Social Assistance)	55 (13.5%)
8. Personal Services (e.g. Arts & Recreation Services; Accommodation & Food Services)	19 (4.7%)

[a]Only organisations with more than 50 employees were included in the study as mentioned in the method section.

Variable Measurement

All of the constructs were assessed using established scales adapted from previous studies. The psychometric properties of the measures were first assessed in SPSS, using exploratory factor analysis (EFA) to assess their unidimensionality, prior to conducting confirmatory factor analysis (CFA). The goodness-of-fit indices[8] (CMIN/DF = 1.52; GFI = 0.90; AGFI = 0.88; RMSEA = 0.04) indicated that the measurement model fitted the data well.

The Extent of Use of SMA Practices

The extent of use of SMA practices was assessed based on the extent of use of 12 different SMA practices including strategic costing (SC), life cycle costing (LCC), activity-based techniques (ABT), TC, quality costing (QC), environmental cost management (ECM), competitive position monitoring (CPM), competitor performance appraisal (CPA), economic value added (EVA), VCA, BSC and customer profitability analysis (CPAN) (Hadid & Al-Sayed, 2021). Hadid and Al-Sayed (2021) measure was chosen as it is the most recent paper published in a highly reputable management accounting journal (i.e. *Management Accounting Research*). In addition, we believe these 12 practices adequately operationalise the SMA definition we adopted in this study.

Respondents were asked to indicate their extent of use of these 12 SMA practices using anchors of '1= not at all' and '5= to a great extent'. The EFA revealed that all 12 items loaded onto 1 dimension and the CFA results show that the factor loadings for all of the items exceeded 0.5 (see Appendix 2).

Organisational Culture

The items used to measure the four dimensions of organisational culture (teamwork orientation, outcome orientation, innovation orientation and attention to detail orientation) were initially developed by O'Reilly et al. (1991) and have been used in a number of studies (Baird et al., 2004, 2007, 2018; Su, Baird, & Blair, 2009). Respondents were asked to indicate the extent to which each item represented the culture within their business unit using a five-point scale with anchors of '1 = Not at all' and '5 = To a great extent'. Specifically, teamwork orientation was measured using three items with EFA indicating that all three items loaded onto one dimension. The CFA was subsequently conducted with one item being removed due to a factor loading lower than the cut-off point of 0.6 (see Appendix 2). Outcome orientation was measured using four items. While EFA revealed that all four items loaded onto the same dimension, one item was removed due to low factor loadings (see Appendix 2). A six-item measure was used to measure the extent of innovation orientation with the EFA revealing that all six items loaded onto one dimension. However, three items were removed as a result of low factor loadings in the CFA (see Appendix 2). Finally, attention to detail orientation was measured using three items with EFA finding that these items loaded onto one dimension and had factor loadings over 0.6 (see Appendix 2).

Competitive Advantage

Competitive advantage was measured using an adapted version of Schilke's (2014) six-item instrument. Specifically, in line with recent studies including Fainshmidt, Wenger, Pezeshkan, and Mallon (2019) and Alshumrani et al. (2022), we adapted Schilke's (2014) scale to treat the six items as a single order construct. Respondents were asked to indicate whether they agreed with each item in respect to their business unit's performance, with anchors of '1 = strongly disagree' and '5 = strongly agree'. All six items loaded onto one dimension and the CFA results show that all six items had factor loadings above 0.5 (see Appendix 2).

Control Variables

Two control variables, organisational size and industry, were included due to their potential effect on competitive advantage. Organisational size was measured based on the number of full-time employees using a range of nominal scales reported in Table 1. Industry was treated as a dummy variable with a score of 1 (0) assigned if organisations were members of a specific industry. For example, if respondents were (not) members of the Financial and Insurance Services industry they were assigned a score of 1 (0). The hypothesised model was tested in respect to each of the industries depicted in Table 1, with the exception of the Extractive, Utilities and Personal Services industries due to their small sample size sector (see Table 5 and Appendix 3).[9]

RESULTS

Measurement Model

Table 2 shows the summary statistics including the mean, standard deviation and the minimum and maximum values for each variable. Table 2 also reveals that the variance inflation factors (VIF) for all of the variables were less than 10, thereby suggesting that multicollinearity was not an issue (Jou, Huang, & Cho, 2014). The results of the CFA analysis have assured the reliability and dimensionality of all of the multi-item constructs (see Appendix 2). In addition, Table 3 shows that the Cronbach's (1951) alpha scores for all of the variables were above or close to 0.7, thereby indicating satisfactory reliability. To evaluate the constructs' convergent validity, the composite reliability and AVE scores were examined, with Table 3 showing that the composite reliability scores for all of the constructs exceeded or were just below the 0.7 threshold (Werts, Linn, & Jöreskog, 1974) while the AVE scores exceeded or were just below the 0.5 threshold (Chin, 1998). Discriminant validity was assessed by comparing the square root of each construct's AVE with the correlations between each construct (see Table 4). As the square roots of the AVEs are greater than the respective correlations between the constructs, discriminant validity was assured (Chin, 1998).

Structural Model

Covariance Based SEM was used to analyse the data with Model 1 (see Table 5) examining the direct effect of the use of SMA practices and the four organisational cultural dimensions (i.e. teamwork orientation, outcome orientation, innovation orientation and attention to detail orientation) on competitive advantage, and Model 2 examining the moderating effect of the four cultural dimensions on the association between the use of SMA practices and competitive advantage.

In regard to Model 1, the five benchmark fit indices (CMIN/DF = 2.22; GFI = 0.99; AGFI = 0.95; CFI = 0.99; RMSEA = 0.05) indicate a good model fit. The results reveal that there is a significant and positive direct association between the use of SMA practices and competitive advantage ($\beta = 0.33$, $p = 0.00$), thereby providing support for *H1*. Three of the four cultural dimensions, including outcome orientation ($\beta = 0.13$, $p = 0.01$), innovation orientation ($\beta = 0.25$, $p = 0.00$) and attention to detail orientation ($\beta = 0.15$, $p = 0.00$), were also found to be significantly and positively directly associated with competitive advantage.

Table 2. Descriptive Statistics.

	N	Mean	Std. Dev.	Minimum Actual (Theoretical)	Maximum Actual (Theoretical)	VIF
Use of SMA practices	408	3.42	0.99	1.08 (1)	5.00 (5)	1.63
Teamwork	408	3.94	0.71	1.00 (1)	5.00 (5)	1.80
Outcome orientation	408	3.89	0.78	1.00 (1)	5.00 (5)	2.11
Innovation	408	3.60	0.77	1.00 (1)	5.00 (5)	1.94
Attention to detail	408	3.90	0.73	1.00 (1)	5.00 (5)	2.22
Competitive advantage	408	3.65	0.75	1.33 (1)	5.00 (5)	NA

Table 3. Results of Cronbach's Alpha, Composite Reliability and Average Variance Extracted.

	N	Cronbach's Alpha Scores	Composite Reliability	Average Variance Extracted
Use of SMA practices (12 items)	408	0.94	0.95	0.62
Teamwork orientation (2 items)	408	0.68	0.67	0.48
Outcome orientation (3 item)	408	0.73	0.74	0.48
Innovation orientation (3 items)	408	0.77	0.74	0.49
Attention to detail orientation (3 items)	408	0.75	0.74	0.49
Competitive advantage (6 items)	408	0.87	0.90	0.61

Table 4. Latent Construct Correlations and Square Root of AVE Between Them.

N = 408	1	2	3	4	5	6
1. Use of SMA	**0.78**					
2. Teamwork orientation	0.32	**0.69**				
3. Outcome orientation	0.40	0.41	**0.69**			
4. Innovation orientation	0.61	0.48	0.68	**0.70**		
5. Attention to detail orientation	0.40	0.59	0.61	0.50	**0.70**	
6. Competitive advantage	0.63	0.52	0.46	0.63	0.54	**0.78**

Note: The diagonal figures in bold represent the square root values of the AVE scores.

In respect to the control variables, organisational size was not significantly associated with competitive advantage ($\beta = -0.03$, $p = 0.42$). Similarly, industry (Financial and Insurance Services) was not significantly associated with competitive advantage ($\beta = 0.06$, $p = 0.06$).[10]

Table 5 reveals that Model 2 exhibited a good fit (CMIN/DF $= 2.74$; GFI $= 0.96$; AGFI $= 0.91$; CFI $= 0.97$; RMSEA $= 0.07$) with the direct association between the use of SMA practices and competitive advantage maintained. Furthermore, Model 2 shows that the association between the use of SMA practices and competitive advantage was positively moderated by teamwork orientation ($\beta = 0.16$, $p = 0.00$), thereby providing support for *H2*. However, the other three dimensions of culture (outcome orientation, innovation orientation

Table 5. Results of SEM Analysis for the Association Between the Use of SMA Practices, Organisational Culture, and Competitive Advantage.

Regression Path	Model 1 ($N = 408$)		Model 2 ($N = 408$)	
	Standardised Beta	p-value	Standardised Beta	p-value
Direct Effects				
Use of SMA practices	0.33	0.00***	0.32	0.00***
Teamwork orientation	0.07	0.14	0.09	0.04**
Outcome orientation	0.13	0.01***	0.13	0.01***
Innovation orientation	0.25	0.00***	0.27	0.00***
Attention to detail orientation	0.15	0.00***	0.15	0.00***
#Organisational size	−0.03	0.42	−0.03	0.39
#Industry	0.06	0.06	0.06	0.08
Interaction effects				
Teamwork orientation x Use of SMA practices	n/a	n/a	0.16	0.00***
Outcome orientation x Use of SMA practices	n/a	n/a	−0.09	0.12
Innovation orientation x Use of SMA practices	n/a	n/a	0.02	0.70
Attention to detail orientation x Use of SMA practices	n/a	n/a	0.03	0.64
#Organisational size x Use of SMA practices	n/a	n/a	0.03	0.41
#Industry x Use of SMA practices	n/a	n/a	−0.02	0.63
Goodness of Fit Statistics				
CMIN/DF	2.22		2.74	
GFI	0.99		0.96	
AGFI	0.95		0.91	
CFI	0.99		0.97	
RMSEA	0.05		0.07	

Notes: Dependent variable = competitive advantage. Industry is treated as a dummy variable with this model focussing on the Financial and Insurance Services industry. We retested this model based on four other industries with the results showing the same significant paths as in Table 5. The results of these models are provided in Appendix 3.

***, ** Statistically significant at 0.01, 0.05 levels respectively (two-tailed).

n/a indicates the absence of coefficient for the deleted path in the revised model.

Control path.

and attention to detail orientation) were not found to moderate the association between the use of SMA practices and competitive advantage, and hence, *H3*, *H4* and *H5* are rejected.

While this finding is surprising it may suggest that different cultural dimensions play different roles in the context of SMA practice. For instance, while we find that teamwork orientation enhances the performance effect of the use of SMA practices (i.e. in respect to competitive advantage), alternatively, other cultural dimensions may have an important role to play in facilitating the use of SMA practices, e.g. outcome orientation influences the use of ABC (Baird et al., 2004). Accordingly, additional analyses were conducted to examine the direct effect of the four organisational culture dimensions on the use of SMA practices. In line with Hadid and Al-Sayed (2021), innovation orientation was found to have a significant positive effect on the use of SMA practices. In addition, we found that attention to detail, was positively associated with the use of SMA practices. Finally, in regard to the two control variables organisational size and industry, neither of them was found to moderate the association between the use of SMA practices and competitive advantage.

DISCUSSION AND CONCLUSION

This study aimed to examine the influence of the use of SMA on competitive advantage and the moderating role of organisational culture (teamwork orientation, outcome orientation, innovation orientation and attention to detail orientation) on such an association. Data were collected from 408 accountants in Australian business organisations using an online survey questionnaire, with SEM applied to analyse the data.

Consistent with previous studies which found a positive association between the use of SMA with organisational financial performance (Alabdulah, 2019; Turner et al., 2017) and overall performance (Aksoylu & Aykan, 2013; Cadez & Guilding, 2008; Kalkhouran et al., 2017), we found a direct positive association between the use of SMA practices and competitive advantage, a crucial performance outcome variable which provides a novel perspective in respect to the SMA-performance relationship. This finding provides empirical support for previous studies which have alluded to the role of SMA practices in assisting organisations in creating and managing value and developing competitive advantage (Bhimani & Langfield-Smith, 2007; Tayles, Bramley, Adshead, & Farr, 2002). Furthermore, amidst concerns that low SMA adoption rates may be attributed to uncertainty regarding the benefits of such practices (Langfield-Smith et al., 2018; Nuhu, Baird, & Appuhamilage, 2017; Phan, Baird, & Blair, 2014), the findings contribute to alleviating these concerns.

In addition, grounded in contingency theory and in response to the call to consider 'how variables combine to create outcomes' (Cadez & Guilding, 2012, p. 485), the study contributes to the contingency-based SMA-performance research by examining the effect of the interaction between the use of SMA practices and organisational culture on competitive advantage. In particular, such analysis contributes to the sparse research focussing on the role of organisational culture in the SMA literature (Hadid & Al-Sayed, 2021). For instance, while Hadid and Al-Sayed (2021) found that organisational culture plays an important direct (i.e. outcome orientation) and indirect (i.e. innovation through management accountant networking) role in facilitating the use of SMA practices, this study extends the literature by highlighting the important role of organisational culture in influencing the success of SMA practices, i.e. enhancing competitive advantage.

In particular, the results suggest that a specific cultural dimension, teamwork orientation, positively moderates the association between the use of SMA practices and competitive advantage, with more (less) teamwork-oriented organisations exhibiting a stronger (weaker) association between the use of SMA practices and competitive advantage. While it was hypothesised that all four dimensions of organisational culture would moderate the association between the use of SMA practices and competitive advantage, no significant moderating effect was found in respect to the other three dimensions, i.e. outcome orientation innovation orientation and attention to detail orientation. Accordingly, future studies could further explore the relationship between these culture dimensions and the use of SMA by employing other methods such as in-depth interviews to provide a more comprehensive insight into these findings.

Acknowledging that the implementation of SMA practices can be a difficult process (Langfield-Smith et al., 2018), our findings provide an insight into the means through which organisations can enhance the success of SMA practices. Specifically, the findings indicate that the effect of SMA practices on competitive advantage is dependent upon the fit between the use of SMA practices and organisational culture, with the teamwork-oriented culture exacerbating the effect of the use of SMA practices on competitive advantage. In the short-term, it is recommended that organisations need to be aware of the prevailing culture currently embedded within their organisations in order to assess the suitability of SMA practices. In particular, as organisations with the right cultural values in place (i.e. teamwork oriented) are expected to achieve a higher extent of SMA success (i.e. competitive advantage), it is recommended that such organisations should use SMA practices to a greater extent. Alternatively, from a long-term perspective, organisations that do not have the right cultural values in place may consider making a conscious effort to develop the cultural values which are found to strengthen the effect of the use of SMA practices on organisations' competitive advantage, i.e. attempt to enhance their emphasis on teamwork orientation. In order to promote a teamwork-oriented culture, organisations should first consider facilitating the formation of teams and clearly defining the roles and responsibilities for each team member. Once teams are formed organisations should encourage frequent communications, information sharing and learning amongst team members. Furthermore, in order to keep team members engaged and work towards a common goal, it is important to give team members a certain level of autonomy in making their own decisions. While these changes may seem intuitive, it is acknowledged that such changes will be difficult due to cultural inertia (Denison, 1990; Hofstede et al., 1990) and hence, may take more than one reporting period to transpire (Langfield-Smith et al., 2018).

While the study makes several contributions to both the literature and practice, it is subject to some limitations which provide potential for future research. First, while a number of strategies have been applied to minimise common method bias, the use of surveys can only allow us to assess associations rather than casual relationships between independent and dependent variables, and there are no opportunities for probing answers. Therefore, future research could employ other methods such as conducting a longitudinal study to provide stronger empirical evidence about the causal relationships between the use of SMA practices, organisational culture and competitive advantage. Second, while we provide an initial insight into the important moderating role of organisational culture (teamwork orientation) in influencing the success of SMA practices (i.e. competitive advantage), given the low sample size in some industries, future research could further explore the study's hypothesised relationship in specific industries. Thirdly, given the limited number of studies that have examined the organisational contextual factors affecting the association between the use of SMA practices and competitive advantage, future studies could consider examining the effect of other contextual factors, such as leadership styles, on the association between the use of SMA practices and competitive advantage. In addition, given this study did not consider organisations with less than 50 employees and utilised a categorical variable to measure organisational size, future studies could provide a more comprehensive insight into the influence of organisational size on the association between the use of SMA practices and competitive advantage. Finally, while this study examines the use of 12 SMA practices as a package, future studies could consider investigating how each specific SMA practice affects organisational performance outcomes and the moderating role of contextual factors including organisational culture on such relationships.

NOTES

1. See details in Literature Review section.
2. See details in Literature Review section.
3. The 12 SMA practices were adopted from Hadid and Al-Sayed (2021). Detailed information about each practice is provided in Appendix 1.
4. The project was approved by the Ethics Committee of the institution where the research was conducted. The data were collected in 2021.
5. A filter question was designed to ask respondents to indicate their job title with a number of options provided, including (a) Accounts Clerk; (b) Auditor; (c) Bookkeeper; (d) Business services accountant; (e) Chief Financial Officer; (f) Corporate Accountant; (g) Cost Accountant; (h) Financial Accountant; (i) Management Accountant; (j) Financial Controller; (k) Other accounting related job title; and (l) Non-accounting related job title. Any respondents who chose 'l' were excluded from the study.
6. A respondent was considered to be a speeder if his/her completion time was less than two standard deviations from the mean completion time.
7. If the respondent clicked the same score for all items in one or more sections.
8. The recommended threshold guidelines are CMIN/DF < 5; GFI > 0.90; CFI > 0.80; AGFI > 0.80; RMSEA < 0.10 (Hair, Anderson, Tatham, & Black, 2010), with values greater than 0.80 considered acceptable for GFI, CFI and AGFI (Abedi, Rostami, & Nadi, 2015, p. 27).
9. The main results provided in Table 5 are based on the Financial and Insurance services industry as it was the largest industry ($n = 123$) amongst the eight industries.
10. The only significant finding in relation to industry was in respect to the Social Services industry which was found to exhibit a significantly lower level of competitive advantage compared to other industries (see part iv in Appendix 3).

REFERENCES

Abedi, G., Rostami, F., & Nadi, A. (2015). Analyzing the dimensions of the quality of life in hepatitis B patients using confirmatory factor analysis. *Global Journal of Health Science*, 7(7), 22–31.

Abernethy, M. A., & Bouwens, J. (2005). Determinants of accounting innovation implementation. *Abacus*, 41(3), 217–240.

Adler, P. S., & Chen, C. X. (2011). Combining creativity and control: Understanding individual motivation in large-scale collaborative creativity. *Accounting, Organizations and Society*, *36*(2), 63–85.

Akenbor, O. C., & Okoye, E. I. (2012). The adoption of strategic management accounting in Nigerian manufacturing firms. *An International Journal of Arts and Humanities*, *1*(3), 270–287.

Akroyd, C., & Kober, R. (2020). Imprinting founders' blueprints on management control systems. *Management Accounting Research*, *46*, 100645.

Aksoylu, S., & Aykan, E. (2013). Effects of strategic management accounting techniques on perceived performance of businesses. *Journal of US-China Public Administration*, *10*(10), 1004–1017.

Alabdullah, T. T. Y. (2019). Management accounting and service companies' performance: Research in emerging economies. *Australasian Accounting, Business and Finance Journal*, *13*(4), 100–118.

Alamri, A. M. (2019). Association between strategic management accounting facets and organizational performance. *Baltic Journal of Management*, *14*(2), 212–234.

Alshumrani, S., Baird, K., & Munir, R. (2022). Management innovation: the influence of institutional pressures and the impact on competitive advantage. *International Journal of Manpower*, *43*(5), 1204–1220.

Ax, C., & Greve, J. (2017). Adoption of management accounting innovations: Organizational culture compatibility and perceived outcomes. *Management Accounting Research*, *34*, 59–74.

Aziz, A. M. (2012). *Strategic role of strategic management accounting towards enhancing SMEs performance in Iraq*. Master's Thesis, University Utara, Malaysia.

Baird, K. M., Harrison, G. L., & Reeve, R. (2007). Success of activity management practices: The influence of organizational and cultural factors. *Accounting & Finance*, *47*(1), 47–67.

Baird, K. M., Harrison, G. L., & Reeve, R. C. (2004). Adoption of activity management practices: a note on the extent of adoption and the influence of organizational and cultural factors. *Management Accounting Research*, *15*(4), 383–399.

Baird, K. M., Hu, K. J., & Reeve, R. (2011). The relationships between organizational culture, total quality management practices and operational performance. *International Journal of Operations & Production Management*, *31*(7), 789–814.

Baird, K. M., Su, S., & Tung, A. (2018). Organizational culture and environmental activity management. *Business Strategy and Environment*, *27*(3), 403–414.

Bhimani, A. (2003). A study of the emergence of management accounting system ethos and its influence on perceived system success. *Accounting, Organizations and Society*, *28*(6), 523–548.

Bhimani, A., & Langfield-Smith, K. (2007). Structure, formality and the importance of financial and non-financial information in strategy development and implementation. *Management Accounting Research*, *18*(1), 3–31.

Brandau, M., Endenich, C., Trapp, R., & Hoffjan, A. (2013). Institutional drivers of conformity – Evidence for management accounting from Brazil and Germany. *International Business Review*, *22*(2), 466–479.

Bromwich, M. (1990). The case for strategic management accounting: The role of accounting information for strategy in competitive markets. *Accounting, Organizations and Society*, *15*(1–2), 27–46.

Cadez, S., & Guilding, C. (2008). An exploratory investigation of an integrated contingency model of strategic management accounting. *Accounting, Organizations and Society*, *33*(7–8), 836–863.

Cadez, S., & Guilding, C. (2012). Strategy, strategic management accounting and performance: A configurational analysis. *Industrial Management & Data Systems*, *112*(3), 484–501.

Cescon, F., Costantini, A., & Grassetti, L. (2019). Strategic choices and strategic management accounting in large manufacturing firms. *Journal of Management and Governance*, *23*(3), 605–636.

Chia, Y., & Koh, H. C. (2007). An exploratory study of the relationship between organizational culture and the adoption of management accounting practices in the public sector. Paper presented at *The Seventh International Conference on Knowledge, Culture & Change in Organisations*, Singapore.

Chin, W. W. (1998). The partial least squares approach to structural equation modelling. In G. A. Marcoulides (Ed.), *Modern methods for business research* (pp. 295–336). New Jersey: Lawrence Erlbaum Associates.

Cronbach, L. J. (1951). Coefficient alpha and the internal structure of tests. *Psychometrika*, *16*, 297–334.

Denison, D. (1990). *Corporate culture and organizational effectiveness.* New York, NY: John Wiley & Sons.

Dixon, R., & Smith, D. R. (1993). Strategic management accounting. *Omega, 21*(6), 605–618.

Drake, A., Haka, S. F., & Ravenscroft, S. P. (2001). An ABC simulation focusing on incentives and innovation. *Issues in Accounting Education, 16*(3), 443–471.

Eichhorn, B. R. (2014). *Common method variance techniques. Cleveland State University, Department of Operations & Supply Chain Management* (pp. 1–11). Cleveland, OH: SAS Institute Inc.

Fainshmidt, S., Wenger, L., Pezeshkan, A., & Mallon, M. (2019). When do dynamic capabilities lead to competitive advantage? The importance of strategic fit. *Journal of Management Studies, 56*(4), 758–787.

Gering, M. (1999). Activity based costing: lessons learned implementing ABC. *Management Accounting, 77,* 26–27.

Hadid, W., & Al-Sayed, M. (2021). Management accountants and strategic management accounting: The role of organizational culture and information systems. *Management Accounting Research, 50,* 1007–1025.

Hair, J., Anderson, R., Tatham, R., & Black, W. (2010). *Multivariate data analysis: A global perspective* (7th ed.). Upper Saddle River, NJ: Pearson.

Hamel, G., & Valikangas, L. (2003). The quest for resilience. *Harvard Business Review, 81*(9), 52–63.

Harman, H. (1967). *Modern factor analysis.* Chicago, IL: University of Chicago Press.

Hart, S. L. (1995). A natural-resource-based view of the firm. *Academy of Management Review, 20*(4), 986–1014.

Henri, J. F. (2006). Organizational culture and performance measurement systems. *Accounting, Organizations and Society, 31*(1), 77–103.

Hofstede, G., Neuijen, B., Ohayv, D., & Sanders, G. (1990). Measuring organizational cultures: A qualitative and quantitative study across twenty cases. *Administrative Science Quarterly, 35,* 286–316.

Janardhanan, N. S., Lewis, K., Reger, R. K., & Stevens, C. K. (2020). Getting to know you: Motivating cross-understanding for improved team and individual performance. *Organization Science, 31*(1), 103–118.

Jordan, P. J., & Troth, A. C. (2020). Common method bias in applied settings: The dilemma of researching in organizations. *Australian Journal of Management, 45*(1), 3–14.

Jou, Y.-J., Huang, C.-C. L., & Cho, H.-J. (2014). A VIF-based optimization model to alleviate collinearity problems in multiple linear regression. *Computational Statistics, 29*(6), 1515–1541.

Joyce, C. (1999). Activity-based costing. *Computerworld, 33*(32), 54–56.

Kalkhouran, A. A. N., Nedaei, B. H. N., & Rasid, S. Z. A. (2017). The indirect effect of strategic management accounting in the relationship between CEO characteristics and their networking activities, and company performance. *Journal of Accounting & Organizational Change, 13*(4), 471–491.

Langfield‐Smith, K. (2008). Strategic management accounting: How far have we come in 25 years? *Accounting, Auditing & Accountability Journal, 21*(2), 204–228.

Langfield-Smith, K., Smith, D., Andon, P., Hilton, R., & Thorne, H. (2018). *Management accounting: Information for creating and managing value* (8th ed.). Sydney: McGraw-Hill Education.

Ma, Y., & Tayles, M. (2009). On the emergence of strategic management accounting: An institutional perspective. *Accounting and Business Research, 39*(5), 473–495.

Mach, M., Dolan, S., & Tzafrir, S. (2010). The differential effect of team members' trust on team performance: The mediation role of team cohesion. *Journal of Occupational and Organizational Psychology, 83*(3), 771–794.

Mannix, E., & Neale, M. A. (2005). What differences make a difference? The promise and reality of diverse teams in organizations. *Psychological Science in the Public Interest, 6*(2), 31–55.

Meneghel, I., Salanova, M., & Martínez, I. M. (2016). Feeling good makes us stronger: How team resilience mediates the effect of positive emotions on team performance. *Journal of Happiness Studies, 17*(1), 239–255.

Merchant, K. A. (1985). *Control in business organizations.* Pittman: Boston.

Naranjo-Gil, D., Maas, V. S., & Hartmann, F. G. (2009). How CFOs determine management accounting innovation: An examination of direct and indirect effects. *European Accounting Review, 18*(4), 667–695.

Nuhu, N. A., Baird, K., & Appuhamilage, A. B. (2017). The adoption and success of contemporary management accounting practices in the public sector. *Asian Review of Accounting*, *25*(1), 106–126.

O'Reilly III, C. A., Chatman, J., & Caldwell, D. F. (1991). People and organizational culture: A profile comparison approach to assessing person-organization fit. *Academy of Management Journal*, *34*(3), 487–516.

Oboh, C. S., & Ajibolade, S. O. (2017). Strategic management accounting and decision making: A survey of the Nigerian Banks. *Future Business Journal*, *3*(2), 119–137.

Oyewo, B., & Ajibolade, S. (2019). Does the use of strategic management accounting techniques creates and sustains competitive advantage? Some empirical evidence. *Annals of Spiru Haret University Economic Series*, *19*(2), 61–91.

Pablo, A. L., Sitkin, S. B., & Jemison, D. B. (1996). Acquisition decision-making processes: The central role of risk. *Journal of Management*, *22*(5), 723–746.

Pavlatos, O., & Kostakis, X. (2018). The impact of top management team characteristics and historical financial performance on strategic management accounting. *Journal of Accounting & Organizational Change*, *14*(4), 455–472.

Phan, T. N., Baird, K., & Blair, B. (2014). The use and success of activity-based management practices at different organisational life cycle stages. *International Journal of Production Research*, *52*(3), 787–803.

Podsakoff, P., MacKenzie, S., Lee, J., & Podsakoff, N. (2003). Common method biases in behavioral research: A critical review of the literature and recommended remedies. *Journal of Applied Psychology*, *88*(5), 879–903.

Pun, K. F. (2001). Cultural influences on total quality management adoption in Chinese enterprises: An empirical study. *Total Quality Management*, *12*(3), 323–342.

Rashid, M. M., Ali, M. M., & Hossain, D. M. (2020). Revisiting the relevance of strategic management accounting research. *PSU Research Review*, *4*(2), 129–148.

Roslender, R., & Hart, S. J. (2002). Integrating management accounting and marketing in the pursuit of competitive advantage: The case for strategic management accounting. *Critical Perspectives on Accounting*, *13*(2), 255–277.

Schein, E. H. (1990). Organizational culture. *American Psychological Association*, *45*(2), 109.

Schilke, O. (2014). On the contingent value of dynamic capabilities for competitive advantage: The nonlinear moderating effect of environmental dynamism. *Strategic Management Journal*, *35*(2), 179–203.

Schneider, B., Brief, A. P., & Guzzo, R. A. (1996). Creating a climate and culture for sustainable organizational change. *Organizational Dynamics*, *24*(4), 7–19.

Shank, J. K. (2007). Strategic cost management: Upsizing, downsizing, and right (?) sizing. In A. Bhimani (Ed.), *Contemporary issues in management accounting* (pp. 355–379). Oxford: Oxford University Press.

Simmonds, K. (1981). Strategic management accounting. *Management Accounting*, *59*(4), 26–30.

Smith, M. (1998). Culture and organisational change. *Management Accounting*, *76*(7), 60–62.

Snell, S. A. (1992). Control theory in strategic human resource management: The mediating effect of administrative information. *Academy of Management Journal*, *35*(2), 292–327.

Stephens, J., Heaphy, E. D., Carmeli, A., Spreitzer, G. M., & Dutton, J. E. (2013). Relationship quality and virtuousness: Emotional carrying capacity as a source of individual and team resilience. *Journal of Applied Behavioral Science*, *49*(1), 13–41.

Su, S., Baird, K., & Blair, B. (2009). Employee organizational commitment: The influence of cultural and organizational factors in the Australian manufacturing industry. *The International Journal of Human Resource Management*, *20*(12), 2494–2516.

Swain, M., & Bell, J. (1999). *The theory of constrains and throughput accounting*. New York: McGraw-Hill.

Tayles, M., Bramley, A., Adshead, N., & Farr, J. (2002). Dealing with the management of intellectual capital: The potential role of strategic management accounting. *Accounting, Auditing & Accountability Journal*, *15*(2), 251–267.

Turner, M. J., Way, S. A., Hodari, D., & Witteman, W. (2017). Hotel property performance: The role of strategic management accounting. *International Journal of Hospitality Management*, *63*(May), 33–43.

Werts, C. E., Linn, R. L., & Jöreskog, K. G. (1974). Intraclass reliability estimates: Testing structural assumptions. *Educational and Psychological Measurement*, *34*(1), 25–33.

Windsor, C. A., & Ashkanasy, N. M. (1996). Auditor independence decision making: The role of organizational culture perceptions. *Behavioural Research in Accounting*, *8*, 80–97.

Yazdifar, H., Askarany, D., Wickramasinghe, D., Nasseri, A., & Alam, A. (2019). The diffusion of management accounting innovations in dependent (subsidiary) organizations and MNCs. *The International Journal of Accounting*, *54*(1), 1950004.

APPENDIX 1

DESCRIPTIONS OF THE 12 SMA PRACTICES (ADOPTED FROM HADID & AL-SAYED, 2021)

1. ABT: Any management accounting technique that uses business unit's activities as its base. For example, Activity Analysis (AA), Activity Cost Analysis (ACA), Activity-based Costing (ABC), Time-Driven ABC, Activity-based Management (ABM) and Activity-based Budgeting (ABB).
2. BSC: Approach to the provision of information to management to assist strategic policy formulation and achievement. The information provided may include both financial and non-financial elements, and cover areas such as profitability, customer satisfaction, internal efficiency and innovation.
3. CPM: The analysis of competitor positions within the industry by assessing and monitoring trends in competitor sales, market share, volume, unit costs and return on sales. This information can provide a basis for the assessment of a competitor's market strategy.
4. CPA: The numerical analysis of a competitor's published statements as a part of an assessment of their key sources of competitive advantage.
5. CPAN: This involves calculating profit earned from specific customers.
6. EVA: Profit less a charge for capital employed in the period. Accounting profit may be adjusted, for example, for the treatment of goodwill and research and development expenditure, before EVA is calculated.
7. ECM: Identification, collection, analysis and use of two types of information for internal decision making: physical information on the use, flows and rates of energy, water and materials (including wastes); and monetary information on environment related costs, earnings and savings.
8. LCC: The appraisal of costs based on the length of stages of product or service's life. Namely: design, introduction, growth, decline and eventually abandonment (marketing perspective).
9. QC: Cost of quality reports is produced for the purpose of directing management attention to prioritise quality problems. The reports focus on the costs associated with the creation, identification, repair and prevention of defects. These costs fall into three categories: prevention, appraisal and internal and external failure costs.
10. SC: Using cost data, strategic and marketing information to develop and identify strategies that will sustain a competitive advantage.
11. TC: Estimating a cost calculated by subtracting a desired profit margin from an estimated or market-based price to arrive at a desired production, engineering or marketing cost, and to design a product which meets that cost.
12. VCA: Use of the value chain model to identify the value adding activities of an entity. This includes value chain costing: An activity-based approach where costs are allocated to the activities required to design, procure, produce, market, distribute and service a product or service.

APPENDIX 2

CFA RESULTS

These are the retained items after CFA. The first item of each scale has no *t*-value since it has a fixed parameter in AMOS.

Items	Loadings	Standardised Error	*t*-value
Teamwork orientation[a]			
Being team oriented (item 2)	0.70	–	–
Working in collaboration with others (item 3)	0.68	0.09	10.62
[a]Item 1 Being people oriented *was removed due to a low factor loading.*			
Outcome orientation[b]			
Having high expectations for performance (item 2)	0.72	–	–
Being results oriented (item 3)	0.72	0.08	11.00
Being action oriented (item 4)	0.64	0.08	11.15
[b]Item 1 'Being achievement oriented' *was removed due to a low factor loading.*			
Innovation orientation[c]			
A willingness to experiment (item 1)	0.76	–	–
Being quick to take advantage of opportunities (item 2)	0.69	0.08	11.93
Risk taking (item 4)	0.65	0.09	11.41
[c]Item 3 'Being innovative', item 5 'Being careful' and item 6 'being rule oriented' *were removed due to low factor loadings.*			
Attention to detail orientation			
Being analytical (item 1)	0.65	–	–
Paying attention to detail (item 2)	0.73	0.10	11.69
Being precise (item 3)	0.71	0.10	11.18
Use of SMA practices			
ABT (item 1)	0.70	–	–
Balanced scorecard (BSC) (item 2)	0.68	0.07	13.65
CPM (item 3)	0.81	0.09	15.09
CPA (item 4)	0.81	0.09	15.07
CPAN (item 5)	0.71	0.08	13.26
EVA (item 6)	0.76	0.08	14.28
ECM (item 7)	0.80	0.09	14.92
LCC (item 8)	0.68	0.08	12.74
QC (item 9)	0.79	0.09	14.69
SC (item 10)	0.77	0.08	14.92
TC (item 11)	0.80	0.08	15.00
VCA (item 12)	0.77	0.08	14.32
Competitive advantage			
We have gained strategic advantages over our competitors (item 1)	0.76	–	–
We have a large market share (item 2)	0.60	0.07	11.51
Overall, we are more successful than our major competitors (item 3)	0.75	0.06	14.88

(*Continued*)

Appendix 2   (Continued)

Items	Loadings	Standardised Error	*t*-value
Our earnings before interest and taxes (EBIT) is continuously above industry average (item 4)	0.75	0.07	14.32
Our return on investment (ROI) is continuously above industry average (item 5)	0.78	0.07	15.50
Our return on sales (ROS) is continuously above industry average (item 6)	0.75	0.07	14.87
Overall Goodness of Fit Statistics			
CMIN/DF	1.47		
GFI	0.92		
AGFI	0.90		
RMSEA	0.04		

APPENDIX 3

RESULTS OF SEM ANALYSIS FOR DIFFERENT INDUSTRIES

i. Manufacturing industry

	Model 1 ($N = 408$)		Model 2 ($N = 408$)	
Regression Path	Standardised Beta	*p*-value	Standardised Beta	*p*-value
Direct Effects				
Use of SMA practices	0.34	0.00***	0.31	0.00***
Teamwork orientation	0.07	0.12	0.09	0.04**
Outcome orientation	0.13	0.01***	0.13	0.01***
Innovation orientation	0.26	0.00***	0.28	0.00***
Attention to detail orientation	0.14	0.01***	0.13	0.01***
#Organisational size	−0.02	0.49	−0.02	0.47
#Industry	−0.04	0.20	−0.06	0.09
Interaction effects				
Teamwork orientation × Use of SMA practices	n/a	n/a	0.16	0.00***
Outcome orientation × Use of SMA practices	n/a	n/a	−0.11	0.08
Innovation orientation × Use of SMA practices	n/a	n/a	0.02	0.65
Attention to detail orientation × Use of SMA practices	n/a	n/a	0.03	0.58
#Organisational size × Use of SMA practices	n/a	n/a	0.03	0.46
#Industry × Use of SMA practices	n/a	n/a	0.04	0.29
Goodness of Fit Statistics				
CMIN/DF	1.51		2.24	

(*Continued*)

Appendix 3   (Continued)

Regression Path	Model 1 (N = 408)		Model 2 (N = 408)	
	Standardised Beta	p-value	Standardised Beta	p-value
GFI	0.99		0.97	
AGFI	0.97		0.92	
CFI	0.99		0.97	
RMSEA	0.04		0.06	

Notes: Dependent variable = competitive advantage.
***, ** Statistically significant at 0.01, 0.05 levels respectively (two-tailed).
n/a indicates the absence of coefficient for the deleted path in the revised model.
Control path.

ii. Other Business Services Industry

Regression Path	Model 1 (N = 408)		Model 2 (N = 408)	
	Standardised Beta	p-value	Standardised Beta	p-value
Direct Effects				
Use of SMA practices	0.33	0.00***	0.33	0.00***
Teamwork orientation	0.07	0.14	0.09	0.04**
Outcome orientation	0.12	0.01***	0.12	0.01***
Innovation orientation	0.26	0.00***	0.28	0.00***
Attention to detail orientation	0.15	0.00***	0.14	0.01***
#Organisational size	−0.02	0.54	−0.02	0.49
#Industry	0.00	0.92	−0.00	0.96
Interaction effects				
Teamwork orientation × Use of SMA practices	n/a	n/a	0.16	0.00***
Outcome orientation × Use of SMA practices	n/a	n/a	−0.10	0.09
Innovation orientation × Use of SMA practices	n/a	n/a	0.02	0.62
Attention to detail orientation × Use of SMA practices	n/a	n/a	0.03	0.58
#Organisational size × Use of SMA practices	n/a	n/a	0.02	0.50
#Industry × Use of SMA practices	n/a	n/a	−0.03	0.52
Goodness of Fit Statistics				
CMIN/DF	1.46		2.21	
GFI	0.99		0.97	
AGFI	0.97		0.92	
CFI	0.99		0.98	
RMSEA	0.03		0.05	

Notes: Dependent variable = competitive advantage.
***, ** Statistically significant at 0.01, 0.05 levels respectively (two-tailed).
n/a indicates the absence of coefficient for the deleted path in the revised modeVl.
Control path.

iii. Distribution Services industry

Regression Path	Model 1 (N = 408)		Model 2 (N = 408)	
	Standardised Beta	p-value	Standardised Beta	p-value
Direct Effects				
Use of SMA practices	0.33	0.00***	0.31	0.00***
Teamwork orientation	0.07	0.14	0.09	0.04**
Outcome orientation	0.12	0.01***	0.11	0.01***
Innovation orientation	0.26	0.00***	0.28	0.00***
Attention to detail orientation	0.15	0.00***	0.14	0.00***
#Organisational size	−0.02	0.53	−0.02	0.48
#Industry	0.00	0.99	0.00	0.83
Interaction effects				
Teamwork orientation × Use of SMA practices	n/a	n/a	0.16	0.00***
Outcome orientation × Use of SMA practices	n/a	n/a	−0.10	0.12
Innovation orientation × Use of SMA practices	n/a	n/a	0.28	0.70
Attention to detail orientation × Use of SMA practices	n/a	n/a	0.03	0.64
#Organisational size × Use of SMA practices	n/a	n/a	0.03	0.41
#Industry × Use of SMA practices	n/a	n/a	0.01	0.63
Goodness of Fit Statistics				
CMIN/DF		0.51		2.03
GFI		0.99		0.97
AGFI		0.99		0.93
CFI		0.99		0.98
RMSEA		0.00		0.05

Notes: Dependent variable = competitive advantage.
***, ** Statistically significant at 0.01, 0.05 levels respectively (two-tailed).
n/a indicates the absence of coefficient for the deleted path in the revised model.
Control path.

iv. Social Services industry

Regression Path	Model 1 (N = 408)		Model 2 (N = 408)	
	Standardised Beta	p-value	Standardised Beta	p-value
Direct Effects				
Use of SMA practices	0.33	0.00***	0.32	0.00***
Teamwork orientation	0.08	0.09	0.10	0.03**
Outcome orientation	0.12	0.01***	0.12	0.01***
Innovation orientation	0.25	0.00***	0.27	0.00***
Attention to detail orientation	0.15	0.00***	0.15	0.00***
#Organisational size	−0.02	0.58	−0.02	0.54.
#Industry	−0.07	0.04**	−0.07	0.04**

(*Continued*)

Appendix 3   (Continued)

Regression Path	Model 1 ($N = 408$)		Model 2 ($N = 408$)	
	Standardised Beta	p-value	Standardised Beta	p-value
Interaction effects				
Teamwork orientation $\times$ Use of SMA practices	n/a	n/a	0.16	0.00***
Outcome orientation $\times$ Use of SMA practices	n/a	n/a	−0.09	0.12
Innovation orientation $\times$ Use of SMA practices	n/a	n/a	0.02	0.70
Attention to detail orientation $\times$ Use of SMA practices	n/a	n/a	0.02	0.64
#Organisational size $\times$ Use of SMA practices	n/a	n/a	0.03	0.41
#Industry $\times$ Use of SMA practices	n/a	n/a	−0.03	0.63
Goodness of Fit Statistics				
CMIN/DF	2.48		2.62	
GFI	0.99		0.96	
AGFI	0.95		0.91	
CFI	0.99		0.97	
RMSEA	0.06		0.06	

Notes: Dependent variable = competitive advantage. The results in relation to Industry 4 are reported in Table 5, while results in relation to Industries 1, 3 and 8 are not able to be produced due to too small sample size.

***, ** Statistically significant at 0.01, 0.05 levels respectively (two-tailed).

n/a indicates the absence of coefficient for the deleted path in the revised model.

Control path.

RESOURCE-BASED COMMITMENT TO A CUSTOMER-CENTERED STRATEGY

Mark Anderson, Shahid Khan, Raj Mashruwala and Zhimin (Jimmy) Yu

ABSTRACT

To create and sustain a resource-based competitive advantage, managers acquire and develop specialized resources as they grow their firms. The authors argue that an important part of committing to a resource-based strategy is a willingness to keep spending on specialized resources during periods when sales and profits are down. The authors seek to validate this conjecture by examining whether such resource-based commitment to a customer-centered strategy results in improved customer satisfaction. The authors use the stickiness of selling, general, and administrative (SG&A) expenses to capture this commitment empirically. The authors first document that future customer satisfaction is positively associated with SG&A cost stickiness, consistent with the premise that the retention of specialized SG&A resources during low demand periods helps firms to build and maintain relationships with customers over time. Next, the authors test whether expected future benefits of customer satisfaction are enhanced when SG&A cost stickiness is higher. The authors find that the positive relation between Tobin's Q and customer satisfaction is positively moderated by SG&A cost stickiness. Finally, the authors test whether earnings persistence, a quality of earnings associated with sustained performance over time, is positively associated with the interaction between customer satisfaction and SG&A cost stickiness. The authors find that it is. Their evidence supporting these predictions is consistent with the conjecture that resource-based

Advances in Management Accounting, Volume 35, 159–180
ISSN: 1474-7871/doi:10.1108/S1474-787120230000035007

commitment reflected in cost stickiness is an important dimension of creating and sustaining a resource-based competitive advantage.

Keywords: SG&A cost behavior; cost stickiness; customer satisfaction; resource-based advantage; earnings persistence; competitive advantage

INTRODUCTION

A company attains a resource-based competitive advantage by developing capabilities that add value to products or services and cannot be easily imitated by competitors (Barney, 1991). Inimitability implies that such capabilities are difficult to replicate because they are acquired and developed over time through costly investments in specialized resources. To create and sustain a resource-based competitive advantage, managers who build resource capabilities during high-demand and growth periods must be willing to retain specialized resources through low demand periods or downturns when the costs of doing so further reduces profitability. This suggests that cost stickiness associated with those specialized resources increases with managers' commitment to a resource-based competitive strategy. In this vein, we use the stickiness of selling, general, and administrative (SG&A) costs (Anderson, Banker, & Janakiraman, 2003) to capture a firm's resource-based commitment to a customer-centered strategy (Miller, 1986; Treacy & Wiersema, 1993). We examine whether higher resource-based commitment enables a firm to build and maintain closer relationships with its customers as reflected in customer satisfaction scores.

The resource-based view (RBV) provides a pivotal framework for describing the basis of a firm's competitive advantage and performance (Barney, 1991; Barney, Ketchen, & Wright, 2011; Slotegraaf & Dickson, 2004; Vorhiers & Morgan, 2005). In the past three decades, numerous conceptual and empirical articles published in marketing and other management disciplines draw on the RBV.[1] These studies concentrate on specialized resources that support intangible assets, such as brands and customer relationships (Srivastava, Shervani, & Fahey, 1998). As much as 70% of a firm's market value comes from its intangible assets (Capraro & Srivastava, 1997), and firm performance is increasingly tied to customer relationships and brand equity (Lusch & Harvey, 1994; Ramaswami, Srivastava, & Bhargava, 2009). Extant research suggests that the greatest benefits accrue when externally focused, customer-based resources are complemented by internal resources (Dutta, Narasimhan, & Rajiv, 1999; Moorman & Slotegraaf, 1999). Customer satisfaction represents the cumulative experience of customers with the company's goods or services (Anderson, Fornell, & Lehmann, 1994). This cumulative experience is a function of resources acquired and developed by the firm to enhance the customer experience and represents an intangible asset with enduring value to the firm (Srivastava et al., 1998). Accordingly, we use customer satisfaction to represent a resource-based competitive advantage.

Recent literature in accounting provides evidence that cost stickiness increases with specialized resource retention associated with building intangible asset value and supporting competitive strategy (Ballas, Naoum, & Vlismas, 2022; Banker, Flasher, & Zhang, 2014; Venieris, Naoum, & Vlismas, 2015). An implication of these studies is that managers' commitment to spending on critical resources through up and down cycles enables firms to build and sustain resource-based competitive advantages. SG&A cost stickiness reflects the costly retention of specialized resources that support customer-centered activities when sales decline (Liu, Liu, & Reid, 2019). Myopic managers, or managers with low commitment to a resource-based strategy, cut SG&A expenditures when sales decrease to preserve short-term profits. Cutting back on these expenditures in a downturn has a negative long-term profit impact if it leads to the erosion of customer-centered resources. Managers that adopt a longer-term view exhibit a greater commitment by retaining specialized SG&A resources in downturns. Therefore, we use SG&A cost stickiness to capture managers' resource-based commitment to a customer-centered strategy.

Our empirical sample is made up of companies that are included in the American Customer Satisfaction Index (*ACSI*) that is widely used in academic research (Anderson & Fornell, 2000; Anderson, Fornell, & Mazvancheryl, 2004). In addition to providing a reliable measure of customer satisfaction, the use of companies in this sample provides assurance that SG&A costs include expenditures on resources that support customer-centered activities. We estimate SG&A cost stickiness on a firm-specific basis following the method described by Weiss (2010). An important dimension of our study is that we go beyond the question whether cost stickiness increases with a commitment to a resource-based strategy to examine whether the beneficial effects of a resource-based competitive advantage are positively moderated by cost stickiness.

We first demonstrate that future customer satisfaction is positively related to SG&A cost stickiness, providing support for our premise that customer satisfaction is supported by costly resource retention in sales-decline periods. Based on previous research that finds that *Tobin's Q*, as a measure of expected future performance, increases with customer satisfaction, we test whether this relation is positively moderated by SG&A cost stickiness and find that it is. Then, because a sustained competitive advantage increases the persistence of earnings, we test whether the persistence of accounting return on assets (*ROA*) increases with the interaction of customer satisfaction and SG&A cost stickiness and find that it does. Thus, we provide evidence supporting the beneficial effects of SG&A cost stickiness with respect to resources that support customer-centered activities.

Our study contributes to the RBV and marketing literature by empirically documenting an association between customer satisfaction and SG&A cost stickiness and by demonstrating that the intangible value of customer assets is enhanced by management decisions that reflect the greater commitment to a customer-centered resource-based strategy. Our study contributes to the managerial accounting literature by examining some of the benefits of SG&A cost stickiness. There is rich set of extant evidence on the determinants of cost stickiness. However, few studies have examined the real outcomes associated with SG&A cost stickiness. Our study provides evidence that resource commitment reflected in SG&A cost stickiness enables firms to build and maintain closer relationships with customers resulting in higher customer satisfaction. We also show that SG&A cost stickiness helps amplify the positive effects of customer satisfaction on future performance.

The remainder of this chapter is organized as follows. In the next section, we review relevant literature and develop our hypotheses. Next, we present our research design followed by sample description and variable definitions. We then discuss the results of estimating our models, and finally conclude.

LITERATURE AND HYPOTHESES

According to the RBV, resources that are valuable, rare, inimitable, and non-substitutable (Barney, 1991) make it possible for businesses to develop and sustain competitive advantages (Armstrong & Shimitzu, 2007; Castanias & Helfat, 1991; Lockett & Thompson, 2001). Managers' deliberate resource allocation decisions create and develop firm-specific resources, such as market-based relationships (Srivastava et al., 1998). Because relational assets are based on factors such as trust and reputation (Barney, 2014), organizations have the potential to develop intimate relations with customers. These relationships may then become difficult for rivals to replicate and have the potential to turn into a unique and valuable competitive advantage for a firm. To build these intimate relationships with customers, organizations invest considerable time, energy, and money to create deep and insightful customer knowledge (Fahey, 1999).

Investments in resources that are used in the customer service process are included in SG&A costs. SG&A can reflect investments in market strategy, market research, customer and social relationships, and human capital (Ballas et al., 2022; Enache & Srivastava, 2018). Building a resource-based competitive advantage through investments in specialized customer-centered resources requires a continuous commitment (Srivastava, Fahey, & Christensen, 2001). This commitment becomes particularly salient when a firm faces a downturn in sales. Managers must decide whether they wish to continue SG&A spending on specialized resources during a downturn or to reduce their SG&A expenses to boost short-term profitability.

Firms vary in their level of commitment to building and retaining long-term resource-based competitive advantages. At one end of the continuum are firms that focus on short-run performance and choose to decrease their SG&A spending proportional to sales in a downturn, thus protecting immediate profits (Deleersnyder, Dekimpe, Steenkamp, & Leeflang, 2009; Tellis & Tellis, 2009). At the other end are firms that maintain SG&A spending on specialized resources even during downturns (Liu et al., 2019). Such firms share the view that neglecting relationships during a downturn will result in a weakening of these relationships, thus reducing profits post-downturn (Lamey, Deleersnyder, Dekimpe, & Steenkamp, 2007). We argue that maintaining SG&A spending on customer-centered resources in a downturn, when competitors may be cutting their spending, can lead to improvements in customer satisfaction over time.

The concept of cost "stickiness" or asymmetric cost behavior, meaning that upward cost elasticity when sales increase is greater than downward cost elasticity when sales decrease in a period (Anderson et al., 2003; Noreen & Soderstrom, 1997), has spawned a stream of literature in management accounting. This literature predicts and provides evidence that cost stickiness increases with adjustment costs for adding and removing resources (Anderson et al., 2003; Banker, Byzalov, & Chen, 2013; Banker & Byzalov, 2014; Golden, Mashruwala, & Pevzner, 2020) and managers' optimism that a downturn is temporary and future sales will increase (Banker, Byzalov, Ciftci, & Mashruwala, 2014). The literature also finds that cost stickiness increases with agency concerns such as empire-building (Chen, Lu, & Sougiannis, 2012).

Following the adjustment cost hypothesis, Venieris et al. (2015) posit that a high level of intangible investments in a firm increases the level of adjustment costs and drives managers to shape more optimistic expectations regarding whether future sales growth will absorb the slack of unutilized resources. They use organization capital as the basis for a firm's intensity of intangible investments and examine the relationship between the cost behavior of SG&A expenses and intangible investments. They find results consistent with their hypothesis that firms with high (low) organization capital exhibit sticky (anti-sticky) SG&A cost behavior.

Banker, Flasher and Zhang (2014) find that firms pursuing differentiation strategies (Porter, 1980) have a higher degree of cost stickiness relative to those pursuing cost leadership. To achieve strategic goals, differentiators invest more in human capital and other resources that provide capabilities in product development, branding, and service to customers specialized to their strategic needs. Such investment creates intangible value that is realized through premium prices in high-demand periods. It is costly for differentiators to cut back on these specialized resources when demand falls because they cannot recapture their investment by trading the resources in secondary markets. On the other hand, cost leaders focus on cost efficiency, pursuing a lean cost structure and low adjustment costs. Ballas et al. (2022) posit and find that a firm's strategic choice is a significant determinant of managerial resource commitment decisions, determining a firm's intensity and direction of the asymmetric cost behavior. They distinguish between defenders and prospectors (Miles, Snow, Meyer, & Coleman, 1978) and find that cost stickiness is associated with a prospector strategy.

Performance measurement tools such as the balanced scorecard (Kaplan & Norton, 1996) include customer-orientation as a distinctive strategic objective. Customer satisfaction is a key generic measure used in the balanced scorecard that links outcomes from the internal business process perspective to the customer perspective and to financial performance (Kaplan & Norton, 1996). Embedded in the balanced scorecard is the notion that spending on internal operations, including manufacturing quality, process controls, on-time deliveries, and pre- and post-sales service, leads to enhanced customer satisfaction. We argue that firms that maintain spending on their internal operations even during sales downturns have a higher likelihood of achieving satisfied customers. Thus, a higher degree of SG&A cost stickiness will be positively associated with improvements in customer satisfaction over time. Accordingly, we state our first hypothesis as follows:

H1. Future customer satisfaction is positively associated with SG&A cost stickiness.

Anderson et al. (2004) develop a theoretical framework that specifies how customer satisfaction affects future customer behavior and in turn, the level, timing, and risk of future cash flows. Firms with high customer satisfaction rely on intimate relationships with customers. Over time, these relationships build the "reputation" of the firm. A good reputation translates into better performance and creates a valuable resource that is difficult to imitate, thus providing the firm with a durable advantage (Carter & Ruefli, 2006). Companies that excel in developing close relationships with customers build long-term customer loyalty. This in turn enables such companies to achieve sustainable financial performance (Heskett & Schlesinger, 1994). Other empirical research confirms a positive relationship between customer satisfaction and future financial performance (Banker & Mashruwala, 2007; Ittner & Larcker, 1998).

Customer satisfaction in a given year results from spending and resource commitments made in the past. We argue that, in order for customer satisfaction to have a continued impact on future performance, managers must maintain resource commitments even in periods of sales declines. Thus, in our second hypothesis, we investigate whether the relationship between customer satisfaction and future performance (as measured by *Tobin's Q*) is stronger when there is greater SG&A cost stickiness. That is, we examine the moderating effect of SG&A cost stickiness in the relationship between customer satisfaction and financial performance.

H2. The positive relation between expected future performance (*Tobin's Q*) and customer satisfaction increases with SG&A cost stickiness.

Earnings persistence is a quality of earnings associated with the ability to sustain earnings performance over time. Advantages attained through customer satisfaction are persistent if the uniqueness of services or products that is valued by customers cannot be easily imitated by competitors. Competitors can respond to price moves almost immediately but it will take them much longer to replicate a firm's brand premium or build strong customer relationships. Thus, customer satisfaction will be associated with a loyal following of customers that will ensure a persistent future cash stream. However, this is only likely to occur when the firm commits to higher spending even in periods of sales downturns. If the firm lets up on its spending when sales decline, then customer loyalty can erode making room for competitors to respond. In our third hypothesis, we examine this conjecture. Specifically, we examine whether earnings persistence increases with the interaction between customer satisfaction and SG&A cost stickiness.

H3. Earnings persistence increases with the interaction between customer satisfaction and SG&A cost stickiness.

RESEARCH DESIGN

Following Weiss (2010), we estimate SG&A cost stickiness at the firm level as the difference between the rate of cost increase for recent quarters with increasing sales and the corresponding rate of cost decrease for recent quarters with decreasing sales.

$$SG\&A \ cost \ stickiness_{i,t} = \log\left(\frac{\Delta SG\&A}{\Delta SALES}\right)_{i,\tau} - \log\left(\frac{\Delta SG\&A}{\Delta SALES}\right)_{i,T} \quad \tau, T \in (t,..,t-11)$$

(1)

where τ is the most recent of the last 12 quarters with an increase in sales and T is the most recent of the last 12 quarters with a decrease in sales. $\Delta SALES_{i,t} = SALES_{i,t} - SALES_{i,t-1}$; $\Delta SG\&A_{i,t} = SG\&A_{i,t} - SG\&A_{i,t-1}$

For customer satisfaction, we use annual values of the *ACSI* from 1993 to 2019 provided by the National Quality Research Center at the University of Michigan. The Index tracks customer satisfaction for many of the largest corporations with operations in the United States across all major economic sectors. For each firm, approximately 250 interviews are conducted with the firm's current customers, using a common questionnaire that contains 17 structured questions and 8 demographic questions with a 10-point rating scale. Overall customer satisfaction (*ACSI*) is operationalized based on three survey measures using a partial least squares (PLS) methodology (Fornell, Johnson, Anderson, Cha, & Bryant, 1996). The estimated weights from PLS are used to construct *ACSI* values from 0 to 100 points which we utilize in our analysis. Across our sample, the values range from 51 to 91 with a mean of 76.9 and a median of 78.0.

We carefully match the *ACSI*'s customer satisfaction data for each firm with its financial data in the FactSet database. Our matching procedures include collecting merger and acquisition decisions from FactSet's firm reports in the main portal and cross-checking with other business media reports. We then match the customer satisfaction data (*ACSI*) before the merger date to the relevant pre-merger financial data in the FactSet database (FactSet keeps financial information for firms before and after the merger and acquisition under separate firm identification numbers). We drop *ACSI* data for government and private organizations from the sample and firms where we could not find a match in the FactSet database. Where there are more than two *ACSI* scores for the same firm due to multiple products lines for a firm, we select the product line with more *ACSI* observations over time.

We use *Tobin's Q* to measure expected firm performance (Anderson et al., 2004) because it is well-grounded in economic theory (Coles, Lemmon, & Meschke, 2012). A firm's Q value is the ratio of its market value to the current replacement cost of its assets. We approximate Q by adding the book value of debt to the market value of equity and dividing the sum by total assets. We use *ROA* as our measure of accounting performance. *ROA* is computed as annual income before tax divided by the annual average assets.

Empirical Models

In our first hypothesis, we examine whether a firm's resource-based commitment to a customer-centered strategy, as proxied by SG&A cost stickiness, leads to greater customer satisfaction in the future. We note that our theoretical development suggests that greater SG&A cost stickiness will lead to improvements or changes in customer satisfaction over time. We include customer satisfaction (*ACSI*) in period $t + 1$ as a dependent variable, while also including *ACSI* in period t as a control variable.[2] We add controls for other economic factors that affect customer satisfaction. We follow Rego, Morgan, and Fornell (2013) who relate market share to customer satisfaction. In their $ACSI_{t+1}$ equation, they include $ACSI_t$ on the right-hand side and they control for economies-of-scale effects and firm-level heterogeneity using firm size (book value of assets), SG&A expense-to-sales, advertising-to-sales, research and development (R&D)-to-sales. They also include *ROA* to control for possible effects of prior firm performance and they include market growth and industry concentration to control for differences between industries. We use similar control variables in our analysis and also include year, industry and country dummies. As the *ACSI* ranges from 0 to 100, we estimate a Tobit model rather than an ordinary least squares model to accommodate the limits on the range of the dependent variable. The empirical model is described below.

$$
\begin{aligned}
ACSI_{t+1} = {} & \beta_0 + \beta_1 SG\&A\ cost\ stickiness_t + \beta_2 ACSI_t + \beta_3 SGA\text{-}to\text{-}Sales_t \\
& + \beta_4 Ln\ Assets_t + \beta_5 Sales\ growth_t + \beta_6 ROA_t + \beta_7 Ad\text{-}to\text{-}Sales_t \\
& + \beta_8 R\&D\text{-}to\text{-}Sales_t + Year\ F.E. + Industry\ F.E. \\
& + Country\ F.E. + \omega_t
\end{aligned}
\tag{2}
$$

Sales$_t$ is net sales revenue and Ln *Assets*$_t$ is the log value of total assets. Variable definitions are provided in Table 1. We include year, industry, and country dummies and estimate versions of model (2) with and without variables representing advertising intensity (*Ad-to-Sales*$_t$) and R&D intensity (*R&D-to-Sales*$_t$).[3]

To test our second hypothesis, that expected future benefits associated with customer satisfaction increase with the degree of SG&A cost stickiness, we estimate an empirical model (OLS) that relates *Tobin's* Q_{t+1} to $ACSI_t$ and the interaction $ASCI_t * SG\&A\ cost\ stickiness_t$. We follow previous literature that relates

Table 1. Variable Definitions.

Sales	Total operating revenues
SG&A	Selling, General and Administrative expense
SGA-to-Sales	The ratio of SG&A to sales
Ln *Assets*	Log of total assets
ROA	Income before tax divided by average total assets
Sales growth	Current period sales minus prior period sales divided by the prior period sales
SG&A cost stickiness	Cost-to-sales in the most recent sales-increasing period minus cost-to-sales in the most recent sales-decreasing period (based on 12 quarters)
ACSI	American Customer Satisfaction Index for the firm
Tobin's Q	The sum of the book value of debt and the market value of equity divided by total assets
Leverage	Long-term debt to total assets
Ad-to-Sales	Advertising expense to sales
R&D-to-Sales	Research and development expense to sales
BTM	Book value of equity divided by market value of common shares

Tobin's Q as a measure of forward-looking performance to *ACSI* (Anderson et al., 2004). We include other variables that may affect *Tobin's Q*, such as Ln *Assets, Leverage, Ad-to-Sales* and *R&D-to-Sales* (Coles et al., 2012) and we include industry, country, and year dummies. *Leverage$_t$* is the ratio of long-term debt to total assets. We estimate versions of the model with and without advertising intensity (*Ad-to-Sales$_t$*) and R&D intensity (*R&D-to-Sales$_t$*). We winsorize the top and bottom 1% of all continuous variables.

$$
\begin{aligned}
\textit{Tobin's } Q_{t+1} = {} & \beta_0 + \beta_1 \textit{SG\&A cost stickiness}_t + \beta_2 \textit{ACSI}_t \\
& + \beta_3 \textit{ACSI}_t * \textit{SG\&A cost stickiness}_t + \beta_4 \textit{LnAssets}_t \\
& + \beta_5 \textit{Leverage}_t + \beta_6 \textit{Ad-to-Sales}_t + \beta_7 \textit{R\&D-to-Sales}_t \\
& + \textit{Year F.E.} + \textit{Industry F.E.} + \textit{Country F.E.} + \omega_t
\end{aligned} \tag{3}
$$

To test our third hypothesis, that earnings persistence increases with the interaction between customer satisfaction and SG&A cost stickiness, we estimate the following OLS model (see Banker, Mashruwala, & Tripathy, 2014).

$$
\begin{aligned}
\textit{ROA}_{t+1} = {} & \beta_0 + \beta_1 \textit{ROA}_t + \beta_2 \textit{ACSI}_t + \beta_3 \textit{SG\&A cost stickiness}_t \\
& + \beta_4 \textit{ACSI}_t * \textit{SG\&A cost stickiness}_t + \beta_5 \textit{ROA}_t * \textit{SG\&A cost} \\
& \textit{stickiness}_t + \beta_6 \textit{ROA}_t * \textit{ACSI}_t + \beta_7 \textit{ROA}_t * \textit{ACSI}_t * \textit{SG\&A cost} \\
& \textit{stickiness}_t + \beta_8 \textit{Ln Assets}_t + \beta_9 \textit{BTM}_t + \beta_{10} \textit{Leverage}_t \\
& + \textit{Year F.E.} + \textit{Industry F.E.} + \textit{Country F.E.} + \omega_t
\end{aligned} \tag{4}
$$

where ROA_{t+1} is return on assets in $t + 1$ and BTM_t represents the book to market ratio in period t. In this specification, the coefficient β_1 captures the persistence of earnings from period t to $t + 1$. We argue that high customer satisfaction combined with a customer-centered strategy that is committed to building and maintaining customer relationships even during sales downturns will enable a firm to report more persistent earnings. Thus, our main coefficient of interest is the coefficient on the triple-interaction term β_7.

SAMPLE AND DESCRIPTIVE STATISTICS

Our sample includes annual observations from 1994 to 2019. There are 299 separate firms with *ACSI* scores that contain financial data in FactSet during this period. Since some firms (23 firms out of 299) are rated more than once by *ACSI* for a year, based on different lines of business, we allow only one observation per firm per year by adopting the following procedure. For 15 firms, we use the *ACSI* score for the line of business that appears most frequently in the 26-year period from 1994 to 2019. For the other 8 firms (out of 23), which have equal numbers of *ACSI* observations over time for two lines of business, we average the *ACSI* score for each year when both lines of business are in the data.

The sample selection is described in Table 2. There are 4,549 *ACSI* observations for the 299 companies. The Weiss (2010) measure of firm-level cost stickiness

Table 2.   Sample Selection Procedure.

	Deleted	Cumulative Observations
Total firm-year observations for 299 *ACSI* followed companies with financial data in FactSet (1994–2019)		4,549
Missing cost stickiness measure – no sales-down in most recent 12 quarters (see Weiss, 2010)	(2,147)	2,402
SG&A expense exceeds sales (see Anderson et al., 2003)	(10)	2,392
Observations dropped due to lead-lag values	(193)	2,199

requires both sales-increase and sales-decrease quarters in the past 12 quarters (including the current quarter). Of the 4,549 observations, 2,147 observations are dropped because there is no sales-down observation in the 12-quarter period ending in the fourth quarter of the year *t*. We follow Anderson et al. (2003) and drop 10 observations where SG&A values exceed sales in a firm-year. Additional observations are dropped to accommodate lead-lag specifications and construction of variables. For estimating equation (2), we have 2,199 observations for 222 firms. We have fewer observations for estimating equations (3) and (4) due to variables needed to construct *Tobin's Q* and *BTM* (book-to-market).

Panel A of Table 3 provides descriptive statistics for the main variables. On average, *sales, SG&A expense,* and *Assets* are $44,943, $7,184, and $64,091 million, respectively, reflecting the large size of companies included in the *ACSI* index. Average *Sales growth* is 5.2% and the average *ROA* is 8.6%, showing that the *ACSI* companies perform well over time. The mean value of the *ACSI* score is 76.9 and the standard deviation is 6.3, indicating that the *ACSI* score is tightly distributed.

Panel B of Table 3 provides Spearman correlations. From a univariate perspective, the *ACSI* score is positively correlated with *SG&A expense, ROA, Tobin's Q,* and measures of advertising intensity *Ad-to-Sales* and R&D intensity *R&D-to-Sales.* Not surprisingly, *Tobin's Q* is highly correlated with *ROA* but none of the other correlations are sufficiently high to cause concerns about multicollinearity in our analysis. Except for interaction terms, the variance inflation factors are less than 10 for all variables in the estimated models.

MODEL ESTIMATION RESULTS

H1 predicts that future customer satisfaction is positively associated with SG&A cost stickiness. Table 4 presents the results of estimating a Tobit model (2) that relates $ACSI_{t+1}$ to *SG&A cost stickiness*$_t$ and $ACSI_t$. We present the results with and without *Ad-to-Sales*$_t$ and *R&D-to-Sales* because these variables are not reported by all firms (we substitute 0 values for missing values of *Ad-to-Sales*$_t$ and *R&D-to-Sales*).

The first column reports the results without *Ad-to-Sales*$_t$ and *R&D-to-Sales*$_t$. The coefficient on *SG&A cost stickiness*$_t$ is 0.0598 (*t*-statistic = 1.84) and the coefficient on *ACSI*$_t$ is 0.7399 (*t*-statistic = 27.49). The significantly positive coefficient

Table 3. Description of Sample Observations.

Panel A. Descriptive Statistics.

	Mean	Std. Dev.	25%	Median	75%	Number
Sales($mil)	44.943	68.976	7,181	18,031	50,208	2,199
SG&A($mil)	7,184	10,114	1,333	3,393	9,564	2,199
SGA-to-Sales	0.202	0.110	0.118	0.200	0.267	2,199
Ln Assets	9.879	1.598	8.864	9.812	10.872	2,199
Sales growth	0.052	0.145	-0.015	0.041	0.101	2,199
ROA	0.086	0.095	0.033	0.077	0.135	2,199
SG&A cost stickiness	-0.071	1.789	-0.978	-0.016	0.926	2,199
ACSI	76.909	6.306	74.000	78.000	81.000	2,199
Tobin's Q	1.589	1.245	0.759	1.156	2.036	2,081
Leverage	0.299	0.215	0.142	0.272	0.410	2,199
Ad-to-Sales	0.013	0.030	0.000	0.000	0.011	2,199
R&d-to-Sales	0.014	0.028	0.000	0.000	0.015	2,199
BTM	0.430	0.394	0.168	0.352	0.622	2,092

Note: See Table 1 for variable definitions.

Panel B. Spearman Correlation Matrix.

	1	2	3	4	5	6	7	8	9	10	11
1. SG&A-to-Sales	1.00										
2. Ln Assets	-0.14*	1.00									
3. Sales growth	-0.01	0.04	1.00								
4. ROA	0.01	-0.12*	0.13*	1.00							
5. SG&A cost stickiness	0.02	-0.01	-0.02	0.03	1.00						
6. ACSI	0.10*	-0.01	-0.04	0.18*	0.05	1.00					
7. Tobin's Q	0.16*	-0.36*	0.13*	0.63*	-0.01	0.14*	1.00				
8. Leverage	-0.03	-0.21*	-0.06*	0.01	-0.05	-0.09*	0.30*	1.00			
9. Ad-to-Sales	0.29*	-0.13*	0.03	0.22*	-0.03	0.18*	0.30*	0.11*	1.00		
10. R&d-to-Sales	0.29*	0.19*	0.05	-0.06*	-0.08*	0.20*	0.07*	-0.17*	0.12*	1.00	
11. BTM	-0.10*	0.34*	-0.05	-0.41*	0.05	-0.02	-0.59*	-0.35*	-0.18*	0.04	1.00

Notes: * denotes significance at the 1% level. See Table 1 for variable definitions.

Table 4. Customer Satisfaction and SG&A Cost Stickiness.

$ACSI_{t+1}$	Coefficient	Coefficient
	(t-statistic)	(t-statistic)
SG&A cost stickiness$_t$	0.0598*	0.0598*
	(1.84)	(1.85)
$ACSI_t$	0.7399***	0.7359***
	(27.49)	(26.91)
SGA-to-Sales$_t$	0.3312	0.1177
	(0.47)	(0.15)
Ln Assets$_t$	−0.0861	−0.1160*
	(−1.47)	(−1.87)
Sales growth$_t$	0.5734	0.5619
	(1.44)	(1.42)
ROA$_t$	0.7800	1.0985
	(1.12)	(1.60)
Ad-to-Sales$_t$		−4.3453**
		(−2.42)
R&D-to-Sales$_t$		10.1521***
		(2.65)
Year effects	Yes	Yes
Industry effects	Yes	Yes
Country effects	Yes	Yes
N	2,199	2,199
Pseudo R-squared	0.3168	0.3174

Notes: This table presents the results of estimating a Tobit model relating customer satisfaction (*ACSI*) to SG&A cost stickiness. See Table 1 for definitions of the variables. The *t*-statistics are based on firm-clustered standard errors (Petersen, 2009).
*, **, and *** denote significance at 0.1, 0.05, and 0.01 using two-tailed tests, respectively.

on *SG&A cost stickiness*$_t$ indicates that customer satisfaction is positively associated with *SG&A cost stickiness*, consistent with *H1*. The coefficient on *ACSI*$_t$ indicates that the *ACSI* scores are persistent over time and that the model may be interpreted as similar to a first-difference specification as opposed to a levels specification. The observed persistence of customer satisfaction is consistent with a sustained resource-based advantage derived from customer relationships.

The results in the second column, with *Ad-to-Sales*$_t$ and *R&D-to-Sales*, are similar to those reported in the first column. The coefficient on *SG&A cost stickiness*$_t$ is 0.0598 (*t*-statistic = 1.85) and the coefficient on *ACSI*$_t$ is 0.7359 (*t*-statistic = 26.91). Interestingly, the coefficient on *Ad-to-Sales*$_t$ is −4.3453 (*t*-statistic = −2.42) while the coefficient on *R&D-to-Sales*$_t$ is 10.1521 (*t*-statistic = 2.65), suggesting that spending on new product development positively impacts changes in customer satisfaction while spending on advertising does not.

Results of both estimations in Table 4 indicate that customer satisfaction improves with managers' commitment to a resource-based strategy as reflected in *SG&A cost stickiness*. We note that the modest size and significance of the *SG&A cost stickiness* variable is understandable given that the *ACSI* scores are tightly distributed and that *SG&A cost stickiness* is a broad measure based on observed differences in changes in all SG&A costs relative to up and down changes in sales

across quarters.[4] With respect to economic significance, a one standard deviation change in *SG&A cost stickiness* is associated with a 0.017 standard deviation
change in *ACSI* or a 0.11 point change in the *ACSI* score.

H2 predicts that the extent to which customer satisfaction is aligned with SG&A
resource retention is positively associated with expected future performance.
Table 5 presents the results of estimating the model in equation (3). The dependent variable is expected future performance measured by *Tobin's* Q_{t+1}, and the primary independent variables of interest are $ACSI_t$, and the interaction of $ACSI_t$
and *SG&A cost stickiness*$_t$. The coefficient on $ACSI_t$ of 0.0412 (*t*-statistic = 2.88) is
consistent with previous research that finds that expected future performance
increases with customer satisfaction (Anderson et al., 2004; Ittner & Larcker,
1998). The coefficient on the interaction term $ACSI_t*SG&A$ *cost stickiness*$_t$ of
0.0027 (*t*-statistic = 1.88) is consistent with *H2* that the positive relation between
expected future performance (*Tobin's Q*) and customer satisfaction increases with
SG&A cost stickiness.

In terms of economic significance, a one-standard-deviation change in the
ACSI score is associated with a 0.208 standard deviation change in *Tobin's Q* or a
nominal change in *Tobin's Q* of about 0.26 when there is no *SG&A cost stickiness*
(the median value of *SG&A cost stickiness* of −0.016 is close to 0). At the 75th
percentile of *SG&A cost stickiness* (value = 0.926), a one-standard-deviation in

Table 5. *Tobin's Q*, Customer Satisfaction, and SG&A Cost Stickiness.

Tobin's Q_{t+1}	Predicted Sign	Coefficient (*t*-statistic)	Coefficient (*t*-statistic)
SG&A cost stickiness$_t$	?	−0.2091*	−0.1984*
		(−1.88)	(−1.82)
$ACSI_t$	+	0.0412***	0.0404***
		(2.88)	(2.87)
$ACSI_t*SG&A$ *cost stickiness*$_t$	+	0.0027*	0.0026*
		(1.88)	(1.82)
Ln *Assets*$_t$	?	−0.1561*	−0.1734**
		(−1.78)	(−2.28)
Leverage$_t$	?	0.5561	0.4805
		(1.64)	(1.32)
Ad-to-Sales$_t$	+		2.5380
			(1.12)
R&D-to-Sales$_t$	+		−3.4888
			(−0.93)
Year effects		Yes	Yes
Industry effects		Yes	Yes
Country effects		Yes	Yes
N		2,081	2,081
R-squared		0.8250	0.8262

Notes: This table presents the result of estimating an OLS model that related *Tobin's Q* to *ACSI* and the
interaction between *ACSI* and *SG&A cost stickiness*. See Table 1 for definitions of the variables. The
t-statistics are based on firm-clustered standard errors (Petersen, 2009).
*, **, and *** denote significance at 0.1, 0.05, and 0.01 using two-tailed tests, respectively.

the *ACSI* score is associated with a 0.222 standard deviation change in *Tobin's Q* or a nominal change of about 0.28. Between the median and 75th percentile of *SG&A cost stickiness*, there is a 6.8% increase in the effect of $ACSI_t$ on *Tobin's Q_{t+1}*. There is a similar change in the magnitude of the effect of *ACSI* between the median value and the 25th percentile of *SG&A cost stickiness* (value = −0.978).

H3 predicts that alignment of a firm's customer-centered resources, represented by customer satisfaction, and resource-based commitment, reflected in *SG&A cost stickiness*, leads to more persistent earnings performance. Table 6 presents the results of estimating the model in equation (4). The dependent variable is ROA_{t+1} (ROA_{t+2} and ROA_{t+3} in alternative estimations), and the independent variables include ROA_t, *SG&A cost stickiness$_t$*, $ACSI_t$, and their interactions.

Our main variable of interest, the three-way interaction ROA_t*$ACSI_t$*SG&A cost stickiness$_t$*, is significantly positive (coefficient = 0.0053, *t*-statistic = 3.26) supporting the hypothesis that earnings persistence increases with the interaction between $ACSI_t$ and *SG&A cost stickiness*. This represents an increase in the persistence coefficient of about 0.385 for a one-unit increase in *SG&A cost stickiness*

Table 6. Earnings Persistence, Customer Satisfaction, and SG&A Cost Stickiness.

Independent variable	$ROA_{i,t+1}$	$ROA_{i,t+2}$	$ROA_{i,t+3}$
ROA_t	0.1141	−0.0643	0.1143
	(0.33)	(−0.13)	(0.32)
$ACSI_t$	0.0015**	0.0023***	0.0036***
	(2.32)	(3.07)	(4.14)
SG&A cost stickiness$_t$	0.0312*	0.0167	0.0176
	(1.75)	(0.97)	(1.09)
$ACSI_t$*SG&A cost stickiness$_t$	−0.0004*	−0.0002	−0.0002
	(−1.79)	(−1.08)	(−1.09)
ROA_t*SG&A cost stickiness$_t$	−0.4008***	−0.3448**	−0.2820*
	(−3.17)	(−2.08)	(−1.67)
ROA_t*$ACSI_t$	0.0031	0.0034	−0.0002
	(0.68)	(0.55)	(−0.05)
ROA_t*$ACSI_t$*SG&A cost stickiness$_t$	0.0053***	0.0047**	0.0036*
	(3.26)	(2.14)	(1.65)
Ln Assets$_t$	−0.0035	−0.0060	−0.0118
	(−0.58)	(−0.83)	(−1.42)
BTM_t	−0.0509***	−0.0315***	−0.0243**
	(−5.21)	(−3.63)	(−2.53)
Leverage$_t$	−0.0334	−0.0175	−0.0013
	(−1.54)	(−0.70)	(−0.05)
Year effects	Yes	Yes	Yes
Industry effects	Yes	Yes	Yes
Country effects	Yes	Yes	Yes
N	2,072	1,939	1,762
R-squared	0.7555	0.7268	0.7302

Note: This table presents the results of estimating models relating *ROA* persistence to cost stickiness and customer satisfaction. The *t*-statistics are based on firm-clustered standard errors (Petersen, 2009). *, **, and *** denote significance at 0.1, 0.05, and 0.01 using two-tailed tests, respectively.

(about equivalent to the change between the median and the 75th percentile or the median and the 25th percentile) at the median value of $ACSI_t$. This positive effect is sustained when persistence is measured with ROA_{t+2} (coefficient = 0.0047, t-statistic = 2.14) and weakly with ROA_{t+3} (coefficient = 0.0036, t-statistic = 1.65).

CROSS-SECTIONAL ANALYSIS

Our results reported above support our research hypothesis that resource commitment to customer-centered activities positively affects future customer satisfaction. However, in certain cases, the statistical significance is weak according to conventional cut-offs, suggesting that the results may be stronger in some segments of the sample than others. Therefore, in cross-sectional tests, we consider sub-groups based on (i) product-market competition, (ii) financial constraints, and (iii) bankruptcy risk.

Our principal thesis is that firms that continue to maintain and build their customer-focused relationships in downturns enjoy higher customer satisfaction over time. Achieving and sustaining high levels of customer satisfaction may be harder in more competitive industries where pricing pressure is high. Firms in less competitive markets deter competition by building and maintaining unique assets. Thus, we may find that the relationship between customer satisfaction and SG&A cost stickiness is stronger when product-market competition is less intense.

We address this empirical question by separating our overall sample into subsamples based on high competition and low competition. We use the Herfindahl-Hirschman Index (*HHI*) to proxy for product-market competition. *HHI* is computed as the sum of squared market shares of each firm competing in the three-digit SIC code in which the focal firm operates. Table 7, Panel A reports the results of estimating our model (1) separately for the two subsamples. In the high-competition subsample, the coefficient on *SG&A cost stickiness* is insignificant at the 10% level. In the low-competition subsample, the coefficient is 0.1579 (t-statistic = 3.68) and significant at a 1% level. These results support our prediction that the relationship between future customer satisfaction and cost stickiness is stronger for firms in less-competitive industries.

Next, we evaluate subsamples based on financial constraints and bankruptcy risk. The financial condition of a firm is likely to impact the resources available to create and maintain firm capabilities. Thus, we expect the relationship to be weaker when a firm faces financial constraints or has greater bankruptcy risk. We measure the financial constraints for each firm by using the Kaplan-Zingales index *KZ-Index*. The *KZ-Index* measures the difficulty in financing a firm's ongoing operations. We calculate the *KZ-Index* using liquidity, leverage, dividends, and *Tobin-Q* information obtained from the FactSet database.[5] We separate our full sample into two subsamples using the median value of the *KZ-Index*: firms facing more financial constraints and those facing fewer financial constraints. Panel B of Table 7 reports the results. For the financially constrained firms, the coefficient on *SG&A cost stickiness* is not significant. However, for the subsample of firms that face fewer financial constraints, the coefficient is 0.0931 (t-statistic = 2.41)

Table 7. Sub-Samples: Customer Satisfaction and SG&A Cost Stickiness.

Panel A. Competition (HHI) Sub-samples.

$ACSI_{t+1}$	High Competition	Low Competition
SG&A cost stickiness$_t$	−0.0072	0.1579***
	(−0.16)	(3.68)
Controls	Yes	Yes
Year effects	Yes	Yes
Industry effects	Yes	Yes
Country effects	Yes	Yes
N	1,095	1,104
Pseudo R-squared	0.3295	0.3108

Panel B. Financial Constraints Sub-samples.

$ACSI_{t+1}$	High Constraints	Low Constraints
SG&A cost stickiness$_t$	−0.0229	0.0931**
	(−0.43)	(2.41)
Controls	Yes	Yes
Year effects	Yes	Yes
Industry effects	Yes	Yes
Country effects	Yes	Yes
N	874	888
Pseudo R-squared	0.3195	0.3164

Panel C. Bankruptcy Risk (Altman Z-Score) Sub-samples.

$ACSI_{t+1}$	High Risk	Low Risk
SG&A cost stickiness$_t$	−0.0168	0.0801**
	(−0.23)	(2.23)
Controls	Yes	Yes
Year effects	Yes	Yes
Industry effects	Yes	Yes
Country effect	Yes	Yes
N	487	1,712
Pseudo R-squared	0.3391	0.3109

Notes: This table presents the results of estimating a Tobit model relating customer satisfaction (*ACSI*) to SG&A cost stickiness. See Table 1 for definitions of the variables. The *t*-statistics are based on firm-clustered standard errors (Petersen, 2009). We control for *SGA-to-Sales*, Ln *Assets*, *Sales growth*, *ROA*, *Ad-to-Sales*, and *R&D-to-Sales*.
*, **, and *** denote significance at 0.1, 0.05, and 0.01 using two-tailed tests, respectively.

and significant at a 5% level. Thus, once again we find that our results are stronger for a cross-section of firms.

Similarly, we use the *Altman-Z* score to separate our full sample into firms that have high bankruptcy risk and those that have low bankruptcy risk. We obtain our *Altman-Z* score from the FactSet database. We assume that firms that have an *Altman-Z* score less than 1.81 have a higher risk of bankruptcy, and firms whose *Altman-Z* score is higher than 1.81 have a lower risk of bankruptcy. We expect to find the relationship between SG&A cost stickiness and next-period customer satisfaction is stronger for firms with lower bankruptcy risk. Panel C of Table 7 reports the results. For higher bankruptcy risk firms, the coefficient is not significant. For lower bankruptcy risk firms, the coefficient is 0.0801 (t-statistic = 2.23) and significant at the 5% level. We note that in this case the cut-off is not arbitrary but based on convention, meaning that the high bankruptcy risk subgroup only includes 487 firms whereas the low bankruptcy risk subgroup includes 1,712 firms. Thus, the removal of less than a quarter of the full sample improves the statistical significance of the results.

ADDRESSING ENDOGENEITY

To ensure the robustness of our results and control for self-selection and omitted variable bias, we conduct tests using Heckman's two-stage regression procedure and propensity score matching (PSM). Following the Heckman procedure, we first calculate the inverse mills ratio IMR to correct the bias resulting from omitted variables. Table 8 reports the results of the second stage regression.

Table 8. Heckman Procedure: Customer Satisfaction and SG&A Cost Stickiness.

	Coefficient	Coefficient
$ACSI_{t+1}$	(t-statistic)	(t-statistic)
SG&A cost stickiness$_t$	0.0605*	0.0611*
	(1.95)	(1.96)
$ACSI_t$	0.7295***	0.7261***
	(29.13)	(28.64)
SGA-to-Sales$_t$	0.8986	0.6946
	(1.19)	(0.81)
Ln Assets$_t$	−0.1117*	−0.1354**
	(−1.93)	(−2.24)
Sales growth$_t$	0.9683**	0.9636**
	(2.57)	(2.58)
ROA$_t$	0.1488	0.4935
	(0.22)	(0.73)
Ad-to-Sales$_t$		−4.1317 **
		(−2.22)
R&D-to-Sales$_t$		9.2216**
		(2.28)
IMR	0.6175	0.2851
	(0.76)	(0.36)
Year effects	Yes	Yes
Industry effects	Yes	Yes
Country effects	Yes	Yes
N	2,092	2,092
Pseudo R-squared	0.3069	0.3074

Note: This table presents the results of estimating a Tobit model relating customer satisfaction (*ACSI*) to *SG&A cost stickiness*. See Table 1 for definitions of the variables. The *t*-statistics are based on firm-clustered standard errors (Petersen, 2009). *IMR* is the inverse mills ratio.
*, **, and *** denote significance at 0.1, 0.05, and 0.01 using two-tailed tests, respectively.

As in model (2), the dependent variable is customer satisfaction (*ACSI*) in period $t + 1$, and the independent variable of interest is *SG&A cost stickiness* in t. The coefficient on *SG&A cost stickiness* is 0.0611 (*t*-statistic = 1.96), significant at a 10% level. We find an insignificant coefficient for the *IMR* variable, and our main results remain consistent with those in Table 4, implying that we do not have a serious self-selection bias issue or omitted variable concern.

In a separate test, we use PSM to mitigate potential self-selection bias. We treat observations as sticky if our measure of cost stickiness is less than 0, and observations as not sticky if cost stickiness is 0 or greater. We match sticky with non-sticky observations using asset intensity, revenue decrease, and country GDP growth rate. We use a caliper of 0.0001 with neighbor 1 to find the best (closest) match for each sticky observation based on propensity scores. The results of estimating model 2 with the matched sample are presented in Table 9. The coefficient on cost stickiness is 0.0909 (*t*-statistic = 2.10), significant at the 5% level. This result is statistically stronger than the result presented in Table 4.

Table 9. Propensity Score Matched Sample: Customer Satisfaction and SG&A Cost Stickiness.

$ACSI_{t+1}$	Coefficient (*t*-statistic)	Coefficient (*t*-statistic)
SG&A cost stickiness$_t$	0.0863**	0.0910**
	(2.00)	(2.10)
ACSI$_t$	0.7527***	0.7479***
	(24.19)	(23.55)
SGA-to-Sales$_t$	−0.1489	−0.5157
	(−0.14)	(−0.42)
Ln *Assets*$_t$	−0.0834	−0.1269
	(−1.11)	(−1.56)
Sales growth$_t$	0.5401	0.5477
	(1.00)	(1.01)
ROA$_t$	0.5377	0.8320
	(0.60)	(0.93)
Ad-to-Sales$_t$		−3.9264*
		(−1.71)
R&D-to-Sales$_t$		13.1964**
		(2.55)
Year effects	Yes	Yes
Industry effects	Yes	Yes
Country effects	Yes	Yes
N	1,066	1,066
Pseudo *R*-squared	0.3207	0.3215

Note: This table presents the results of estimating a Tobit model relating customer satisfaction (*ACSI*) to *SG&A cost stickiness*. See Table 1 for definitions of the variables. The *t*-statistics are based on firm-clustered standard errors (Petersen, 2009).
*, **, and *** denote significance at 0.1, 0.05, and 0.01 using two-tailed tests, respectively.

CONCLUSION

The resource-based theory considers how investments in resources that are not easily imitated provide a competitive advantage. The marketing literature builds on resource-based theory to examine how companies achieve competitive advantage through investments in customer-centered resources. The accounting literature considers how deliberate resource allocation decisions affect cost behavior. Our study merges these fields by investigating whether a firm's resource-based commitment to a customer-centered strategy enables a firm to build and maintain closer relationships with their customers resulting in higher customer satisfaction. Our study represents an initial examination of the effects of resource retention in sales-decline periods on firm performance from a resource-based perspective.

With customer satisfaction representing a resource-based competitive advantage, we use the stickiness of SG&A costs to measure the tendency of firms to retain customer-centered resources in decline periods. We recognize that SG&A cost stickiness is a broad measure because SG&A expenditures are made to support a variety of activities including those that are specifically targeted to enhancing the customer experience. Nonetheless, we do find evidence supporting our prediction that customer satisfaction is associated with the stickiness of SG&A costs, based on the premise that companies must retain specialized resources that have been acquired and developed to support a resource-based competitive advantage.

While many studies investigate predictions about factors that influence cost stickiness, few studies examine the effects of cost stickiness on firm performance. A primary prediction in the accounting literature is that managers retain resources in sales-down periods to avoid adjustment costs of retrenching and then reacquiring resources when sales pick up in the future. Our analysis suggests that managers also consider the need to retain specialized resources that have been acquired and developed to provide a resource-based advantage. If such resources could be bought and sold easily in the market, they would not provide such an advantage. Our analysis supports the predictions that the competitive advantage represented by customer satisfaction has a stronger influence on expected future performance when SG&A cost stickiness is higher, and the prediction that sustained performance measured by the persistence of earnings is greater when cost stickiness is higher.

Future research may build on these ideas and improve on this analysis by examining costs that are more specifically related to a resource-based advantage. Moreover, we have noted that some of our empirical results are weak in terms of statistical significance. This could potentially result from limited power of our tests to detect a relationship, either due to relatively small sample size or due to small variation in our key variables over time. We provide evidence that the results are stronger in certain segments of the data, including a lower competition segment and segments with fewer financial constraints. We encourage future researchers to examine this research question in other settings to substantiate and validate our findings.

NOTES

1. At the time of this writing, Barney (1991) has 91,828 Google citations.
2. Thus, we capture changes in customer satisfaction without the restrictive assumption in a changes specification that would artificially set the coefficient on customer satisfaction in period t to equal one. Since we include the lagged value of $ACSI$ as a control variable, we do not include firm fixed effects when estimating this model. Nonetheless, using lagged values of $ACSI$ as a control variable enables us to control for time-invariant firm characteristics that drive customer satisfaction.
3. We substitute 0 for missing values of advertising or R&D spending.
4. A finer analysis would isolate specific costs associated with customer relations and other resources dedicated to improving the customer experience.
5. KZ-$Index$ is calculated as follows: $-1.001909*$(cash ratio) $+ 3.139193*$(debt ratio) $-39.36780*$(dividend ratio) $- 1.314759*$(liquidity ratio) $+ 0.2826389*$($Tobin's\ Q$).

ACKNOWLEDGMENTS

The authors gratefully acknowledge helpful comments and suggestions by Jim Cannon, Dan Weiss, two anonymous reviewers, discussants and conference participants at the 2016 European Accounting Association Annual Congress, the 2016 Canadian Academic Accounting Association Annual Conference, and the 2018 American Accounting Association Management Accounting Section Midyear Meeting.

REFERENCES

Anderson, M. C., Banker, R. D., & Janakiraman, S. N. (2003). Are selling, general, and administrative costs "sticky"? *Journal of Accounting Research, 41*(1), 47–63.

Anderson, E. W., & Fornell, C. (2000). The customer satisfaction index as a leading indicator. In A. S. Rust & R. L. Oliver (Eds.), *Handbook of service marketing and management* (pp. 255–267). London: Sage Publications.

Anderson, E. W., Fornell, C., & Lehmann, D. R. (1994). Customer satisfaction, market share, and profitability: Findings from Sweden. *Journal of Marketing, 58*(3), 53–66.

Anderson, E. W., Fornell, C., & Mazvancheryl, S. K. (2004). Customer satisfaction and shareholder value. *Journal of Marketing, 68*(4), 172–185.

Armstrong, G., & Shimitzu, K. (2007). A review of approaches to empirical research on the resource-based view of the firm. *Journal of Management, 33*(6), 959–986.

Ballas, A., Naoum, V. C., & Vlismas, O. (2022). The effect of strategy on the asymmetric cost behavior of SG&A expenses. *European Accounting Review, 31*(2), 409–447.

Banker, R. D., & Byzalov, D. (2014). Asymmetric cost behavior. *Journal of Management Accounting Research, 26*(2), 43–79.

Banker, R. D., Byzalov, D., & Chen, L. T. (2013). Employment protection legislation, adjustment costs and cross-country differences in cost behavior. *Journal of Accounting and Economics, 55*(1), 111–127.

Banker, R. D., Byzalov, D., Ciftci, M., & Mashruwala, R. (2014). The moderating effect of prior sales changes on asymmetric cost behavior. *Journal of Management Accounting Research, 26*(2), 221–242.

Banker, R. D., Flasher, R., & Zhang, D. (2014, August). *Strategic positioning and asymmetric cost behavior*. Working paper, Temple University.

Banker, R. D., & Mashruwala, R. (2007). The moderating role of competition in the relationship between nonfinancial measures and future financial performance. *Contemporary Accounting Research, 24*(3), 763–793.

Banker, R. D., Mashruwala, R., & Tripathy, A. (2014). Does a differentiation strategy lead to more sustainable financial performance than a cost leadership strategy? *Management Decision, 52*(5), 872–896.

Barney, J. (1991). Firm resources and sustained competitive advantage. *Journal of Management, 17*(1), 99–120.

Barney, J. (2014). How marketing scholars might help address issues in resource-based theory. *Journal of the Academy of Marketing Science, 42*(1), 24–26.

Barney, J., Ketchen, D., & Wright, M. (2011). The future of resource-based theory: Revitalization or decline? *Journal of Management, 37*(5), 1299–1315.

Capraro, A., & Srivastava, R. (1997). Has the influence of financial performance on reputation measures been overstated? *Corporate Reputation Review, 1*(1), 86–93.

Carter, S. M., & Ruefli, T. W. (2006). Intra-industry reputation dynamics under a resource-based framework: Assessing the durability factor.*Corporate Reputation Review, 9*(1)

Castanias, R., & Helfat, C. (1991). Managerial resources and rents. *Journal of Management, 17*(1), 155–171.

Chen, C. X., Lu, H., & Sougiannis, T. (2012). The agency problem, corporate governance, and the asymmetrical behavior of selling, general, and administrative costs. *Contemporary Accounting Research, 29*(1), 252–282.

Coles, J. L., Lemmon, M. L., & Meschke, J. F. (2012). Structural models and endogeneity in corporate finance: The link between managerial ownership and corporate performance. *Journal of Financial Economics, 103*(1), 149–168.

Deleersnyder, B., Dekimpe, M. G., Steenkamp, J., & Leeflang, P. (2009). The role of national culture in advertising's sensitivity to business cycles: An investigation across continents. *Journal of Marketing Research, 46*(5), 623–636.

Dutta, S., Narasimhan, O., & Rajiv, S. (1999). Success in high-technology markets: Is marketing capability critical? *Marketing Science, 18*(4), 547–568.

Enache, L., & Srivastava, A. (2018). Should intangibles be separately reported or comingled with operating expenses? *Management Science, 64*(7), 3446–3468.

Fahey, L. (1999). *Competitors: Outwitting, outmaneuvering, and outperforming.* New York: Wiley.

Fornell, C., Johnson, M. D., Anderson, E. W., Cha, J., & Bryant, B. E. (1996). The American customer satisfaction index: Nature, purpose, and findings. *Journal of Marketing, 60*(4), 7–18.

Golden, J., Mashruwala, R., & Pevzner, M. (2020). Labor adjustment costs and asymmetric cost behavior: An extension. *Management Accounting Research, 46*, 100647.

Heskett, J. L. & Schlesinger, L. A. (1994). Putting the service profit chain to work. *Harvard Business Review, 72*(2), 164–174.

Ittner, C. D., & Larcker, D. F. (1998). Are nonfinancial measures leading indicators of financial performance? An analysis of customer satisfaction .*Journal of Accounting Research, 36*(1), 1–35.

Kaplan, R. S., & Norton, D. P. (1996). Linking the balanced scorecard to strategy. *California Management Review, 39*(1), 53–79.

Lamey, L., Deleersnyder, B., Dekimpe, M. G., & Steenkamp, J. (2007). How business cycles contribute to private-label success: Evidence from the United States and Europe. *Journal of Marketing, 71*(1), 1–15.

Liu, X., Liu, X., & Reid, C. D. (2019). Stakeholder orientations and cost management. *Contemporary Accounting Research, 36*(1), 486–512.

Lockett, A., & Thompson, S. (2001). The resource-based view and economics. *Journal of Management, 27*(6), 723–754.

Lusch, R., & Harvey, M. (1994). Opinion: The case for an off-balance sheet controller. *Sloan Management Review, 35*(winter), 101–105.

Miles, R. E., Snow, C. C., Meyer, A. D., & Coleman, H. J. Jr. (1978). Organizational strategy, structure, and process. *Academy of Management Review, 3*(3), 546–562.

Miller, D. (1986). Configurations of strategy and structure: Towards a synthesis. *Strategic Management Journal, 7*(3), 233–249.

Moorman, C., & Slotegraaf, R. (1999). The contingency value of complementary capabilities in product development. *Journal of Marketing Research, 36*(2), 239–257.

Noreen, E., & Soderstrom, N. (1997). The accuracy of proportional cost models: Evidence from hospital service departments. *Review of Accounting Studies, 2*(1), 89–114.

Petersen, M. A. (2009). Estimating standard errors in finance panel data sets: Comparing approaches. *Review of Financial Studies*, *22*(1), 435–480.

Porter, M. E. (1980). *Competitive strategy: Techniques for analyzing industries and competitors*. New York: Free Press.

Ramaswami, S. N., Srivastava, R. K., & Bhargava, M. (2009). Market-based capabilities and financial performance of firms: Insights into marketing's contribution to firm value. *Journal of the Academy of Marketing Science*, *37*(2), 97–116.

Rego, L. L., Morgan, N. A., & Fornell, C. (2013). Reexamining the market share–customer satisfaction relationship. *Journal of Marketing*, *77*(5), 1–20.

Slotegraaf, R., & Dickson, P. (2004). The paradox of a marketing planning capability. *Journal of Academy of Marketing Science*, *32*(4), 371–385.

Srivastava, R. K., Fahey, L., & Christensen, H. K. (2001). The resource-based view and marketing: The role of market-based assets in gaining competitive advantage. *Journal of Management*, *27*(6), 777–802.

Srivastava, R. K., Shervani, T. A., & Fahey, L. (1998). Market-based assets and shareholder value: A framework for analysis .*The Journal of Marketing*, *62*(1), 2–18.

Tellis, G. J., & Tellis, K. (2009). Research on advertising in a recession. *Journal of Advertising Research*, *49*, 304–327.

Treacy, M., & Wiersema, F. (1993) Customer intimacy and other value disciplines. *Harvard Business Review*, *71*(1), 84–93.

Venieris, G., Naoum, V. C., & Vlismas, O. (2015). Organization capital and sticky behavior of selling, general and administrative expenses. *Management Accounting Research*, *26*, 54–82.

Vorhiers, D., & Morgan, N. (2005). Benchmarking marketing capabilities for sustainable competitive advantage. *Journal of Marketing*, *69*(1), 80–94

Weiss, D. (2010). Cost behavior and analysts earnings forecasts.*The Accounting Review*, *85*(4), 1441–1471.

DOES RELATIVE PERFORMANCE INFORMATION IMPROVE PERFORMANCE IN REMOTE WORK ARRANGEMENTS?

Abbie L. Daly and Dimitri Yatsenko

ABSTRACT

Firms use Relative Performance Information (RPI) to improve employee performance; however, differences in employees' remote work environments call into question whether RPI improves performance in remote work arrangements. By manipulating RPI provision across sections, the authors examine whether RPI improves performance in remote work arrangements using a field experiment in introductory accounting courses taught during the COVID-19 pandemic. The authors found that RPI improves performance in a remote work setting, as students receiving RPI achieved higher exam scores and increased their exam scores to a greater extent than students who did not receive RPI. The authors also found that lower performers improved performance more than higher performers in response to RPI, and the effect of RPI was more pronounced in those closest to meaningful thresholds. These results inform practice on the expected benefits of implementing RPI in a remote work setting.

Keywords: COVID-19 pandemic; relative performance information; remote work; employee performance; social comparison theory; accounting students

Advances in Management Accounting, Volume 35, 181–201
Copyright © 2023 by Emerald Publishing Limited
All rights of reproduction in any form reserved
ISSN: 1474-7871/doi:10.1108/S1474-787120230000035008

INTRODUCTION

RPI improves employee performance by motivating increased effort in traditional work environments, including in settings in which RPI is not used for compensation purposes (e.g., Anderson, Crowell, Sponsel, Clarke, & Brence, 1983; Hannan, Krishnan, & Newman, 2008; Hannan, McPhee, Newman, & Tafkov, 2013; Kramer, Maas, & Rinsum, 2016; Nordstrom, Lorenzi, & Hall, 1991; Tafkov, 2013; Yatsenko, 2022). However, increasingly, modern professional and administrative work is performed remotely. The COVID-19 pandemic has further necessitated a large swath of the workforce to work remotely, after which many employees and firms expect remote work to continue after the pandemic (Global Workplace Analytics, 2021; Harvard Business School Online, 2021). Instead of responding to RPI with increased effort, remote employees can blame unflattering relative performance on differences in access to technology, and home living arrangements, such as space availability, family obligations, access to additional furniture or equipment, etc. RPI in this setting could not only fail to motivate employees but could even demotivate the lower performers, causing overall employee performance to decline (Berger, Klassen, Libby, & Webb, 2013; Hannan et al., 2008). Due to the increased prevalence of remote work arrangements and doubts about the impact of RPI in such arrangements, we investigate whether RPI improves performance in remote work arrangements.

In typical remote work arrangements, employees work remotely from other offices, their homes, or other locations, such as a coffee shop, instead of commuting to the local office. Even before the pandemic, the prevalence of employees working remotely, including telecommuting from home, had increased over the last decade and was expected to accelerate further. Hooks and Higgs (2002) identified working from home as an established phenomenon for professional services firm employees, with approximately 20% reporting working from home during typical business hours at least once per week. The Bureau of Labor Statistics (2020) reports that 37% of employees in management, business, and financial operations occupations and 33% of those in professional and related occupations did some or all of their work from home in 2019. COVID-19 has accelerated the remote work trend, with 21% to 26% of *all* employed persons working from home during 2020, as the Bureau of Labor Statistics (2021) reported.

Remote work is a crucial topic for the accounting profession, where employee turnover has been a persistent problem (Larkin, 1995). In the professional accounting workforce, Almer and Kaplan (2002) found that flexible work arrangements, including remote work arrangements, lead to higher job satisfaction and lower turnover intentions for CPAs. In addition, Pasewark and Viator (2006) found that much of this turnover is among individuals trying to satisfy the demands of both work and family, for whom flexible work arrangements effectively reduce this turnover. Throughout the pandemic, remote work was crucial for individuals balancing work and childcare responsibilities. Thus, accounting firms may benefit from lessons learned during the pandemic regarding new ways to embrace remote work arrangements.

Prior research generally shows a positive effect of RPI on performance in collocated workers and an increase in performance in workers switching to remote work. Based on these studies, information about peers' performance gained from RPI may increase workers' awareness of the achievable performance levels in such arrangements. This information would then elicit increased effort from those working remotely that may have otherwise blamed the remote work arrangement for their performance, but through RPI, learn that others can overcome any obstacles to working remotely.

However, there is reason to question whether RPI will improve performance in remote work arrangements. According to the social comparison theory, which explains the positive effect of RPI on performance, workers should complete a similar task in a similar environment and compare themselves to similar peers (Goethals & Darley, 1977; Harkins & Jackson, 1985; Wheeler, Koestner, & Driver, 1982; Zanna, Goethals, & Hill, 1975). Notably, the environment varies in remote work arrangements because of workers' differences in access to technology, home life, and other related aspects of remote work. Workers may use these environmental differences to explain unflattering relative performance. As social comparisons threaten self-esteem, workers are likely to attribute unflattering relative performance to factors other than themselves. Remote work provides more potential factors to explain differences in performance. Because of this attribution, workers may not engage in the effort-increasing competitive behavior that results in the increased performance documented in prior research (Hannan et al., 2008, 2013; Kramer et al., 2016; Nordstrom et al., 1991; Tafkov, 2013; Yatsenko, 2022). Prior research suggests that providing RPI in this setting could cause weaker performers to give up, causing employee performance to decline (Berger et al., 2013; Hannan et al., 2008). Thus, it is an empirical question whether RPI improves performance in remote work arrangements.

We conducted a field experiment using students to investigate whether RPI improves performance in a remote work arrangement brought about by the COVID-19 pandemic. Specifically, we evaluate performance in synchronous online introductory accounting courses during the pandemic, in which instructors either refrained from making any relative comparisons in their classes or posted each student's ordinal rank after each exam.[1] The universal nature of the remote work arrangement is a strength of our design as we avoided the self-selection into remote work arrangement inherent in many previous studies (e.g., Bloom, Liang, Roberts, & Ying, 2015; Gajendran & Harrison, 2007). In previous studies, management selected workers to work remotely or workers who volunteered to work remotely: both approaches limit the ability to draw inferences to the general workforce. During the pandemic, many workers that would not have otherwise been selected or volunteered for remote work arrangements were thrust into them. Therefore, this setting allowed us to measure the performance of individuals working remotely without the selection effect inherent in prior studies.

This setting also permitted us to investigate additional research questions regarding the effect of RPI on performance. First, our setting permitted us to investigate the effect of RPI on the performance of workers at different performance levels. While some studies found that the highest and lowest performers respond the most to RPI (e.g., Azmat & Iriberri, 2010), other studies found that top performers become complacent while the weakest performers tend to give up (e.g., Berger et al., 2013; Hannan et al., 2008). In our setting, where the cost of giving up is high, we predict that low performers will benefit more from RPI than high performers.

Our setting also enabled us to investigate whether RPI affects workers differently based on how close they are to a meaningful threshold. Prior research showed that competitiveness increases in proximity to an objective performance standard (e.g., Garcia, Tor, & Gonzalez, 2006; Garcia, Tor, & Schiff, 2013; Vandegrift & Holaday, 2012). In our setting, letter grade cutoffs provide such objective standards. We predict that the positive effect of RPI on performance will increase with proximity to these objective standards.

We found that RPI increases performance in a remote work setting. Specifically, students who received RPI outperformed students who did not receive RPI, and students who received RPI improved their scores to a greater degree than students who did not receive RPI. We also found that lower performers benefited more from RPI than higher performers, and students closer to a meaningful threshold benefited more from RPI than students further from a meaningful threshold. Overall, we found a strong positive effect of RPI on remote workers, with the most substantial effect on lower performers, alleviating a concern of lower performers giving up in response to RPI. Our results also suggest that introducing meaningful thresholds in the presentation of RPI provides workers with a next objective standard to strive toward.

This study contributes to the accounting literature on the effect of RPI on performance (e.g., Anderson et al., 1983; Hannan et al., 2008, 2013; Kramer et al., 2016; Murthy & Schafer, 2011; Nordstrom et al., 1991; Tafkov, 2013; Yatsenko, 2022). First, we contribute beyond these studies by considering whether RPI improves performance in remote work arrangements. It is crucial to investigate the effectiveness of RPI for such arrangements because remote work is growing in prevalence, and workers may not engage in effort-increasing competitive behavior in this setting. Despite potential environmental differences in remote work arrangements, RPI still improves performance. Notably, by using a setting that permits measuring the performance of individuals working remotely without selection effects, this study also contributes to the literature on remote work arrangements (e.g., Apgar, 1998; Bailey & Kurland, 2002; Bloom et al., 2015; Gajendran & Harrison, 2007; Gajendran, Harrison, & Delaney-Klinger, 2015; McCloskey & Igbaria, 2003; Pinsonneault & Boisvert, 2001).

Second, we contribute to the mixed results of prior studies investigating the effect of RPI on performance for workers at different performance levels. In our setting, the cost of giving up is high, as repeating a class carries a significant monetary penalty. We document more substantial effects of RPI on lower performers in remote work arrangements and do not document complacency in high performers. Using a setting where the cost of giving up is high, we provide insight into one reason for the mixed results of prior studies.

Lastly, we contribute to the accounting literature on the effect of RPI on performance by investigating the use of meaningful thresholds in the presentation of RPI. Through semi-structured interviews, Carroll and Marginson (2021) found that using RPI with meaningful thresholds affects managers' behavioral responses, such as gaming practices. In our setting, where letter grade cutoffs provide meaningful thresholds in the presentation of RPI, we investigate the effect of such thresholds on performance. We found RPI to be increasingly influential with the nearness of workers' performance to an objective standard. Specifically, workers who missed an objective standard by a small margin improved their performance more in response to RPI than workers who missed the performance standard by a larger margin.

These results inform practice on the expected benefits of implementing a RPI feedback system for remote work arrangements. Based on the findings, RPI is effective in remote work arrangements, even when workers face significant differences in environmental factors. Practitioners may also appreciate the positive effects of RPI on lower performers and no evidence of complacency in high performers. In contexts with a binary outcome (e.g., meeting a deadline, landing a client), the finding that workers closest to the next meaningful threshold are most affected by RPI may be of interest, as the increased effort that results in the desired outcome is more practically imperative than the increased effort that may not be sufficient to reach the desired outcome.

LITERATURE REVIEW AND HYPOTHESES DEVELOPMENT

We examine the impact of RPI, information that is not used for compensation, in a remote work setting. The literature on remote work arrangements, where workers were either selected by management or volunteered to work remotely, has shown a positive relation between such arrangements and performance (see Allen, Golden, & Shockley, 2015 for a review). Gajendran and Harrison (2007) conducted a meta-analysis and found that telecommuting is positively associated with supervisor-rated or objectively measured job performance. Furthermore, Gajendran et al. (2015) found that supervisors evaluated telecommuters higher than non-telecommuters. Bloom et al. (2015) found that employees who volunteered to work from home and then were permitted to do so increased their objectively measured performance compared to those who were not permitted to work from home. These results are often attributed to the improved productivity that comes with fewer disruptions when doing tasks remotely (Bailey & Kurland, 2002; McCloskey & Igbaria, 2003; Pinsonneault & Boisvert, 2001) and through increased work hours made possible by time saved from not commuting (Apgar, 1998).

The literature on RPI has shown that RPI improves performance in traditional work settings (Anderson et al., 1983; Hannan et al., 2008, 2013; Kramer et al., 2016; Murthy & Schafer, 2011; Nordstrom et al., 1991; Tafkov, 2013; Yatsenko, 2022). Notably, research has shown the positive effects of RPI even when RPI is not used for compensation.[2] These studies found that RPI improves performance through social comparison theory, whereby RPI highlights incorrect decisions, increases awareness about attainable performance levels, and increases cognitive activity (Festinger, 1954). Recipients react to this social comparison information by increasing their competitive behavior (Hannan et al., 2008, 2013, 2019;

Kramer et al., 2016; Tafkov, 2013; Yatsenko, 2022). This increased competitive behavior manifests in increased effort, as individuals set out to demonstrate that they are just as capable as their peers if only they expend as much effort as their peers, leading to increased performance.

Because performance is a function of ability and effort, a difference in ability, effort, or both can explain a difference in performance between oneself and one's peers. When workers receive RPI, attribution theory suggests they are motivated to attribute higher peer performance to higher peer effort. This self-enhancing effort attribution preserves the workers' self-view of possessing comparable or superior ability and results in the competitive behavior predicted by social comparison theory and documented in prior research (Murthy & Schafer, 2011; Tafkov, 2013; Yatsenko, 2022). When considering remote work arrangements, RPI provides those working remotely with information about their peers' performance, increasing their awareness of the possible performance levels for such arrangements. This information may elicit increased effort from those working remotely that may have otherwise blamed the remote work arrangement for their performance, but through RPI, learn that others have overcome any obstacles to remote work. Thus, we predict RPI will positively affect performance in remote settings, consistent with previously documented positive effects in face-to-face settings.

However, there is a reason to question whether RPI will improve performance in remote work arrangements due to differences between remote and traditional work settings. An assumption of the Social Comparison Theory, which explains the performance-enhancing effects of RPI, is that workers complete a similar task in a similar environment. The environment varies in remote work arrangements because of workers' differences in access to technology, home life, and other environmental factors. Attribution theory suggests that workers exhibiting low relative performance will be more likely to attribute their performance to these environmental differences. In contrast, workers exhibiting high relative performance will be more likely to attribute their high relative performance to their effort or abilities (Miller & Ross, 1975; Zuckerman, 1979). Individuals prefer comparing their performance to peers similar on related attributes (Goethals & Darley, 1977; Seta, 1982; Wheeler et al., 1982; Zanna et al., 1975). For example, Zanna et al. (1975) found that participants prefer to compare their performance to that of a group similar to themselves on attributes participants believed to be related to the underlying ability. Similarly, Wheeler et al. (1982) found that participants who ranked 6th out of 9 could feel better about their rank by comparing themselves only to those participants who practiced the same amount as they did.

Thus, prior research suggests that individuals attempt to control for all determinants of performance when comparing themselves to peers. They may also attempt to control for differences in the work environment by attributing any unfavorable comparisons to those differences. By attributing their low relative performance to environmental factors, these workers may not engage in the effort-increasing competitive behavior predicted by social comparison theory, precluding performance increases. These possible differences in the environment may provide more avenues to attribute differences in performance away from ability, which creates tension in extending prior research results to a remote setting.

However, consistent with prior research, we predict a positive effect of RPI on performance in a remote setting.

H1. **RPI will positively affect performance in remote work arrangements.**

Next, we examine whether the effect of RPI on performance differs by performance level. Prior studies investigating the effect of RPI on performance for workers at different performance levels report mixed results. When studying the effect of RPI on performance for high school students, Azmat and Iriberri (2010) found that students at the tails of the distribution (i.e., the highest and lowest performers) respond the most to RPI. However, prior research has also shown that in repeated contests, top performers become complacent, while the weakest performers tend to give up, especially if there is an explicit option to do so (Berger et al., 2013; Hannan et al., 2008; Martin, Thomas, & Yatsenko, 2022). These findings suggest that RPI may affect higher and lower performers differently. RPI may exacerbate the complacency of high performers by providing relative information confirming their favorable relative standing in the peer group, thus, demotivating further effort, and can lead low performers to give up by highlighting the gap between them and their peers.

While prior experimental research found evidence of a demotivating effect of RPI on the weaker performers, potentially leading to giving up or reducing effort, we argue that in settings where giving up is costly, weaker performers will react to RPI by increasing effort. In work settings where ceasing effort can lead to disciplinary measures, including termination, the cost of ceasing effort is very high. Thus, an initial reaction to poor relative performance may be increased effort, leading to higher performance, especially because low performers have more room to increase performance than high performers. Thus, for a setting where the cost of giving up is high, we predict that low performers will benefit more from RPI than high performers.

H2. **Low performers will benefit more from RPI than high performers.**

Next, we investigate whether RPI affects workers differently based on how close workers are to an objective performance standard or a meaningful threshold, which brings the desired reward. Festinger (1954) posits that individuals have a "unidirectional drive upward" when comparing abilities. Research supporting this idea has shown that individuals engage in upward comparisons when trying to improve their performance (e.g., Friend & Gilbert, 1973; Suls & Tesch, 1978; Wheeler & Koestnerj, 1984). Prior research has also shown that competitiveness increases in proximity to a standard, whether the number one ranking or another meaningful threshold, such as a cutoff point on a scale (Garcia et al., 2006, 2013; Vandegrift & Holaday, 2012). These studies found that the unidirectional drive upward increases with the proximity to a standard, suggesting that workers will be more competitive as they approach the next performance standard.

Regarding RPI, Carroll and Marginson (2021) found that using meaningful thresholds in the presentation of RPI affects managers' behavioral responses, such as gaming practices. These results suggest that using meaningful thresholds in the presentation of RPI creates multiple different comparison groups for managers at different performance levels. Furthermore, based on the premise that when the winner cohort is small, individuals perceive low pressure for social comparison, Knauer, Sommer, and Wohrmann (2017) found that firms can increase employee effort (and performance) by increasing the proportion of winners. Meaningful thresholds in the presentation of RPI increase the proportion of "winners" by providing workers at different performance levels with different objective standards to strive toward.

These studies suggest that using meaningful thresholds in the presentation of RPI provides multiple different comparison groups for workers comparing themselves with others who rank better. Because the effort-increasing behavior of RPI also derives from increased competitiveness, we predict that RPI will enhance the competitive behavior exhibited by workers approaching a performance standard.

H3. **The positive effect of RPI on performance will increase with proximity to an objective standard.**

RESEARCH DESIGN

We tested our hypotheses in introductory accounting courses taught in the Fall 2020 semester, when almost every class at the university was taught online due to COVID-19. A significant benefit of using data from this semester is the lack of self-selection into online courses that would be inherent in other semesters.[3] Students did not choose course modality, enabling us to capture the effects of our intervention in the general student population, as opposed to only in the population of students who self-select into online courses.

Sample

Our sample contains 513 undergraduate students at a public university in the Midwestern United States; 307 students enrolled across 10 introduction to financial accounting course sections and 206 students enrolled across 7 introduction to managerial accounting course sections. Students are typically in their first or second year at the time of taking these classes and would be about 19 years old. These two classes are required for all business majors in the college of business, including accounting. There are more male than female students in the college; however, there is no reason to expect a gender imbalance across sections.[4] There is no forced curve grade policy for the courses, and the exam grades are not curved. Neither course teaches ranked performance metrics, such as RPE or RPI. Nine instructors teach the sections; the authors of this chapter are not the instructors of any section in the sample.[5] Our sample only includes students who completed the course and have taken every exam in the course.[6]

Manipulation and Dependent Variables

We manipulated the RPI provision between sections of introductory financial and managerial accounting. We chose these courses because these courses use a standard structure, cover the same material for each class, have few differences between instructors, and have high enrollments that enable sufficient data collection to test our hypotheses. We randomly assigned provision or non-provision of RPI between sections by asking instructors of introductory financial and managerial accounting courses to either refrain from making any relative comparisons in their classes (No RPI condition) or post each student's ordinal rank after each exam based on that exam's performance, privately to each student via Canvas, a course management platform (RPI condition). Thus, we provided students with Private RPI, and students did not know the identities of students ranked higher or lower than them.[7] Prior research finds Public RPI leads to a stronger effect compared to Private RPI (Tafkov, 2013).

Every section in our sample had four exams during the semester, which resulted in students in the RPI condition receiving their ordinal rank four times a semester, one after each exam they took, including the final exam. The last exam is the final exam. Each exam only covers approximately one-fourth of the material in the course, and there is no comprehensive exam. The sections did not give a common exam; each instructor created their exams, primarily comprised of multiple-choice questions. In a field setting, we cannot control for every difference, so we control for section effects in the analysis to help alleviate concerns that differences between sections drive the results.

Students were unaware that RPI would (or would not be) provided prior to the first exam. This design allows us to compare the exam performance before RPI is provided to anyone (first exam) with after RPI is provided to those in the RPI condition (second, third, and fourth exams). Thus, we compare exam performance between treatments, within treatments over time, and evaluate how the differences in exam performance changed over time between treatments. Fig. 1 provides a visualization of the timing of each RPI instance.

Our first dependent variable is the level of exam scores for each exam and using the average scores on exams 2–4. Our second dependent variable is the changes in exam scores between exams, as depicted in Fig. 1.

RESULTS

Descriptive Statistics

Fig. 2 shows exam scores by condition. Table 1 presents descriptive statistics for exam 1, a control exam for every section since students took exam 1 before anyone received RPI, and exams 2–4, after one group received RPI, and the other did not. Focusing on how exam scores changed between exam 1 and subsequent exams, we note that scores in the No RPI group have declined from an average of 79.16% to an average of 74.53%, while scores in the RPI group increased from 75.94% to 78.41%.

As we manipulate the provision of RPI on a section level, we employ several approaches to mitigate the effects of students being in a section on our analyses. First, we use mixed-effects linear models to evaluate whether the average exam scores in sections that received RPI differ from those in sections that did not receive RPI. Mixed-effects linear models are well suited for analyzing clustered

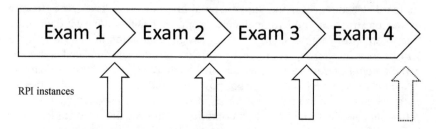

Fig. 1. RPI Timing and Changes in Exam Scores. *Notes*: Students in the RPI condition received their ordinal rank four times a semester, one after each exam. Exam 4 is the final, non-comprehensive exam. As courses end after the final and there are no performance measures after the final exam, we focus on the three instances of RPI (exams 1–3), after which students' performance is measured with a subsequent exam. Thus, there are three changes (CHANGE) in scores between exams:

CHANGE 1 = Exam 2 – Exam 1
CHANGE 2 = Exam 3 – Exam 2
CHANGE 3 = Exam 4 – Exam 3

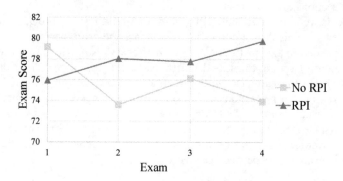

Fig. 2. Exam Scores by Condition. *Notes*: Performance on exam 1 serves as a control, as neither group received RPI until after exam 1 (based on exam 1 performance).

data in small samples (McNeish & Stapleton, 2016a, 2016b). Second, we cluster standard errors by section, which adjusts standard errors for section effects. Third, we evaluate the effect of RPI using both levels of exam scores, including a model that controls for student ability using their scores on exam 1, and changes in exam scores.

H1 – Differences in the Levels of Exam Scores by Condition

The first set of mixed-effects linear models examines whether exam scores for each of the four exams differ between sections with and without RPI. The model includes a by-section intercept, which averages exam scores by section, thus

Table 1. Descriptive Statistics. Exam Scores (Standard Deviation) by Exam and Condition.

	SCORE Exam 1 (Control)	*SCORE* Exam 2	*SCORE* Exam 3	*SCORE* Exam 4	Average *SCORE* on Exams 2–4
No RPI **n = 285**	79.16 (11.78)	73.58 (15.91)	76.15 (13.41)	73.88 (12.90)	74.53 (11.25)
RPI **n = 228**	75.94 (17.24)	78.05 (12.11)	77.75 (12.12)	79.73 (15.79)	78.41 (10.95)
Total	77.73 (14.53)	75.57 (14.54)	76.72 (12.86)	76.48 (14.54)	

Notes: SCORE is a percent score on each exam from 0 to 100. *RPI* is a binary variable coded as 1 if a student is in the RPI condition and 0 otherwise. Table 1 presents simple averages by a student.

controlling for any section effects, and uses section-level clustered robust standard errors. We run this model separately for each exam. Notably, we do not expect differences between the RPI and No RPI sections on the first exam because no RPI was provided to any section prior to the first exam. Thus, comparing the average performance on exam 1 by condition serves to identify potential differences between sections.

Table 2 presents the results of this model.[8] Consistent with our expectations, we found no difference in performance between RPI and No RPI sections on exam 1 ($p = 0.23$, two-tailed), suggesting students are similar across sections assigned to different conditions. We found students in sections with RPI performed significantly better than students in sections without RPI on exam 2 ($p = 0.02$, one-tailed) and exam 4 ($p = 0.03$, one-tailed), but we did not find a difference on exam 3 ($p = 0.29$, one-tailed). Prior research shows that top performers become complacent in repeated contests (e.g., Berger et al., 2013). These results

Table 2. Mixed-effects Linear Model: Effect of RPI on Scores by Exam.

Coefficient (*p*-value)	Exam 1 (Control)	Exam 2	Exam 3	Exam 4
RPI	−3.58	4.62	1.69	5.81
	(0.23)	**(0.02)**	**(0.29)**	**(0.03)**
Intercept	79.01	73.43	76.00	73.87
	(0.00)	(0.00)	(0.00)	(0.00)
Model fit (Wald χ^2)	1.43	4.12	0.33	4.03
Clusters (sections)	17	17	17	17
Students	513	513	513	513

Notes: Bolded *p*-values indicate hypothesized effects and are one-tailed. Non-bolded *p*-values are two-tailed. The model includes a by-section intercept and uses clustered robust standard errors by section. Table 1 presents simple averages by a student. Averages in Table 1 differ from coefficients in Table 2 because the model in Table 2 includes a by-section intercept. The by-section intercept averages student score within each section and then averages those averages to estimate the model intercept and coefficient on RPI. *SCORE* is a percent score on each exam from 0 to 100. *RPI* is a binary variable coded as 1 if a student is in the RPI condition and 0 otherwise.

suggest that a complacency effect may exist, as students become complacent for exam 3, having improved on exam 2. However, the complacency effect dissipated for the final exam, as students increased effort following the lower performance on exam 3.

The second mixed-effects model provides a more direct test of *H1* by testing the average differences between conditions across all exams by averaging scores on exams 2–4 and then controlling for performance on exam 1. Controlling for exam 1 performance accounts for differences in individual student ability. This mixed-effects linear model also includes a by-section intercept, which averages exam scores by section, thus further controlling for any section effects, and uses section-level clustered robust standard errors.

Table 3 presents the results of estimating the effect of RPI on average exam scores on exams 2–4 when controlling for performance on exam 1 and section effects. As expected, we observe a significant positive coefficient on exam 1 score ($b = 0.31$, $p < 0.01$, two-tailed), indicating past performance positively correlates to future performance. More importantly, we found RPI increased the average exam score by 5.18 percentage points ($p = 0.01$, one-tailed), after controlling for the exam 1 score, which proxies for individual student ability.

H1 – Differences in the Changes in Exam Scores by Condition

In addition to finding higher exam scores in RPI sections, it is also crucial to examine whether the rate of improvement is different in students receiving RPI compared to students not receiving RPI, as we should see differential improvement if RPI prompts higher effort. Thus, we use the third mixed effects model to examine the changes in exam scores, which is another way of controlling for individual student ability, and a way to examine whether individual student performance improves at a higher rate in response to RPI. We run a mixed-effects linear model regressing the changes in exam scores on *RPI*, so that the dependent variable is the three changes between each student's exam scores, per Fig. 1. This

Table 3. Mixed-effects Linear Model: Effect of RPI on Average Score.

Coefficient (p-value)	AVESCORE
RPI	5.18
	(0.01)
Exam1Score	0.31
	(0.00)
Intercept	49.54
	(0.00)
Model fit (Wald χ^2)	113.45
Clusters (sections)	17
Students	513

Notes: Bolded p-value indicates hypothesized effects and is one-tailed. Non-bolded p-values are two-tailed. The model includes a by-section intercept and uses clustered robust standard errors by section. *AVESCORE* is an average percent score on exams 2–4 (Exam 2 + Exam 3 + Exam 4)/3 and ranges from 0 to 100. *Exam1Score* is a score on exam 1, ranging from 0 to 100. *RPI* is a binary variable coded as 1 if a student is in the RPI condition and 0 otherwise.

model contains three observations (changes in scores) per student, which necessitates the inclusion of a by-student intercept in the mixed effect model to address the non-independence of three changes in scores per student. The model includes a by-student intercept, which averages the changes by student, thus controlling for potential section effects, and uses clustered robust standard errors by section.

Table 4 presents the results of this model. We found that students in the RPI sections increased their scores between exams by an average of 3.03 percentage points more than students in the No RPI sections ($p = 0.02$, one-tailed). As a robustness check, we split the model by the type of class – financial and managerial accounting. We continue to observe a significant effect within both financial (3.40 percentage points, $p = 0.01$, one-tailed) and managerial (3.26 percentage points, $p < 0.01$, one-tailed) courses. We did not find a difference between financial and managerial accounting sections in the effect of RPI on the changes in exam scores ($b = 0.14$, $p = 0.93$, two-tailed, untabulated).

Overall, we found support for *H1* in both levels and changes analyses. Thus, we conclude that the introduction of RPI led students in sections with RPI to outperform those without RPI on average in both absolute scores and relative improvement between exams. These results suggest that RPI improved students' performance on exams throughout the course. These results are encouraging because they suggest that even when environmental differences exist because of a remote work arrangement, workers may still attribute their low relative performance to their own effort and engage in effort-increasing competitive behavior in response to RPI.

H2 – Differences in Effects of RPI Between Lower Versus Higher Performers

H2 predicts that low performers will benefit more from RPI than high performers. We test *H2* using the same changes mixed-effects linear model as discussed above, but we split students into quintiles based on their performance on exam 1. The first quintile consists of students in the top 20% of exam 1 scores, while the fifth

Table 4. Mixed-effects Linear Model: Changes in Scores.

Coefficient (*p*-value)	**All Sections**	**Financial Accounting**	**Managerial Accounting**
RPI	3.03	3.40	3.26
	(0.02)	**(0.01)**	**(< 0.01)**
Intercept	−1.76	−3.46	0.41
	(0.04)	(< 0.01)	(0.60)
Model fit (Wald χ^2)	4.90	5.09	12.96
Clusters (sections)	17	10	7
Students	513	307	206
Observations (changes in scores)	1,539	921	618

Notes: Bolded p-values indicate hypothesized effects and are one-tailed. Non-bolded p-values are two-tailed. The model includes a by-student intercept and uses clustered robust standard errors by section. RPI is a binary variable coded as 1 if a student is in the RPI condition and 0 otherwise. The dependent variable (CHANGE) is the three changes between each student's exam scores (SCORE), per Fig. 1, which results in three observations (changes in scores) per student.

quintile consists of students in the bottom 20% of exam 1 scores. As predicted by *H2*, we expect bottom quintiles to benefit from RPI more than top quintiles.

Table 5 presents our results. The intercept in each regression corresponds to the average changes in exam scores for students who did not receive RPI, as compared to exam 1 score, thus, a negative intercept indicates an average decline in exam score compared to exam 1 score. We found positive effects of RPI in the first (b = 1.51, p = 0.05, one-tailed), third (b = 3.17, p = 0.02, one-tailed), and fifth quintiles (b = 7.30, p < 0.01, one-tailed), a marginally significant positive effect in the second quintile (p = 1.78, p = 0.08, one-tailed), but no significant effect in the fourth quintile. Notably, in the fifth quintile, we observed a positive effect of a much larger magnitude than in any other quintile, suggesting that the lowest-performing students improved their subsequent performance the most in response to RPI.

In addition to showing that top performers quickly become complacent in repeated contests, prior research also shows that the weakest performers tend to give up (e.g., Berger et al., 2013; Martin et al., 2022). However, we found that even the low performers engage in effort-increasing competitive behavior in response to RPI, which is inconsistent with the concern that RPI has a discouraging effect on effort in lower performers. Consistent with a complacency effect between the second and third exams, these results suggest that a complacency effect may exist, not necessarily for the top performers but more generally for individuals who have achieved their goals. It is reasonable then that RPI affects the fifth quintile the most, but also that RPI significantly affects the third quintile because the college has specific GPA requirements.[9]

H3 – Differences in Effects of RPI with Proximity to an Objective Standard

H3 predicts that RPI will have a stronger effect on performance as performance gets closer to an objective standard. In our setting, letter grade cutoffs provide the

Table 5. Changes in Scores Split by 1st Exam Performance Quintiles.

Coefficient (*p*-value)	1st Quintile	2nd Quintile	3rd Quintile	4th Quintile	5th Quintile
RPI	1.51	1.78	3.17	1.97	7.30
	(0.05)	**(0.08)**	**(0.02)**	**(0.16)**	**(< 0.01)**
Intercept	−3.94	−3.27	−1.95	0.00	−0.01
	(0.00)	(0.00)	(0.04)	(0.99)	(0.99)
Model fit (Wald χ^2)	2.88	1.94	4.13	0.99	13.81
Clusters (sections)	17	17	17	17	17
Students	95	109	102	97	110
Observations (changes in scores)	285	327	306	291	330

Notes: Bolded *p*-values indicate hypothesized effects and are one-tailed. Non-bolded *p*-values are two-tailed. The model includes a by-student intercept and uses clustered robust standard errors by section. RPI is a binary variable coded as 1 if a student is in the RPI condition and 0 otherwise. The dependent variable (CHANGE) is the three changes between each student's exam scores (SCORE), per Fig. 1. 1st quintile consists of the top 20% of students, and the 5th quintile consists of the bottom 20% of students, as measured by 1st exam performance.

objective standard to work toward, as increasing one's performance to move to the next grade range is more rewarding than increasing one's performance inside a range.[10] Thus, we expect the positive effect of RPI on performance to increase with proximity to the next letter grade cutoff.

We use a mixed-effects linear model with exam scores on exams 2–4 as the dependent variable. This mixed-effects linear model also includes a by-student intercept, controlling for three observations per student, and uses section-level clustered robust standard errors. To test whether RPI will have a stronger effect on performance as performance gets closer to an objective standard, we create a variable showing how close a student was to the next grade cutoff on a given exam (*Near*) and interact this variable with the provision of RPI.[11] The resulting interaction term, *Near * RPI*, is our variable of interest, as a significant positive coefficient would indicate stronger effects of RPI with proximity to the next objective standard.

Table 6 presents our results. Consistent with *H3*, we found a positive and significant interaction between *RPI* and *Near* ($b = 0.24$, $p = 0.05$, one-tailed). In untabulated robustness tests, the interaction coefficient continues to stay significant if we control for exam 1 score ($p \leq 0.04$, one-tailed), limit this analysis to scores below the highest threshold, or limit the analysis only to those students who had a higher standard to work toward ($p = 0.01$, one-tailed).

Table 6. Mixed-Effects Linear Model: Effect of RPI on *Score*.

Coefficient (*p*-value)	*SCORE*
Intercept	79.29
	(0.00)
RPI	2.18
	(0.19)
Near	−1.89
	(0.00)
*RPI * Near*	0.24
	(0.05)
Model fit (Wald χ^2)	886.58
Observations	1,539
Students	513

Notes: Bolded *p*-value indicates hypothesized effect and is one-tailed. Non-bolded *p*-values are two-tailed. The model includes a by-student intercept and uses clustered robust standard errors by section. *RPI* is a binary variable coded as 1 if a student is in the RPI condition and 0 otherwise.

Near is the difference between the score on the exam and the closest higher grade cutoff, which proxies for an objective standard or target (*Near* = Target − *Score*). For example, if a student scored 89.5 on an exam, we assume that the student was targeting a score of 90, which is the next higher-grade cutoff, and *Near* assumes the value of 0.50. Similarly, if a student scored 79.5 on an exam, *Near* assumes the value of 0.50, as we assume that the student was targeting a score of 80. As described in footnote 10, the standards are grade cutoffs from the grading rubric in each class, as the next grade represents the next aspirational standard relative to the realized score.

*RPI * Near* interaction term is our variable of interest in testing *H3*, as it captures the differential effect of RPI on exam scores as they get closer to the next highest grade cutoff.

SCORE is a percent score on each exam from 0 to 100. The model includes only scores on exams 2–4, as students received RPI feedback only after Exam 1.

Sensitivity Test: Hybrid Participation

Four of 17 sections permitted a limited number of students to attend one or more class sessions in-person while teaching online simultaneously to the rest of the class (3 sections with RPI and 1 section without RPI). Feedback from instructors suggests in-person student participation was infrequent, and most students participated only online. We asked instructors to identify students who participated in person in the anonymous data, and we removed the 41 students identified by instructors from our analysis as a robustness check and continued to find support for our predictions.

CONCLUSION

Modern professional and administrative work is increasingly performed remotely, with 37% of employees in management, business, and financial operations occupations and 33% of those employed in professional and related occupations, doing some or all of their work from home in 2019, even before the COVID-19 pandemic increased the share of remote work further. An essential question in remote work arrangements is whether traditional management control tools, such as RPI, will continue to be effective. Prior research generally shows a positive effect of RPI on performance in collocated workers and an increase in performance in workers switching to remote work. Because there is reason to question whether RPI will improve performance in remote work arrangements, we investigate whether RPI improves performance in remote work arrangements in a setting where the entire cohort had to switch to remote work due to COVID-19.

Using introductory accounting courses taught in the Fall of 2020, a semester in which almost every class at the university was taught online due to COVID-19, we found RPI improves performance in remote work. Specifically, we found that students receiving RPI achieved higher exam scores and showed greater improvement on exams than those who did not receive RPI. Furthermore, we found that the improvement in exam scores from RPI was the most extreme for those initially performing the lowest (i.e., in the fifth quintile), and the effect was more pronounced in students close to the next grade cutoff. Overall, we found RPI was effective in remote work arrangements, particularly in lower performers and those closest to the next objective performance standard.

These results inform practice on the expected benefits of implementing RPI in remote work arrangements. Our results support the use of RPI to improve employee performance in remote work arrangements, including for workers who would not have otherwise been selected or volunteered for them. Furthermore, our finding that RPI is more effective for lower performers and those closest to the next objective performance standard provides additional insight for practice to target specific groups using RPI.

This study makes several contributions to the literature. First, we extend the literature on RPI (e.g., Anderson et al., 1983; Hannan et al., 2008, 2013; Kramer et al., 2016; Murthy & Schafer, 2011; Nordstrom et al., 1991; Tafkov,

2013; Yatsenko, 2022) by examining whether RPI improves performance in remote work arrangements.

Second, by using a setting without selection effects, we contribute to the literature on remote work arrangements (e.g., Apgar, 1998; Bailey & Kurland, 2002; Bloom et al., 2015; Gajendran et al., 2015; Gajendran & Harrison, 2007; McCloskey & Igbaria, 2003; Pinsonneault & Boisvert, 2001). Our findings suggest that RPI, an element of the management control system, positively affects workers' performance in remote settings, similar to how it would in traditional settings.

Third, we contribute to the mixed results of prior studies investigating the effect of RPI on performance for workers at different performance levels. Some studies found that the highest and lowest performers respond the most to RPI (e.g., Azmat & Iriberri, 2010), while other studies found that top performers become complacent while the weakest performers tend to give up (e.g.,Berger et al., 2013; Hannan et al., 2008). We found that RPI strongly affects lower performers in a remote setting with high costs of giving up, which may help reconcile the mixed results of prior studies.

Fourth, we contribute to the accounting literature on the effect of RPI on performance by investigating the use of meaningful thresholds in the presentation of RPI. We found RPI to be increasingly influential with the nearness of workers' performance to an objective standard so that workers who are closer to meeting an objective standard improve their performance more in response to RPI than workers who are further from the performance standard.

We also provide insights for practice and the classroom. Our results suggest RPI increases performance for lower performing online students, a result that may be extended to remote workers. More research is needed to assess effort directly (e.g., hours on task, use of tutoring resources, etc.) and to investigate the effects of RPI in high-stakes settings such as job environments. Additionally, we highlight that the lowest performers may respond most strongly to RPI. Thus, in practice, implementing RPI may increase the effort and performance of lower performers up to and over the minimum expected performance. In the classroom, RPI provision would have similar effects on students, benefiting the lowest performers the most and potentially helping them to clear the bar. While the current study finds RPI to be effective in improving performance on exams comprised primarily of objectively graded multiple-choice questions, we also believe RPI would be effective with essay-type exams requiring subjective performance evaluation to the extent recipients of RPI trust the objectivity of the evaluator.

A limitation of our study is the reliance on grade cutoffs to identify meaningful thresholds. If students had other meaningful thresholds that they worked toward, such thresholds would introduce noise in our data. Future research can compare differences in the effects of RPI for those working remotely with those not working remotely. Future research can also compare differences in the effects of RPI for higher versus lower performers in a low versus a high-stakes setting. Given the concerns about employee turnover in the accounting profession, future research can investigate any effects of providing RPI for remote work arrangements on employee job satisfaction and turnover intentions. Finally, future research can investigate whether providing RPI affects employees' likelihood of opting into remote work arrangements.

NOTES

1. Four sections out of 17 allowed limited in-person participation, and one section was asynchronous online. Results are robust to sensitivity tests (included in the results section) that consider hybrid participation and the asynchronous online section.

2. Prior research on efficient contracting examines RPI as a way to remove common uncontrollable factors from relative performance evaluation, or RPE (Frederickson, 1992; Holmstrom, 1982; Kandel & Lazear, 1992). In the setting examined in this chapter, RPI is not used for compensation or reward, as one agent's outcome is independent of peers' outcomes.

3. The Institutional Review Board (IRB) of the university where data were collected approved this study.

4. For the 2020–2021 academic year, the college was comprised of 68% males and 32% females.

5. Sixteen sections are taught on Zoom at set days and times, and one section is taught asynchronously online. Our inferences are unchanged if we drop the online section.

6. The withdrawal rate from courses does not differ by condition. In sections without RPI, 8.74% of initially enrolled students have dropped out, while in sections with RPI 8.36% of initially enrolled students have dropped out, with the difference not statistically significant ($p = 0.91$, two-tailed, untabulated). Thus, there is no evidence that RPI caused students to withdraw at different rates.

7. Specifically, in the RPI condition, students' ranks were posted in Canvas with the following explanation: "This displays your rank in the class based on your performance on Exam N." Instructors then sent a message to the students stating that in addition to their exam scores, that the ranking in Canvas shows how their score compares to that of their classmates, whereby rank 1 means that their Exam N score was the top score in the class, etc. Furthermore, the message stated that the same information will be provided after subsequent exams.

8. Table 1 presents simple averages by a student. Averages in Table 1 differ from coefficients in Table 2 because the model in Table 2 includes a by-section intercept. The by-section intercept averages student score within each section and then averages those averages to estimate the model intercept and coefficient on RPI.

9. Both courses are required for all majors in the college; admission to the college requires a 2.8 GPA and graduation requires a 2.5 GPA.

10. Fifteen of the seventeen sections used the standard letter grade cutoffs of 93% or above for an A: 90% to 93% for an A-, 87% to 90% for a B+, and 83% to 87% for a B, etc. with the lowest possible passing grade of D- for scores above 60%. Two of the seventeen sections used a slightly different scale of 92% or above for an A: 90% to 92% for an A-, 88% to 90% for a B+, and 82% to 88% for a B, etc. with the lowest possible passing grade of D- for scores above 60%. In calculating the highest target, we use actual grade cutoffs for each section.

11. For example, if a student scored 89.5 on an exam, then we assume that the student was targeting a score of 90, which is the next higher-grade cutoff, and assign value of 0.50 to *Near*. Similarly, if a student scored 79.5 on an exam, then we assume that the student was targeting a score of 80, and assign value of 0.50 to *Near*.

ACKNOWLEDGMENTS

We thank the faculty and staff of the Accounting department at the University of Wisconsin-Whitewater for their help in making this study possible. We thank

Avishek Bhandari, Clay Partridge, Tyler Thomas, Ke Xu, and the 2022 Accounting, Behavior, and Organizations conference participants for their helpful comments. We also thank two anonymous reviewers for their assistance in improving the chapter.

REFERENCES

Allen, T. D., Golden, T. D., & Shockley, K. M. (2015). How effective is telecommuting? Assessing the status of our scientific findings. *Psychological Science in the Public Interest, 16*(2), 40–68.

Almer, E. D., & Kaplan, S. E. (2002). The effects of flexible work arrangements on stressors, burnout, and behavioral job outcomes in public accounting. *Behavioral Research in Accounting, 14*, 1–34.

Anderson, D. C., Crowell, C. R., Sponsel, S. S., Clarke, M., & Brence, J. (1983). Behavior management in the public accommodations industry: A three-project demonstration. *Journal of Organizational Behavior Management, 4*(1–2), 33–66.

Apgar, M. (1998). The alternative workplace: Changing where and how people work. *Harvard Business Review, 76*(3), 121–136.

Azmat, G., & Iriberri, N. (2010). The importance of relative performance feedback information: Evidence from a natural experiment using high school students. *Journal of Public Economics, 94*, 435–452.

Bailey, D. E., & Kurland, N. B. (2002). A review of telework research: Findings, new directions, and lessons for the study of modern work. *Journal of Organizational Behavior, 23*, 383–400.

Berger, L., Klassen, K. J., Libby, T., & Webb, A. (2013). Complacency and Giving Up Across Repeated Tournaments: Evidence from the Field. *Journal of Management Accounting Research, 25*, 143–167.

Bloom, N., Liang, J., Roberts, J., & Ying, Z. J. (2015). Does working from home work? Evidence from a Chinese experiment. *The Quarterly Journal of Economics, 130*(1), 165–218.

Bureau of Labor Statistics. (2020). American Time Use Survey – 2019 Results. Retrieved from https://www.bls.gov/news.release/atus.nr0.htm

Bureau of Labor Statistics. (2021). Employment Situation. Retrieved from https://www.bls.gov/bls/news-release/empsit.htm#2021

Carroll, E., & Marginson, D. (2021). Relative performance information and social comparisons: Exploring managers' cognitive, emotional, and dysfuntional behavioral processes. *Management Accounting Research, 53*, 1–15. doi:10.1016/j.mar.2021.100768

Festinger, L. (1954). A theory of social comparison processes. *Human Relations, 7*(2), 117–140.

Frederickson, J. R. (1992). Relative performance information: The effects of common uncertainty and contract type on agent effort. *The Accounting Review, 67*(4), 647–669.

Friend, R. M., & Gilbert, J. (1973). Threat and fear of negative evaluation as determinants of locus of social comparison. *Journal of Personality and Social Psychology, 41*, 328–340.

Gajendran, R. S., & Harrison, D. A. (2007). The good, the bad, and the unknown about telecommuting: Meta-analysis of psychological mediators and individual consequences. *Journal of Applied Psychology, 92*(6), 1524–1541. doi:10.1037/0021-9010.92.6.1524

Gajendran, R. S., Harrison, D. A., & Delaney-Klinger, K. (2015). Are telecommuters remotely good citizens? Unpacking telecommuting's effects on performance via I - Deals and job resources. *Personnel Psychology, 68*(2), 353–393.

Garcia, S. M., Tor, A., & Gonzalez, R. D. (2006). Ranks and rivals: A theory of competition. *Personality and Social Psychology Bulletin, 32*, 970–982.

Garcia, S. M., Tor, A., & Schiff, T. M. (2013). The psychology of competition: A social comparison perspective. *Perspectives on Psychological Science, 8*(6), 634–650.

Goethals, G. R., & Darley, J. M. (1977). Social comparison theory: An attributional approach. In J. M. Suls & R. L. Miller (Eds.), *Social comparison processes: Theoretical and Empirical Perspectives* (pp. 259–278). Washington, DC: Hemisphere.

Global Workplace Analytics. (2021). Work-At-Home After Covid-19 - Our Forecast. Retrieved from https://globalworkplaceanalytics.com/work-at-home-after-covid-19-our-forecast

Hannan, R. L., Krishnan, R., & Newman, A. H. (2008). The effects of disseminating relative performance feedback in tournament and individual performance compensation plans. *The Accounting Review*, *83*(4), 893–913.

Hannan, R. L., McPhee, G. P., Newman, A. H., & Tafkov, I. D. (2013). The effect of relative performance information on performance and effort allocation in a multi-task environment. *The Accounting Review*, *88*(2), 553–575.

Hannan, R. L., McPhee, G. P., Newman, A. H., & Tafkov, I. D. (2019). The informativeness of relative performance information and its effect on effort allocation in a multitask environment. *Contemporary Accounting Research*, *36*(3), 1607–1633.

Harkins, S. G., & Jackson, J. M. (1985). The role of evaluation in eliminating social loafing. *Personality and Social Psychology Bulletin*, *11*(4), 457–465.

Harvard Business School Online. (2021). HBS Online survey shows most professionals have excelled while working from home. Retrieved from https://online.hbs.edu/blog/post/future-of-work-from-home

Holmstrom, B. (1982). Moral hazard in teams. *The Bell Journal of Economics*, 324–340.

Hooks, K. L., & Higgs, J. L. (2002). Workplace environment in a professional services firm. *Behavioral Research in Accounting*, *14*, 105–127.

Kandel, E., & Lazear, E. P. (1992). Peer pressure and partnerships. *Journal of Political Economy*, *100*(4), 801–817.

Knauer, T., Sommer, F., & Wohrmann, A. (2017). Tournament winner proportion and its effect on effort: An investigation of the underlying psychological mechanisms. *European Accounting Review*, *26*(4), 681–702.

Kramer, S., Maas, V. S., & Rinsum, M. V. (2016). Relative performance information, rank ordering and employee performance: A research note. *Management Accounting Research*, *33*, 16–24.

Larkin, J. M. (1995). Managing employee turnover is everyone's business. *National Public Accountant*, *40*(9), 34–36.

Martin, R., Thomas, T., & Yatsenko, D. (2022). *To give up or not to give up: The effect of contract frame and target difficulty on effort provision and performance?* Working Paper, Utah State University, University of Wisconsin – Madison and University of Wisconsin – Whitewater.

McCloskey, D. W., & Igbaria, M. (2003). Does "out of sight" mean "out of mind"? An empirical investigation of the career advancement prospects of telecommuters. *Information Resources Management Journal*, *16*(2), 19–34.

McNeish, D. M., & Stapleton, L. M. (2016a). The effect of small sample size on two-level model estimates: A review and illustration. *Educational Psychology Review*, *28*(2), 295–314.

McNeish, D. M., & Stapleton, L. M. (2016b). Modeling clustered data with very few clusters. *Multivariate Behavioral Research*, *51*(4), 495–518.

Miller, D. T., & Ross, M. (1975). Self-serving biases in the attribution of causality: Fact or fiction? *Psychological Bulletin*, *82*(2), 213–225.

Murthy, U. S., & Schafer, B. A. (2011). The effects of relative performance information and framed information systems feedback on performance in a production task. *Journal of Information Systems*, *25*(1), 159–184.

Nordstrom, R., Lorenzi, P., & Hall, R. V. (1991). A review of public posting of performance feedback in work settings. *Journal of Organizational Behavior Management*, *11*(2), 101–124.

Pasewark, W. R., & Viator, R. E. (2006). Sources of work-family conflict in the accounting profession. *Behavioral Research in Accounting*, *18*, 147–165.

Pinsonneault, A., & Boisvert, M. (2001). The impacts of telecommuting on organizations and individuals: A review of the literature. In N. J. Johnson (Ed.), *Telecommuting and virtual offices: Issues and opportunities* (pp. 163–185). Hershey, PA: Idea Group Publishing.

Seta, J. J. (1982). The impact of comparison processes on coactors' task performance. *Journal of Personality and Social Psychology*, *42*(2), 281–291. doi:10.1037/0022-3514.42.2.281

Suls, J. M., & Tesch, F. (1978). Students' preferences for information about their test performance: A social comparison study. *Journal of Applied Social Psychology*, *8*, 189–197.

Tafkov, I. D. (2013). Private and public relative performance information under different compensation contracts. *The Accounting Review, 88*(1), 327–350.

Vandegrift, D., & Holaday, B. (2012). Competitive behavior: Tests of the n-effect and proximity to a standard. *Journal of Neuroscience, Pyschology, and Economics, 5*, 182–192.

Wheeler, L., Koestner, R., & Driver, R. E. (1982). Related attributes in the choice of comparison others: It's there, but it isn't all there is. *Journal of Experimental Social Psychology, 18*(6), 489–500.

Wheeler, L., & Koestnerj, R. (1984). Performance evaluation: On choosing to know the related attributes of others when we know their performance. *Journal of Experimental Social Psychology, 20*, 263–271.

Yatsenko, D. (2022). Productivity effects of shared peer effort and relative performance information. *Management Accounting Research, 56*. doi:10.1016/j.mar.2021.100779

Zanna, M. P., Goethals, G. R., & Hill, J. F. (1975). Evaluating a sex-related ability: Social comparison with similar others and standard setters. *Journal of Experimental Social Psychology, 11*(1), 86–93.

Zuckerman, M. (1979). Attribution of success and failure revisited, or: The motivational bias is alive and well in attribution theory. *Journal of Personality, 47*, 245–287.